# China and Global Capitalism

## List of Previous Publications

*The British New Left* (1993)

*The Transformation of Chinese Socialism* (2006, 2007)

*Reflections on China's Reform Trajectory* (2008)

*China I, II, and III* (edited, 2000)

*Was Mao Really a Monster? The Academic Response to Mao: The Unknown Story* (edited with Gregor Benton, 2009)

*Women: The Longest Revolution* (edited with Li Yinhe and Tan Shen, 1997)

# China and Global Capitalism

## Reflections on Marxism, History, and Contemporary Politics

*Lin Chun*

CHINA AND GLOBAL CAPITALISM
Copyright © Lin Chun, 2013.

First published in 2013 by
PALGRAVE MACMILLAN®
in the United States—a division of St. Martin's Press LLC,
175 Fifth Avenue, New York, NY 10010.

Where this book is distributed in the UK, Europe and the rest of the world,
this is by Palgrave Macmillan, a division of Macmillan Publishers Limited,
registered in England, company number 785998, of Houndmills,
Basingstoke, Hampshire RG21 6XS.

Palgrave Macmillan is the global academic imprint of the above companies
and has companies and representatives throughout the world.

Palgrave® and Macmillan® are registered trademarks in the United States,
the United Kingdom, Europe and other countries.

ISBN: 978–1–137–30125–3

Library of Congress Cataloging-in-Publication Data is available from the
Library of Congress.

A catalogue record of the book is available from the British Library.

Design by Newgen Knowledge Works (P) Ltd., Chennai, India.

First edition: December 2013

10 9 8 7 6 5 4 3 2 1

# Contents

# Preface

This small book addresses the question of China in the modern world and its evolving relationship with global capitalism, past and present. It also considers future possibilities for China in redefining that relationship, given that history does not have an end state. Only by situating the country in the historical and international context of its revolutionary, socialist, and post-socialist transformations can a national political economy increasingly embedded in the global market (and hence the Chinese [self-]positioning in that integration) be properly understood. The purpose is to look into whether a renewed Chinese social model, as an alternative to the eco-social impasse of standard modernization and with potential universal implications, is still possible. Critical of either economically or culturally deterministic approaches, the argument focuses on the power of transformative politics.

Part I explains the general framework of the book, revisits Marx's conception of history and "Oriental society," and reviews relevant issues in more recent historical and comparative economic history debates. Part II presents a critical assessment of the lessons from both eras of Chinese socialism and reform as resources for a reorientation. Part III returns to Marxism and its contemporary self-reflexive moves in rethinking world history.

Parts of chapters 1, 2, and 8 are reworked versions of an article written in 2009 and published in *Inter-Asia Cultural Studies* (13(3), 2012). I thank Taylor & Francis for their permission. I remain most grateful to the conference participants for their valuable discussions of different forms of that article in the University of Wisconsin, Madison, June 2009, Zhejiang University, July 2009, and Stanford University, May 2011, in particular Catherine Lynch, Tom Lutze, Sooyoung Kim, Lisa Rofel, Wang Ban, Chen Kuan-Hsing, Viren Murthy, Lv Xinyu, and Zhong Xueping. Chapter 6 is an extension of a paper I presented at a Makerere Institute of Social Research workshop in August 2012, where I benefited greatly from a lively debate.

My heartfelt appreciation goes to my editors, critics, and friends, especially Farideh Koohi-Kamali and Sara Doskow, at Palgrave, as well as Newgen Knowledge Works for their unfailing support, patience, and careful work, Katherine Livingston for saving me from the embarrassment of too many errors in English, and Cao Nanwei for taking on the job of compiling the index; Perry Anderson, Henry Bernstein, and Mahmood Mamdani for critical comments on various parts of various earlier drafts; Rebecca Karl for pressing on clarity, Abha Sur for introducing works and ideas from our part of the world, Lin Shan and Paul Forman for generous logistic help, and Rosa and Cao Tianyu for continuous intellectual stimulation. I also thank Cui Zhiyuan and Wang Shaoguang for their sharing of information over years in the spirit of knowledge commons and dot communism.

Maurice Meisner, who in a book review points to an air of utopianism in my discussion of a "democratic socialist market," remarks that such a project is nevertheless "historically plausible," and, "without utopian hopes, people would not only lose their will to make history, but also cripple their ability to judge the history that is being made for them." I was enormously moved by his generosity and vision. This book is dedicated to his memory.

# Part I

# 1
## Positioning China in World Capitalist Development

The question of how to view the position of China in the world in general and with respect to the development of capitalism as a world system in particular is certainly not one of a fixed place of a static entity in a predestined global order. It rather is one of how China has evolved while interacting with other cultures and nations in the modern era dominated by the rise and decline of global capitalism.

What is China? What does *zhongguo* or the "Middle Kingdom" signify? This question, asked by generations of scholars inside and outside China, admits of no definitive answer. Yet a few common sense premises apply. Above all, the (self) identity of China is intrinsically plural and always in flux. This is especially so with respect to its more recent history, a history of immensely complicated revolutionary and developmental experiences undergone by a multiethnic, multiregional, and multifaceted people transforming one of the world's oldest and largest civilizations or states. Then, given those monumental transformations, given China's vast internal diversity and diverse external influences, and given the country's traditionally competitive local powers, neither the Chinese state nor Chinese society can ever be treated as a coherent monolith—there is never anything like a singular, authentic "Chineseness" to speak of. Even at its material cultural origin, what later came to be known as Sino civilization was based on an intricate interweaving of a variety of prehistorical cultures. With a written record of social, political, and technoeconomic developments over four to five millennia, China is, as always, one country of many worlds.

This propensity to elasticity and formidability of both national outer boundaries and inner delineations is certainly not unique to China, nor is the local tendency of "territorialization within the state" (Cartier 2002). Our concern here with respect to China is with "which China" and with who speaks for it, and why in the necessary language of class and power as related to political predominance and ideologically charged contestation for "discursive hegemony" (Gao 2008: chs.7 and 8; Vukovich 2012: 15–16). The everincreasing intensity and extent of communication and mass migration in the ongoing transitions in China, as in the world, only impart to personal and collective identities a permanent sense of fluidity.

In a corrective bifurcation of linear national history, China, and along with it modern Chinese nationalism, is in an influential scholarship viewed as a "false unity" of study to be "decentered" (Duara 1997). By contrast, provincial narratives informed by regional and global trends have flourished. This fruitful "localist turn," however, should be tempered so as not to undermine perspectives regarding the structural integrity of China's modern project of national and social liberation. After all, the historical significance and contemporary relevance of that overall project are certainly not antithetical to the multiplicities of the Chinese situations. Their theorized synthesis is the real "object" absent from the intellectual paradigms of area and postcolonial studies, in which the totalizing force of capital and capitalism is downplayed (Harootunian 2002: 153). "Decentering national history" could also backfire when a positivist mode of investigation prioritizes the local and particular over the national, however bifurcated the analysis might, as it should, be. Without an appreciation of both the complexity and the entirety of modern Chinese developments, the very meaning and analytical insight of locality and unevenness would be lost.

There are intrinsic difficulties in attempting to grasp the idea of China in familiar social science language.[1] Not even postimperial China fits the model of nation-state well. The model was born of the emergence of modern capitalism in Europe, requiring a unified national market and government initially achieved through financial-military means. The modern Chinese state has also never conformed to the received nationalist logic that "the political and the *national unit* should be *congruent*" (Gellner 1983: 1). The sinological notion of *tianxia* represents a nonspatial cosmology that claims "all under heaven" to embrace races and cultures, including intermittent minority rule over the empire and its constant amalgamation. It was the rise of revolutionary nationalism after the first Opium War of 1840 which forced China to be integrated into the world market, indeed along with it internationalism of alliance with oppressed peoples within and without China proper, that conferred on the modern Chinese identity a cohesive self-consciousness. This new and superseding sense of collective identity came into being in terms of the "Chinese nation" and the "Chinese people" through China's twentieth-century revolutions. The replacement of the last dynastic court with China's first republican government resulted from the republican revolution of 1911 was the outcome of a unique "historical compromise." It was achieved, following the events around an armed uprising, by political incorporation among the revolutionaries, constitutionalists, army strongmen and imperial reformers (Zarrow 2005: ch.2).[2] China's territorial integrity had heretofore been preserved under the revolutionary banner of a unified "republicanism of five nations" (Han, Hui, Mongo, Tibet, and Manchu).

The communists continued to struggle for national independence, but their revolution was also simultaneously and radically a social one. The enemies of the communist revolution were defined in the party program as "imperialism, feudalism, and bureaucratic capitalism" in reference to what was formulated as China's "semicolonial and semifeudal" conditions (first in Lenin's *Democracy and Narodism in*

*China*, 1912). Fighting against foreign domination in collusion with a domestic *ancien regime*, the revolution built up its forces from the rural margins with mixed ethnicities. The fact that the revolution aimed not only at liberating an integrated Chinese nation from the imperialist powers but also at liberating its internal minorities from traditional ruling class chauvinism predetermined the constitutional foundation of the People's Republic of China. This political-institutional situation turned out to be as much a vital asset as a stigma for the PRC, in that its present day territories were a heritage from the seventeenth-century Qing empire (though with considerable diminution). Likewise, the innovative quasi-federal system of multileveled autonomous regional governments could be as much a blessing as a curse. The repossession of Hong Kong (1997) and Macao (1999) as China's "special administrative regions" was an additional manifestation of the elasticity of a formally unitary state's external and internal boundaries.

It should be useful to note here a distinguished feature in China's attitude toward the outside world. Attributable partly to its historical tradition of inward looking, and partly its modern political commitment, however compromised here and there, China, "unlike the major European states, has not tried to colonize areas of the world poorer or weaker than itself." In broad comparisons, "unlike pre-World War II Japan, it has not waged ruthless warfare against its neighbors…Unlike the United States, it has not set up military bases all over the world…or sent in troops whenever 'security interests' seemed threatened. Unlike the Soviet Union, it has not engaged in a massive arms race with the world's other 'superpower,' nor has it installed client governments in nations on its border" (Schweickart 2011: 174). Likewise, concerning patterns of sea power, "in sharp contrast to the European powers and their colonial-settler descendants, China did not seek to construct an overseas empire. This difference has had profound consequences for the global distribution of national property rights over the oceans' resources" (Nolan 2013: 80). The "China threat" propaganda is indeed baseless. However, as China has increasingly participated in the global competition for resources, which has its own logic, a reminder of its nonexpansionist tradition is important. Interestingly enough, instead of this Chinese virtue in contrast with Western imperialism and colonialism, attention is paid to Chinese peculiarity. A lack of the "normal" breakdown of the empire common to the Eurasian trajectories violates the conception of "nation" as the antithesis of "empire." For Euro-based intellectual sensitivities, this temporal-spatial duality of the two forms seems a sheer anachronism. Their conflation, both descriptively (of an awkward and backward political entity) and conceptually (about disparities between the Sino zone and Europe), indicates impeded development and is utterly wrong historically: "empire" signifies premodernity and despotism in contrast with the sovereign modern "nation" capable of progress and democracy. To criticize the Eurocentric "historical narratives that identify modernity with the nation-state" and then the nation-state with capitalism, as Wang Hui clarifies, is to take issue with the whole "China/West binary" in which China (and its "sphere of influence") is denied rightful historical recognition as neither "nation" nor "empire" (Wang 2007: 16–18; 2011: 73–85). In a frequently quoted condescending statement, Lucien Pye's China is no more than "a civilization pretending to be a nation-state" (1992: 1162).[3] This depiction endures and is occasionally used admiringly (e.g., Martin Jacques's "civilization-state" in 2011), but the notion of Chinese "deviation" has a deep seated implication regarding the country's inadequacy or insufficient modernity.

Overlooked in these binaries is the fact that the nation-state model is itself parochial, obsolete, and complacent. It fails to account for at least three overwhelming phenomena of our own times. First, multinational states have become a norm. Second, imperialism can hijack democratic powers, turning a democracy into the incompatible form of empire.[4] And third, there is always the categorical difference between oppressed and oppressor nations as between defensive and aggressive nationalisms. Having bypassed imperial disintegration, the secular, independent, and socialist PRC Constitution nevertheless symbolizes the country's incontestable modern accomplishment. Commitment to the centrality of the "people" is a definitive modern marker of a sovereign political community, be it branded a culture, a civilization, or a (multi)nation-state. This renders dichotomies posing a paradigmatic Europe against a deficient China hypocritical and meaningless.

In the same vein, "China" seems not to fit any of our received taxonomies of "purer" social formations. For one thing, in contrast with the Soviet system, new China was preoccupied with its own conditions as a rural based political economy. Even in its pursuit of industrialization, China resisted Stalinist approaches in formulating its own policies and methods of governance. Moreover, despite close affinities and ties with national liberation movements and postcolonial nation building, China's revolutionary and postrevolutionary paths were set apart historically and decisively from developments in the countries in the capitalist third world. These complications, reinforcing existing prejudices in European sinology and American area studies, have played into the disciplinary "ghettoization" (term borrowed from Hough 1977 about Sovietology) of China scholarship. Meanwhile, the tendency to look for pathological symptoms in the case of China persists. Exclusion and self-exclusion are both at work in this ideological delegitimation. It conveniently projects "abnormality" and "particularity" to validate the "normal" and "universal." The idea of "normalizing" the Chinese polity in the reformist ideology is precisely about global integration into a capitalist universe.

If "China" is both concrete and elusive in its signification, global capitalism at the other end of the relationship is ubiquitously tangible. In its "epochal conditions," formed, developed, and stabilized in the last several centuries, nations and societies have since found themselves. These global conditions interact with specific local situations through economic, political, military, and ideological sources of power (Mann

1986: 2, 22–30), as well as demographic, geographical, and ecological forces. Capitalism is therefore totalizing as a mode of production and extraction, but is simultaneously fragmented by conflicting classes, states, markets, and other structural components and agents working for or against the system.

For Marx, the epoch of capitalist global transformation for the first time connected the disjoint economies and cultures with which world history began. The historical distinction of this epoch is brilliantly summarized in the *Communist Manifesto*: capitalism constantly revolutionizes production while transforming pre-capitalist relations. The bourgeoisie, emanating from Europe, by rapidly improving productive instruments and means of communication, draws all nations into the world market. The need for market expansion chases the bourgeois class over the entire surface of the globe—it must nestle everywhere, settle everywhere, and establish connections everywhere, inventing a world after its own image. Colonial violence is not the focus of the *Manifesto*, but Marx and Engels emphatically note the "free trade" of cheap commodities requiring the "heavy artillery" that "batters down all Chinese walls" ([1848]1998: 38–40). There is no lack of either moral condemnation or instrumental rationalization in their writings on the capitalist global conquest. They denounce colonial barbarity as manifested in looting and destruction of native societies and the killing, enslaving, and trading of indigenous people overseas. The "civilization mongers" "drink nectar from the skulls of the lesser breed," as the direct producers are compelled to become exploited and expropriated slaves or wage laborers selling themselves. The capitalist primitive accumulation is thereby compiling a page "in the annals of mankind in letters of blood and fire" ([1867]1971: 146, 738; in Avineri 1969: 93).

Of the main conceptualizations within the Marxist framework of capitalist global expansion, "uneven and combined development" stands out. This thesis is concerned with the potential "privilege of backwardness" initially depicted by the Russian *narodnik* and confirmed by the Bolshevik theorists.

Given the prospect of the proletarian revolutions stirring up the capitalist strongholds, socialism instigated at the "weak links" of imperialist chains can catch up economically with more advanced regions (Trotsky 1959; Rosenberg 1996; Veblen 1990: 253). The logic of the margin overtaking the core through compressing more regular developmental stages in this perspective anticipates the idea of shifting power centers of the global system. When a flourishing China led the way in outputs, Europe was backward at the global periphery. Later, the decline of China and rise of Europe offered another case of uneven development in world history. Once a center becomes too rigid to be open to learning and adaptation, when stability turns into inflexibility or stagnation, it loses its advantages and begins to develop vulnerabilities. The time then comes for a new center to form and grow (see case analysis in Amin 1980).

In the world system theory, scrutiny of capitalism begins with the "long sixteenth century" (1350–1650), when it began to grow globally. The history of this systemic formation is shown to be a process of relentless capital accumulation, not only domestically but also through colonization, intraimperialist wars, unequal exchange between rich and poor countries, and deprivation and subordination of the peripheries (Amin 1976; Frank 1978; Wallerstein 2004). In the same vein, "space" is an appealing analytical tool of "historical-geographical materialism." Capitalist "spatial fix" in its double denotation refers to borderless capital flows in the form of physical investment as well as to the function of relaxing or transferring crises. In the vein of the earlier insights, the "uneven geographical development" of "accumulation by dispossession" driven by the capitalist class and state in search of sustained profits is highlighted (Harvey 2006: 42–46, 90–109; 2010; Arrighi 2009).[5]

In particular, as an adventure of hegemony building, capitalist development relies on regional and global power networks. These networks enable ever freer movement of evermore financialized international capital (Arrighi 1994: ch.1, 96ff; 2007: 89–96, 140–161). The observation regarding the financialization of capitalism has its intellectual origin in the classic Marxist analysis of financial capital, overaccumulation, and imperialism by Rosa Luxemburg (*The Accumulation of Capital*) among others. These trends, augmented by a virtual economy and "casino capitalism" (Strange 1986) largely severed from real material production in the post–Bretton Woods era, have peaked to engender a series of financial crises. The lost fiscal capability without gold standard and international balance of payment have enabled primarily the United States to freely enlarge and export its inflation, credit and deficit, along with liberalization of transaction in speculative investments. This "new global financial architecture" facilitates easy international transfer of liquid "surplus fictitious capital" to wherever it can be most profitable (Harvey 2010: 16, 30).

Among non-Marxist thinkers, capitalism is generalized as a convergent modern "commercial economy" and the end form of historical evolution. Its problems are variously recognized but are seen as overshadowed by its necessity or advantages—accelerated production and circulation, spread of liberal values, individual rights and market democracy, or international balance of power. A more interesting approach is to trace business cycles of capitalism in the light of periodic "creative destructions," which, following Marx, are seen as strikes generated from within the system's own technological and innovative successes. Such cycles could even lead to a socialist conversion, like it or not, through the regulatory apparatus, corporatist accommodation and labor unionization (Schumpeter 1962). In an especially critical perception of modern capitalism as a socially destructive transformation, the stark utopia of the "self-adjusting market" is seen as potentially "annihilating the human and natural substance of society." A predictable "double movement" of social self-defense is thus bound to arise (Polanyi 2001: 3, 45ff, part III). This critique is directly resonant with respect to China's present developmental costs and social tensions; market integration and commodification of labor and society in general appear to have gone farther in China than in most other ex-communist states and transitional economies. Needless to add that, having experienced an indigenous revolution and thoroughly anticapitalist radicalism, the Chinese should not have needed any such exposition from a foreign source.

For our concern here with China's past and future trajectories in terms of its position in the world system or its evolving relationship with the global capitalist political economy, particularly worth noting is also Fernand Braudel's distinction between market and capitalism. For him, both are about accumulative augmentation of material and monetary wealth, as well as short and long distance trade constitutive of locally and globally nested productive and commercial activities. But "capitalism" is not merely a "market economy" and dependent on a specific structural constellation of state promotion and protection (1980: 31, 34, 48; 1992: 232–238). Instead of the "surplus value" central to the Marxist notion of "economic base," this non-Marxist observation confirms the importance of proactive or reactive functions of the state in the "superstructure"—never mind if these metaphors have long been abandoned by the Marxists themselves. Braudel is relevant also because this distinction is most splendidly vindicated in the Chinese traditional economy: for all its sophisticated agriculture, advanced specialization, and artisanship, and extensive trading practices long antedating European capitalism, China had not evolved into a capitalist structure of its own. That is, there can be no assured developmental linkage assumed between commodity production and capitalism, between merchant and industrial capital, or more specific to the case of China, between a "Smithian growth" and capitalist industrialization.

Furthermore, capitalism in its monopolistic tendencies is repressive for a competitive market economy. The dystopia of an "antimarket capitalism" realistically features the monopoly of private and state capital alike, which could stifle competition by taking over and dominating the business world.[6] To prevent the monopoly of "the interests of profit earners," which "always involve a widening of the market and a narrowing of the competition," Adam Smith presupposes a visible role of the sovereign who activates and regulates intercapitalist competition for the market to function in "the general social interest" (quoted in Arrighi 2007: 47–49, 166).

It doesn't matter if Smith has been "overread" in different interpretations. The consensus that state capacity remains a crucial factor in development, despite evermore invasive global constraints, does not require any classical authorization. Governments in the West employed hard and soft means to expand markets and extract resources from colonies in an earlier era; and forms of "developmental state" in the East dominated success stories in late development. "Capitalism only triumphs when it becomes identified with the state, when it is the state" (Arrighi 2007: 92). In the history of capitalism, the notions of "trade" and "conquest" are often interchangeable. In Europe itself at the dawn of capitalism, market integration was less frequently disrupted by any "unlimited" state than by states being too restricted. The necessary contributions of the state to economic growth turned out to be "the centralization of government, the reduction of decentralized rent-seeking, and the creation of viable markets." Only then could Europe initiate its "centuries-long process of catching up in welfare and technology with the most advanced economy of the time, Ming-Ching China" (Epstein 2000: 169–171).

Capitalism has so far survived its recurring economic and political crises, including the two horrendous world wars and ongoing cold and hot wars. Its forward and backward movements have continued to shape and be shaped by the oppositions and resistances intrinsic to the system. In a straightforward historical perspective, the typical trajectory of industrial capitalism that originated in Europe is not, for all its reach in a transnational order of epochal parameters, a "natural" course repeatable elsewhere. Rather, the capitalist epoch circumscribes national and local developments. The misreading of Marx's conception of history into a linear "stage theory" universally followed thus makes no sense and has long been rejected in serious Marxist circles. That reformers in China picked it up to validate their departure from a socialist course is only a sign of intellectual poverty and political bankruptcy. In the end, historical capitalism itself must be properly conceived of as a dynamic, fluctuating, and open contour of transformations. It has been made, remade, and challenged or defied by locally kindled events and sequences, especially (and tautologically) those that proved to be world-historical, such as the social revolutions. Within the capitalist epoch each society finds itself in its relational interactions with the global movement. This two-way traffic reflects both the openings and constraints of the system.

That is, to situate China (as any other developing countries) in the world and world history cannot be a matter of measuring its temporal distance from any standard modernization projection of liberal capitalism. The real question is not one of how latecomers may achieve "modern norms" by overcoming their inherent flaws or making up missed opportunities. It is about any possibility, let alone desirability, of the third world emulating the first. The latter's historically specific advantages and morally tainted methods are all too palpable to ignore. Moreover, as epochal parameters evolve and power centers shift, capitalism's genesis and expansion do not follow any iron law of development. The essence of the process is only its structural synchrony and spatial unevenness. The "mainstream civilization" of capitalist universality of development, and values, institutions, and teleology—as illusorily celebrated by the intellectual elites in "transitional societies"—does not really exist. In fact, China's (and for that matter any other nation's) position in the globe is defined not only by the epochal conditions but also by its ability to modify those conditions. Such abilities, likely to be magnified in those momentous historical conjunctures, are what tend to be overlooked in a defeatist discourse of capitalist unavoidability on the one hand and escapist, self-congratulatory narratives of the local, particular, and hybrid on the other.

An important conceptual implication of this dialectical relationship is that if any society must be understood in terms of its interactive positioning in a world of capitalist globalization, then it is by reason of that relentless linkage or "interculturality" alone that there is no people without history.[7] World history has to be taken "as a whole, a totality, a system" of interconnections in interconnected causal chains extending beyond individual populations. The conception of any "historyless people" is therefore a disdained fiction. Every people has a history, including those seemingly irrelevant to a particular historical course leading to the formation of industrial capitalism and hence wiped out in the process; and every history is intelligible with respect to other histories and to entire historiography (Wolf 2010: 385).

Insisting that capitalism is historical, Marxism refuses the ideological closure of conflating it and modernity (Meszaros 2008: 55). It is against the tensions and contradictions within the capitalist modern paradigm that history becomes unlocked. Consider evolutionary effects of construction and destruction and revolutionary breaks as well as decay and counterrevolutionary reversals. Marx, not to mention Mao Zedong, who actually launched a preventive Cultural Revolution, warned against the perversion of revolution through which "the old muck" of the past could be restored (1867). Consider also overlapping temporalities and spatialities within modernity, most remarkably noncapitalist modern developments. In critical theory, medieval theologies maintain a modern presence, and this "necessary anarchism" is also paradoxically "analogous to postmodern sensibilities" (Cole and Smith 2010: 28). Taken together, the Weberian secular world time as a sociological signifier is neither merely accumulative nor unidirectional. It is marked by nonlinear trajectories, compressions, leaps, and bounds. It is punctuated by alterations, turnovers, retreats, and contretemps. History cannot be and has not been either deterministic or singular. To pluralize time, as to diversify modernity, is inherent to any honest historiography. Just as "social space" is a "means of control, and hence of domination, of power" (Lefebvre 1974: 26), "it matters who owns time" (Buck-Morss 2010: 68–69), time as a matter of historically specific social relations. The broken time of politics catalyzes the present simultaneity of past and future, making Whig history even in its newest pretensions untenable. Before we proceed to more concrete discussion, it is worth accentuating that the sense, if not the science, of history must be without teleological illusions—history has no end, and progress can be self-negating. Confined to its structural yet ultimately transformable parameters, the age of capitalism is but an open course of struggles and possibilities.

# 2

# Debating History: From "Oriental Society" to "Great Divergence"

For positioning China in the modern world in terms of its relationship with capitalism as a historical materialist account, a few academically or politically influential concepts of traditional China deserve our special attention. Marx and Engels adopted the language of "Oriental society" from Europe's worldly thinkers. Along with it they inherited some of the main assumptions and categories of (early) modern European imaginations of Asia, most of which have been proven to lack factual or interpretative reliability. Marx wrote extensively about the "Eastern question," not limited to geographic Asia, although his intellectual focus had always been on capitalism rather than societies deemed precapitalist, except for those useful for understanding capitalism's own genesis. From his political journalism on distant social formations, the best known analysis is the emblematic "dual judgment," combining demands of morality and rationality, that he employed for the representative case of British rule in India: the British treatment of India was simultaneously a colonial crime and an instrument of history, for, by breaking down the native social structure and relations, it produced "the only *social* revolution ever heard of in Asia" (Marx in Avineri 1969: 93). Engels shared much of that view and, beyond Asia, saw the suppressed Slavs in southern Europe, for example, as Hegel's "residual fragments of peoples" turning into "fanatical standard-bearers of counter-revolution." In the event, the Germans and others who held the Slavs in bondage "became the main vehicle of historical development" (Engels [1849]1977: 233).

A central concept in Marx's theorization of the East is the "Asiatic mode of production" (AMP). This concept, rightly "buried" many times, has endured much political and intellectual fascination. Elaborated in *A contribution to the critique of political economy* in 1859, the AMP implies two basic characteristics: stagnation and despotism. Behind them lay the entire tradition of European social philosophy after a romantic episode in which Enlightenment thinkers (led by Voltaire) were in awe of the East and China as a model for Western imitation. A "generalized slavery" of "absolute equality" and "Asian servility" under "Oriental despotism" became common references in the Occidental discourse about the Orient, from Montesquieu to Condorcet, Hegel to Marx (Dawson 1964: ch.1). Although Marx did not depart decisively from the Hegelian perception of nonhistoric peoples, he and Engels were resolutely supportive of the nationalist struggles for Irish, Polish, Jewish, and indeed Chinese liberation.

But Marx goes deeper to offer a socioeconomic explanation of the timeless Orient in its political economy: the absence of private land and hereditary nobility, and hence of class division, is "the key to the secret of the *unchangeableness* of Asiatic *societies*... in such striking contrast with the constant dissolution and refounding of Asiatic *State*." Despite cyclical dynastic changes, "the structure of the economical elements of society remains untouched by the storm-clouds of the political sky" ([1867]1971: 352). In a chapter on "precapitalist economic formations" of the *Grundrisse*, Marx's focus moves from "the absence of property in land" to "the self-sustaining unity of manufacture and agriculture." Such unity as the basic organizational rationale of village communities "contains all the conditions for reproduction and surplus production within itself." As such, "the Asiatic form necessarily hangs on most tenaciously and for the longest time" ([1857-]1973: 486).

Unlike (pre-)Mughal India, China is not a primary case for the formulation of AMP. But it is placed in the same bin for its presumed structural similarities with India. The news in the 1850s and 1860s, however, was that the "rotting semi-civilization" as a "living fossil" immune to change had now been "brought into contact with the open air" by "the English cannon of 1840" (Marx in Avineri 1969: 188ff). And Marx found no difficulty linking the Chinese unrest with the "next uprising of the people of Europe" ([1853]1979a: 93). "Chinese socialism may, of course, bear the same relation to European socialism as Chinese to Hegelian philosophy," as Britain's dirty drug war stirred up a place "vegetating in the teeth of time." So when the "European reactionaries" on their next flight through Asia reach the Chinese wall, "perhaps they will read the following inscription: *Republique Chinoise: Liberte, Egalite, Fraternite*" (Marx in Avineri 1969: 49–50)! Predicting colonial backlash, this instinctive twist in thinking about revolutionary changes in Oriental society is truly remarkable. Half a century later, Lenin lived to watch the actual "awakening of Asia" in China's republican revolution of 1911 when "cultured Europe" turned out to be reactionary while the "barbaric Asians" progressive. The international battles were fought "between the counter-revolutionary imperialist West and the revolutionary nationalist East" ([1913]1977a: 65; [1913]1977b: 99–100). Certainly more than a passing observation, this judgment anticipated an entirely new conception of history in which the East will take the lead.

The concept of AMP was heatedly debated in the former Eastern bloc. In China, the great social history debate of the 1920s and 1930s over the nature of Chinese society was most influential (Dirlik 1978: 191–207; 1994: 24ff). Later, in a very different context, there was a wave of revisiting the concept right after the Cultural Revolution (Rapp 1987; Brook 1989; Sullivan 1990). Both debates were politically charged and geared toward defining a historical conjuncture and the pressing tasks it posed for political actors. The communist revolutionary program was at stake in the earlier case, and the imminent reform project was the urgent concern in the latter. More recently the AMP, as an unacknowledged specter in a growing revisionist historiography, has been perversely brought back to once again serve a political purpose. Almost anticlimactic, the weird revival of Cold War anticommunism has not even produced new terms. Dead ideological labels echoing convenient descriptors of the Asiatic mode, such as "totalitarianism" and "bureaucratic tyranny," are found useful. Specifically, the new age historians dismiss the Chinese historical experiences of class struggle between landlords and the landless alongside poor tenants and middle peasants. Consequently, they ignore the political and economic ties forged since the mid-nineteenth century between the imperialist-bureaucratic powers and China's multifaceted institution of landlordism, even if at the time large landholding was not very common in certain regions and rural poverty was not caused solely by unequal land ownership (Yang 2009). For them the contradiction throughout Chinese history is exclusively between an autocratic state and a (classless) population. Sure enough, in an "Asiatic" story, class analysis is misplaced, "feudalism" a wrong term, and the land revolution superfluous or altogether mistaken.

In the Chinese communist theory, "feudalism," adapted from European and Japanese usage, is a politically and linguistically handy label for denoting China's rural social relations. Whether elements of a typical feudal system had ever developed in China is largely irrelevant, insofar as the term signals the country's major social-class structure for revolutionary mobilization. Without implying a destined capitalist replacement of feudalism in a pseudo Marxist orthodox of universal societal sequencing, the term was not only conceptually permissible but also strategically necessary in the articulation of communist ideology and programs at the time. With crystal clarity, it was recognized that "the contradiction between imperialism and the Chinese nation and the contradiction between feudalism and the great masses of the people are the basic contradictions in modern Chinese society" (Mao [1939]1991: ch.2).

The present contention is over "class," a keyword with respect to the realities of a capitalistic transition in China that is nevertheless silenced in the reformist ideology pretending to be apolitical. But Deng Xiaoping's "no argument" and developmentalist policies have themselves been hailed as ideological fundamentals. The revisionist enterprise is to direct current public indignation from class subjugation and exploitation to state control and violence, as though the two are not related. In a restored "Oriental despotic" perspective, the main social contradiction in China today is between an illegitimate (because its leaders are not elected) communist state and individual citizens as private property holders and market actors (who would presumably opt out of the Communist Party). Yet polarization and conflicts between capital and labor, the possessed and deprived, or "winners" and "losers" in a ruthless marketplace are impossible to deny. The point is that even if this dubious state-citizen antagonism does contain some important truth, only a truthful class analysis can reveal the most critical factor in the state-capital alliance. Clearly, debating the AMP in China has not been about the empirical or conceptual validity of the original model but about its immediate political function. Marx's diagnosis of the perpetual reproduction of a closed mode of production as a hindrance to progress and foundation of despotism has been seized on as a powerful weapon by the critics, Marxist and anti-Marxist alike, of past and present regimes in Chinese history.

Both the empirical and the conceptual bases of the AMP are indeed shaky. In the case of China, an extensive historical and archival record confirms that private landowning developed early and widely, as did a landed aristocracy. China's blooming markets along with a partially commercialized peasant economy in much of the imperial era were among the most advanced in the premodern world (cf. a survey of literature in Wang X. 2011). Such local commercialization, viewed by some as a form of merchant or commercial (as opposed to industrial) capitalism, was achieved without destroying an ancient moral economy, integrating separate markets of short and long distance trade, and creating a gluttonous "bourgeois" class. This allowed some marvelous productive and social gains beyond the reach of the central state. Although Marx seemed to become aware of the existence of private landownership in China (Meisner 1963: 103), his focus remained on the household organization combining small scale agriculture and domestic industry as the feature of AMP as of the primitive communal formations in general.

Concerning state power, the "hydraulic society" thesis (Wittfogel 1957) is largely rejected for being ideologically driven and factually groundless in large parts of the South Asian and Eurasian empires. It does strike a chord in China, where grand irrigation schemes surpassed earlier Indian projects, for instance, in scale and organization. But defense, because of China's rough nomadic north, was a lasting and probably even greater budgetary and administrative burden for the imperial government. An interesting comparison would be the European monarchies' use of war routinely, with or without border issues, to finance their states and palaces. While they did face certain institutional challengers at home (churches or parliaments), these states were really "absolutist" as warmongers. Interstate wars together with colonial conquests gave rise to financial capitalism (Tilly 1984; 1992).[1] Thus the functionality of "despotism" confining to the East is incoherent. Modern variants of the "fiscal-military state" (Glete 2001) certainly still dominate international politics today, only a hundred times more powerful.

The notion of untrammeled Oriental rulers is equally biased. Except for perhaps a few periods under newly established minority reigns that had to be extraordinarily controlling to consolidate power, the historical Chinese empire was by and large ruled loosely given its vast and diverse territories. Traditional local autonomy had a socio-geopolitical root in the condition that, as the saying goes, "the heaven is high and the emperor far away." Moreover, the emperors could be multiply constrained, not least by their ministers and advisers. Instead of the institutional checks and balances found in Europe, it was bureaucracy that had developed most in China. The governing Confucian ideal of political order, which by the way never gained monopoly over the legalist and other native political philosophies, stressed moral ruling—however vague or deceptive that notion might be. The gentry-scholar officials, supposed to follow the *li* or Confucian rite and be upright as the guardians of morality and legitimacy, were responsible for interpreting the "mandate of heaven." This mandate was part of the cultural mechanism of meritocracy and limiting state power.

Descriptively then, Marx is proven to be triply wrong by a truer and fuller history. After all, the "Orient" did have its own dynamics of change (negating stagnation); changes might and did take a form other than industrial capitalism (negating the industrialism-capitalism equation); and imperialist interventions could and did obstruct indigenous development (negating both the thesis that Asian societies need external shocks for social change and the instrumentalist rationalization of colonialism). The scenario calling for imperialist intervention remains disastrous in an ostensibly postcolonial world. However, Marx also has a luminous historical intuition that runs counter to the gist of an Asiatic mode: he had no problem predicting revolutions in Asia that could spark and advance the international communist movement.

Conceptual criticisms of the AMP concentrate on its prescriptive discrepancies. There are at least two major theoretical objections. First, in the Marxian construal of world history, the "pre-capitalist" Asian societies are mostly passive, awaiting capitalist integration. Relying on a sharp dichotomy between Occidental dynamism and Oriental immobility, the concept of AMP is a disturbing instance of complacency in Marxism. It leaves little room for any genetic potential of either noncapitalist development or independent non-Western development of a capitalist character. It also precludes capitalist stagnation or regression other than cyclic crises and eventual demise. Moreover, the lack of a conceptual distinction between non- and pre-capitalism also gives Marx's worldview a teleological overtone. In the still dominant modernization theory under the obvious influence of Marxism, noncapitalist development is inconceivable. Capitalism in our self-indulgent modern knowledge becomes the only path to, or the only form of, modernity.

The other objection relates to the conceptual logic of "mode of production" itself. The concept of Asiatic mode is variously applied as an Oriental equivalent of other primitive systems (ancient, Germanic, Slavonic, etc.), as the earliest and most primitive of all systems, or as an exceptional "sixth" system.[2] It is in any case an outcast vis-à-vis the paradigmatic modes of production—primitive, slave, feudal, capitalist, and communist (Marx [1857]1964; Marx and Engels [1846]1968: 7–13). While each of the typical and successive modes before future communism stands in a dialectical relationship with the one replacing itself, the Asiatic mode in its characterizations is missing the emerging contradiction between its forces and relations of production that is seen as required for any upward transition. Relying on external force for change and hence off the regular track of societal evolution, the notion of AMP lacks the coherence needed for a successful conceptual construction in the same analytical framework. If "the dialectics of historical development are not operative in Asia," Marx's theory of history is diluted by logical inconsistency (Avineri 1969: 5–6, 13).

More specifically, if state monopoly over rent is indistinguishable from tax and tribute, or if the state (and its bureaucracy) is both the landlord and the sovereign under which divisions between exploiting and producing classes cannot be specified (Marx [1894]1993: 790–791), then the Asiatic mode can hardly be validated in accordance with the general formulation of mode of production; its logic contradicts that distinguished Marxist terminology (Hindess and Hirst 1977: 178–182, 192ff). This criticism, however, may not affect the concept's other signification—in Marx's usage it also refers to the historical epochs corresponding, but not confined, to the specific processes of production, circulation, and distribution (Bernstein 2013: 316). The concept of "tributary mode of production," introduced by Samir Amin (1976) and espoused by some influential theoretical anthropologists and historians, has a mitigating effect on the difficulties of conceptualizing certain non-Western and hence marginalized experiences of social organization and evolution. Addressing mainly the controversial issue of the universality of feudalism, the tributary mode "sets takers against the producers of tribute and gives rise to military and political competition both within and between the contending classes" (Wolf 2010: 386). Seeing the tribute-paying mode as the most widespread form of pre-capitalist class societies, Amin emphasizes the separation of the peasantry and the ruling class, which monopolizes political functions of state and economic functions of extraction. "This circumstance makes it impossible to reduce production relations to legal property relations, and compels us to see production relations in their full, original significance" (1976: 15–16). That is, since class division is viewed as underdeveloped in Asiatic societies, a closer use of the tributary mode is to denote that "the state controls *both the means of production and the ruling class*, and has 'unlimited disposal over the total surplus labor of the population'" (Rudolf Bahro quoted in Banaji 2010: 23). Similarly proposed is a "peasant mode of production" in which forms of simple commodity production are based on patriarchal management of family and subsistence labor. This "recast version" of the tributary regimes "can help resolve the problem of the Asiatic mode of production, both vindicating Marx's sense of history's peculiarities and superseding his own obsolete model" (Banaji 2010: 94–102, 356). Another, different reference of the tributary system is specific to the historical East Asian regional order centered in the Chinese cosmological authority over a precarious jurisdiction with or without hard territorial borders of the empire. It embraced the emperor's "barbarian" subjects, semi-independent vassals and smaller neighbors in a tributary fold of protection, subordination, and coexistence.

Back to Marx, it is notable that AMP has a temporal, more than spatial, connotation. The signifier "Asiatic" turns out not to limit the concept to geographic Asia; AMP refers to a specific mode of production in a transhistorical process that may find resonance anywhere, from Mexico and Peru to Celtic Europe. An example is Marx's famous analogy characterizing insulated and self-sufficient French rural families and villages as "equal magnitudes" like a "bag of potatoes" endlessly reproducing themselves. Their inability of self-representation was what explained Louis Bonaparte's coup as meeting their need for an absolute overlord ([1852]2005: 84–85). Likewise, Lenin sees a Russian affinity in the Tsarist semi-Asiatic empire, which mirrored "the oppressive features of Asiatic bondage" (in Lowe 1966: 58–60).

As Eric Hobsbawm points out, the succession of historical modes of production in Marx's analysis is merely observational, "perhaps not in any particular predetermined order" due to any predestined internal dynamics ([1964]2011: 136, 151). Theoretically nonexistent private property in the Asiatic mode, for instance, masks actual tribal/communal property, which could be conducive to variously "more despotic or more democratic" types of state ([1964] 2011: 148). Feudalism, as a typical example, originated in a conjunction of Germanic military conquest and conquered Roman agricultural settings. It was not a result of a social revolution induced by internal contradictions of slavery. There was thus no sequential logic relating the slave and feudal formations. As noted, if Marx had any concern with "pre-capitalist" societies, it would be only for their explanatory value with respect to the origins of capitalism, structural or contingent. In fact, since only feudalism had undergone a transition to capitalism, it is probably the only mode prior to capitalism that attracted his theoretical attention. After the *Manifesto* he did not, after all, return to any outlining of lawlike mechanisms of the breakdown of preclass communities or their passage to a higher mode of production (Hobsbawm

[1964]2011: 156, 171). Largely without a causal link to capitalist development, the Orient is insignificant in the Marxist conception of history.

But why is capitalism so important in the Marxist perspective? Is the concept dispensible in our modern understanding of "capitalism" and "modernity" being readily interchangeable? Capitalism is about unprecedented productive capabilities and, for liberals as much as Marxists, individual rights and political democracy. The difference, of course, is that the grand historical materialist narrative is not only about the vicissitudes of the genesis, development, and globalization of capitalism; it is also about capitalism's historicity—its predictable crises, eventual demise, and future replacement. The alternative to capitalism, which should include not only historically known non- and anticapitalist experiences but also and especially present struggles and potential imaginaries, is where the most useful debate begins. This search, however, requires an epistemological breakthrough in the modern knowledge production and its symbolic domination. For what is historically contingent has been turned into inevitable: "History" becomes "nature," and the existing order is naturalized in our unconscious "habitus" (Bourdieu 1977: 164), undoubtedly nurtured also by conscious ideological socialization.

Not unnoted in valuable critiques but never eliminated from relevant debates are the following habitual conflations: First, market and capitalism are conflated, to the neglect of highly developed markets without an archetypal capitalist trajectory in "premodern" China, India, Indochina, and the Arab world, for example. Second, industrialism and capitalism are conflated, the result being blindness not only about old mercantile capitalism in which artisans and workers are not generally transformed into factory wage labor but also about an increasingly financialized capitalism dependent on a virtual economy. At issue is not deindustrialization in any postindustrial economies that outsource manufacturing to "emerging markets" but the place of socialist industrialization in a real economy (which I discuss in the next chapters). This then leads to the third conflation, of capitalism and development, which precludes socialist modernization among other developments not conforming to capitalist standards. These conflations, in line with the dominant intellectual preoccupation with capitalist modernity, produce a circularity that brings us all the way back to the historically and intellectually rejected confusions between development and westernization, westernization and modernization, and modernization and capitalism.

The enduring lure of the Marxian Orient is visible even in the radically anti-Eurocentric debate initiated by the celebrated California school in comparative economic history. Comparing mainly Qing China with Georgian-Victorian England, scholars trace an advanced "Asian Age" prior to 1800 to explain the rise of Europe and decline of China/Asia as leading producers and technological inventors in the world. The "great divergence" between the two paths was marked by the industrial revolution, which overtook any previously more advanced economies around the turn of the nineteenth century. The premise of the validity and superiority of capitalism in historical progress is not usually questioned in this fascinating inquiry. Consequently, not doing away with the customary threshold of industrial capitalism, the intervention cannot really unravel the entrenched "Asiatic" perceptions. Despite a tailored *lingua franca* bypassing the "mode of production," much in the discredited dispositions about Oriental defects lingers.

The classic Weberian riddle therefore persists: What explains the Chinese failure to launch an industrial revolution (with all its supposed material and moral benefits), leaving this world-historical milestone uniquely to the Europeans? This generic question is repeatedly asked in different ways concerning different features of the phenomenon, from wealth and productivity to culture, science, and technology. The post–Cold War atmosphere of liberal capitalist triumphalism has only invigorated the riddle. This time, though, an answer may no longer be implied in the question itself, which overlooks fundamentals about capitalism being financially, socially, and ecologically unsustainable.

Max Weber's own response is exemplary. He holds that in the absence of a Roman-law-type institutional development in political and economic organization, including free labor, there "did not exist in China the legal forms, or the sociological basis, of the permanent capitalist enterprise." This was due partly to the continental scale of Chinese power and partly to the lack of professionalism needed for a rationalization of the gentry-bureaucracy. A centralized yet patrimonial state and its trade regimes suppressed any nascent bourgeoisie and wider commercialization and overtaxed or monopolized the circulation of certain essential goods. Weber's cultural thesis invoking the Protestant ethos and work ethic to underscore the inner connection between Christianity and capitalism is a rebuff of the conservative Confucian literati (Weber 1968a: 100–104; 1978: 196, 202, 315–336). Echoing Marx, he also notes that Oriental cities were places of luxury consumption, mandarin rituals, and court politics rather than production, guilds, and civil associations. They were of a different species from autonomous towns or workshops and commerce in ancient and early modern Europe and the Mediterranean (Weber 1968b: 290–292, 327; 1986; Skinner 1977). The fact that Weber knew little about the East, it is argued, does not even slightly reduce the value of his insight. China's economically advanced global position on the eve of European takeoff "only further sharpens the question why Europe and not China achieved an industrial revolution" (Runciman 1978: 288).

The Weberian diagnosis emphasizing the lack of liberal institutions that could have fostered better market functions and of a bourgeoisie class in China has a large following in institutionalist expositions as well as their critiques (Rosenthal and Wong 2011). Beside constitutionalism, legality, and property rights, a reward mechanism for competition and innovation is also deemed missing within a traditional land system and social organization of self-sustaining petty production—recall Marx's initial diagnosis. Lacking the right incentives and forces to stimulate productivity and curb monopolies, China is said to have rewarded parasitic classes and nonproductive investment. Meanwhile, the culturalist explanation identifies Chinese ways of thinking as having blocked a mathematically and experimentally based cognitive-scientific revolution along with its productive and technological applications (Needham 1976: sec.19; Elvin 2004; Goldstone 2008). Other obstacles considered are state restrictions both on oceanic adventures beyond showing off or bestowing imperial wealth and on foreign commercial participation; ancestral worship, clanship, and an inheritance tradition that perpetually fragmented family stocks by not favoring the oldest son (as in Western Europe, where stability and accumulation of property favored reinvestment) (Levy 1963: chs 3 and 5); agricultural conservatism sustained by irrigation dependent rice cultivation and multiple cropping, which held back division of labor; and many climatic, geographic, and demographic factors. Regularly mentioned are also devastations of recurring social upheavals in the dynastic history rooted in a systemic tendency of rural surplus labor being cut off from the means of production by land concentration, landlessness, and destruction of subsistence farming.

The China puzzle, dismissed as misconceived by critics of Eurocentrism, has nevertheless stimulated fruitful investigations. The Chinese reformulation in the communist debate is the problematic of so-called embryonic capitalism— whether, when, how, and why an endogenous capitalism had emerged (as early as in Song China, as some argue; others choose the Ming-Qing period) and later been derailed by the reactionary and intertwining foreign and domestic powers. Brought to light are questions concerning such matters as land rights, class relations, the difficult growth of a national bourgeoisie, and state weaknesses. Separation of capital accumulation and productive investment, with money going mostly to land purchase and usury, is singled out to explain the general lack of an industrial impulse. This was a reason for government attempts, rarely successful, to control commercial transactions as land concentration was detrimental to both production and taxation. This is also where the conventional Chinese stress on agriculture differed from methods of both physiocrats and mercantilists in Europe. It was a policy on which secured revenue, fiscal stability, and a grain reserve system that used price mechanism to balance good and bad harvests had to depend. China, after all, was not a colonial empire sitting on overseas extraction. By the same token, the worsening collusion of landed/money-owning classes and local officials/warlords in the early part of twentieth century destroyed the agricultural base of the Chinese economy and rural society. Together with a deepening national crisis, China was inevitably on the road to a revolution that would liberate its legendary, yet then-stifled, productive forces.

In the non-Chinese scholarship, Mark Elvin points to China's "high-level equilibrium trap," denoting a disparity between abundant, cheap labor and scarce physical resources, especially land. Given the severe demographic strain, he argues, the transaction cost was simply too high for any major technological adaption to be rational (Elvin 1973: 314ff). Similarly, Philip Huang describes the Yangzi Delta since the fourteenth century as undergoing a parallel process of increasing total output and diminishing marginal returns in household farming. He depicts it (after Clifford Geertz) as "involutionary growth without development," a paradox of quasi-capitalist production relations of commercial agriculture based on a pre-capitalist level of productivity and income (Huang 1990: 11–18, ch.5). Kenneth Pomeranz looks further into the ecological-economic bottlenecks that halted regional proto-industrialization south of the Yangzi (*Jiangnan*) around 1800. This contrasts sharply with early capitalist Europe, where comparable ecological pressures were relieved through colonization. The windfall of the New World provided the major European economies with both a population outlet and a source of land intensive primary products (Pomeranz 2000: 22, 239, 287–288).[3]

Such a quantitative involution without qualitative transformation, in the eyes of the "Euro-Marxists," can be
explained only by China's backward petty agrarian management incapable of either efficient capital investment or
needed technological upgrading. In particular, right of use
without formal ownership allowed small farmers to stay on
the land through evermore intensive labor input and to keep
reproducing themselves. *Jiangnan* was thus in no position to
compete with the more socialized economies like England's
in which legal clarity regarding property relations protected
right-holders and offered productively progressive incentives
(Brenner and Isett 2002). Clearly owing a debt to Marx's
original insight on closed village communities, this argument requires some unpacking. It is one thing to prioritize
ownership relations, a position shared by Marxists and market liberals in explaining the nature of a political economy.
It is quite another, however, to insist on the centrality of
a legal-political framework for the orderly operation of
any economy, which may not require "clarified" property
rights for private domination claimed by the neoclassical
institutionalists.

Also illuminating is the tale of underdeveloped financial
tools and markets in China, which is paradoxically attributable to the country's hegemonic position in East Asia. Unlike
Europe, where the frequency of wars necessitated a sophisticated credit system (Ertman 1997), the Chinese empire
in dominance and relative peace did not need to borrow.
Its eighteenth-century imperial administrators even set up
pawnshops as lenders. Yet, without a comparable pressure
to finance wars, China even at the height of its growth failed
to establish a balanced scheme of tax rates and collection
(hence the capitalist form of political representation of tax-
payers). Nor did it forge a unified fiscal structure, independent monetary policy, or public budgeting, which though had
been more or less compensated by well-functioning informal
arrangements of personal relations, family ties, partnerships,
and clansmen networks.[4] The reform attempt in the high
Ming period to establish a single tax in silver based on a

national survey of landowning was ineffective. In terms of industrialization the Chinese advantage of comparative peace and stability became a developmental disadvantage. Skilled banks and lending activities in central and coastal China notwithstanding, deficient financialization was as much a barrier to capital accumulation as fiscal sovereignty. In contrast, financialization and fiscal sovereignty were the factors that boosted capitalism in Europe (Rosenthal and Wong 2005: 14–18).

As European merchants in Asia could not draw on the ready reserves of credit they were used to at home, they sought recourse to American silver. China (along with India) then found itself a "bottomless pit" for the precious metals in circulation. The influx of silver and its monetization were so vital to a now open Chinese economy that China began to suffer from currency dependency on foreign supply and off-shore exchange rates. This situation became not only economically but also politically costly. If capitalism was "*deliberately* thwarted by the state" in China (Braudel 1984: 217, 490–491, 520), that state was itself undermined by the monetary arbitrage of the silver standard determined in the rising capitalist world (Frank 1998: 134–139; Han 2009: 152–161, 295).[5] The Chinese anguish had exactly the same source as European profits and power. The cosmic sum of reparations in silver coins that Western and Japanese imperialism violently imposed on China through (drug) wars, looting, and unequal treaties is also an indispensable part of the story.

In addition to but also in spite of whatever had been underway in the preceding centuries with respect to class reconfiguration, social autonomy, machine use, and policy reforms, a sharp drop in agricultural surplus 1800–1820 appeared to hit hard. Whether China's decline (even before its Western encounter) was historically destined, and whether the Chinese record is read in a positive light (emphasizing achievements in public infrastructure and disaster relief, for example) or in a negative one (focusing on features such as autocracy), the nature and capacity of the state greatly matter. This point might be seen as an original contribution from the otherwise flawed model of AMP. The waning of a once strong and resourceful central state—never mind whether it was also part of the problem—deprived China of a political requisite for industrialization.

The new economic historians are beginning to shift the ground of the debate by removing the "Why not China?" question. A practical strategy is to destandardize the European patterns of change, asking "Why England/ Europe?" regarding the industrial revolution and "Why not England/Europe?" regarding non-Western achievements. To address the latter question it is noted, for example, that there was "a stable and integrated political order" more or less maintained by a meritocratic bureaucracy in China since around 1100 (Wong 1997: 72ff, 290). More boldly, focusing on state building, the Chinese are viewed as having invented the "modern state" with Qin (221–206 BC), its first unified, though also short lived, dynasty. The Qin unification of Chinese civilization (as opposed to mere territories) took the annals of Spring and Autumn and Warring States to accomplish. By that time, then, the Chinese state already "had many if not all of the characteristics that Max Weber defined as quintessentially modern." The "great Han system" in the next 400 years continued the Qin system and developed a rational bureaucracy that later was replicated by virtually all modern governments (Fukuyama 2011: 125–126, 134–138). The Chinese recruiting system was far more "modern" than Western ones subsequent to the Roman empire, having abandoned hereditary aristocracy centuries before Europe did and adopted civil examinations designed to be class blind. For centuries, China not only was the world's largest economy and trader, it also had sophisticated laws, rules, and administrative apparatus. Government policies and microregulations were in place, aided by standardized measurement of goods, a single currency, and a transportation network of land and water routes in all directions.

The classical puzzle is thus reversed to address "Why China?" as opposed to "Why not China?" and "Why Europe?" Evidence gathered in an eye opening literature portrays a Tang-Song and/or Ming-Qing Chinese economy and society as, in parts or overall, far more advanced than the Europeans in their prolonged "dark age."

The methodological "internalists," on the other hand, reject any comparative evaluation. They focus on what China has accomplished independently regardless of any European resemblance. Claiming anything authentically "native" or developmentally *sui generis*, however, can be tricky.[6] Even if morally appealing and intellectually coherent, internalism is nonoperational in the first place. The capitalist global parameters have increasingly and inexorably blurred demarcations between indigenous and exogenous. China's economic difficulties and political turmoil around the dynastic transfer from Ming to Qing, for instance, were by no means insulated from the seventeenth-century world crisis. The Chinese and global monetary systems were closely linked with each other, as evidenced by the serious inflation in China at the time caused by the depletion of silver inflow (Wakeman 2009: 27–35). The Sino-East Asian intermingling would be another example, which makes any judgment "independent" of regional stimulus unfeasible. After all, "the world and the region have been at the heart of the nation," and "only by integrating outside and inside can we view history in its fullness" (Duara 2009: 1, 17). Neither China nor Europe can be extracted from their respective historical positions and cross cultural references, given the ever-intensified dual process of "transnationalization" (the development of global cities and transnational classes, for example) and "translocalization" (above all, migration) (Dirlik 2011a: 294).

If industrial capitalism is considered more broadly than in its modern European manifestations, many expectations based on the European experience would have to be abandoned. Above all, magnificent "premodern" (according to the European chronology) modernity is found in China and quite a few other places in the East, near and far from a

European standpoint. According to some widely cited (though not always consistent) statistics regarding comparative economic performance, the volume of trade between Europe and Asia/the Middle East was much higher than that within Europe throughout the medieval and early modern eras. There had been more than one Silk Road and also numerous other trading routes flourishing around Asian, Arab, and Mediterranean ports and cities since the time of the Han dynasty. The Orient came to be the "greatest of all" among the world's economic regions; and China for most of the first two millennia was the largest "national" economy and market (Braudel 1984: 484ff; Arrighi 2007: 321).[7] Until 1820, the Chinese and Indian economies combined are believed to have accounted for more or less half of global production. They for instance dominated the production of finished textiles, which were to become one of the flagship trades in industrializing Europe. Competitive pressures from Asia were so great that the British had to achieve a "cotton revolution" by finding new production techniques. The search culminated in the spinning machine; the spread of spinning, together with the use of coal—which enabled the invention of the steam engine—eventually caused the shift of the world's economic center from Asia to Europe (Parthasarathi 2011: ch.6). At the peak of this "Asian age," serious scholars believe, the Asians with their two-thirds share of the global population produced four-fifths of the total global output. And the one-fifth of the global population in Europe still could not claim all of the remaining one-fifth output, which included contributions from the Africans and Americans (Frank 1998: 172–173; Nolan 2011). According to Pomeranz among others, Qing China at its splendor also reached a level of gross wealth and, in its wealthiest areas, living standards and life expectancies equivalent to or higher than those in England at the same time (2008: 96).

These contentions are not beyond controversy. Disputed, for example, is whether peasant China generally maintained only a subsistence level throughout its premodern history. Economic unevenness and widespread rural poverty were features of life, which partly explains endless peasant revolts. Still, the "Asian Age" contentions have confirmed what was authoritatively endorsed at the time as an overall assessment. Adam Smith wrote in *The Wealth of Nations* that "China is a much richer country than any part of Europe," even though there were already signs of its entering stagnation because of such problems as low wages, poverty and inadequate foreign trade ([1776]1976: 30, 70–71, 210).[8]

The debate concerning the why and why not questions focuses in the end on the economy itself. China might have been trapped in a "high-level equilibrium" or "involution." Its bountiful labor supply along with resource constraints might have limited its developmental options. In these circumstances it was only rational for people to economize on their assets rather than adopt labor-saving mechanization or capital intensive corporations (Elvin 2008: 87). Ultimately, if one compares capitalized windmills in the Netherlands, for instance, with human-oxen power in the Yangzi Delta, why should China want, or be expected, to go for industrialization? As Jan Luiten van Zanden puts it, while European entrepreneurs were forced to adopt machines in order to cut labor costs, "China didn't 'miss' the industrial revolution—it didn't need it" (2011).[9] In this view, in other words, there was nothing surprising or questionable about China not taking the path Europe took. It is only in the light of the Dutch or English initiatives that the Chinese trajectory looks puzzling: a developed commodity economy totally unprepared for an industrial breakthrough.

But useful in the comparative background would also be an overall picture of historical industrial capitalism as a process of primitive accumulation, internally through the horror of proletarianizing peasants or urban exploitation such as is portrayed by Dickens and externally through the cruelty of violent colonization or slave labor and trade. Continuously and increasingly, industrial capitalism has also been beset by resource depletion and other eco-environmental crises. Immanuel Wallerstein is not off the mark in saying that nothing is regrettable in the fact that "China, India, the Arab world and other regions" have not gone forward to capitalism; they are thus "better immunized against the toxin" (1999: 179–181). There was surely no shortage of native toxins under the old regimes, from repression to underdevelopment. But the alternative does not have to be capitalist industrialization.

Scholars draw a contrast between two models of "empire" that seem to have followed different historical logic and developmental paths. The term should be taken as free of the "empire versus nation" misconception indicated in the previous chapter. Unlike a divided Europe, the Chinese empire was for the most part politically unified and in certain respects centralized. Unlike European militarism and expansionism, China was largely inward looking and reactive to border incursions or foreign encounters. Unlike the feudal system of land concentration that paved the way for a capitalist transformation by driving the peasants to wage labor, China's petty land right and family farming conjoined with small handcraft workshops kept the direct producers on the land. Sophisticated household production also protracted a broadly self-sufficient economy and stable imperial ruling order. Culturally, if European empires had a worldview of conquests and dominance, the mandarin metaphilosophical vision stood for universal inclusiveness and civilization (Wang, G. 2006; Zhao 2011). Some of these contrasts might be partial or exaggerated, given the downplayed Sino factors of internal warfare, large landowning, class conflicts, or a parasitic agrarian bureaucracy. Nevertheless, this line of empirical reasoning is more plausible and useful than a recent trend in Chinese language publications that idealizes some of the observable demarcations noted above. Traditionalists go so far as to project a long standing and self-contained Chinese empire as "virtuous" "credible," "harmonious," and just. Lacking a critical edge, such a generalized projection betrays historical reality and enhances an illusory replay of sinological otherness. If the empire was so harmless or admirable, what could have justified and explained China's heroic and costly modern transformations?

A clarification is in order. In our modern understanding, the invention of "Asia" (as the beginning of Hegelian world history) is only part of the invention of "Europe" (as the end of that history) and, in turn, the European reinvention of the globe. In due course, the invented Asiatic stereotype proves unfounded, if only because of the capacity of the Chinese and other marginalized peoples for novelty, development, and revolutionary change. However, the Eurocentric, modern-centric and capitalist-centric outlook remains a dominant ideology. Divergence and convergence here are primarily not cultural but political matters, as legitimacy or superiority is bestowed not so much on the West per se as on capitalism, which is the essence of the West. This reminds us of the intensity and urgency of the politics of comparison, as best elucidated in the AMP and comparative history debates.

To deconstruct our spatial identities, the Eurasian narratives are of particular interest. The "European miracle" should be seen as only a part of the wider Eurasian phenomenon (Goody 2010). This "interactive zone" of "parallel integration" of West and East illustrates how and why essentialist contrasts between European and Asian exceptionalisms are flawed (Lieberman 2009: chs.5 and 6). "Great divergence" cannot be the whole story. Insofar as China's early development of commodity production is recognized, for instance, it would be necessary to place that development in a universal framework of socioeconomic evolution. Countries in the East can, as some have done, develop their own variants of "capitalism" without an industrial bourgeoisie and independently of the varieties of capitalism in the West. Capitalism might have taken a different form in the Middle Kingdom long before the nineteenth-century shock of Western impact. The same could be said about agricultural and industrial civilizations alike across conventional chronological and geographical divides. An additional conceptual implication is that the perceived divergence is still an instance of capitalism as an overarching global system, internal to modernity as a landmark of world history. The "great divergence" between Europe and Asia notwithstanding, it has always been accompanied by convergence in historical courses. The real divergence in terms of socialist modernity is examined in Part II.

# Part II

# 3

# Chinese Socialism and Global Capitalism

Marx did not foresee the socialist revolutions in economically backward national settings—the Leninist initiative broke the imperialist chains to create the first Soviet regime in Russia in 1917 and, through an entirely different path, the Maoist strategy of mobilizing rural forces brought the communists to power in China in 1949. The economic deterministic tenor is palpable in Marx's major works, as his critics agree. For him, in the last analysis people would not be free from the "realm of necessity" without a material foundation of abundance. And even a successful socialist revolution would not be able to hold up against the remnants or return of the old social structures and relations. For a comparatively less developed country such as Germany in his time, "the successive phases of its normal development" by "the economic law of motion of modern society" could not be skipped by either "bold leaps" or "legal enactments." This, in the strongest terms he once employed, is intrinsically "not a question of the higher or lower degree of development of the social antagonisms that result from the natural laws of capitalist production. It is a question of these laws themselves, of these tendencies working with iron necessity towards inevitable results." With respect to the necessary modern transformation, "the country that is more developed industrially only shows, to the less developed, the image of its own future" (1867).

Marx is here speaking about industrial and economic advances, not capitalism. The two, as was argued in Part I, are different as separable historical processes and in terms of reference and should not be conflated conceptually. Moreover, pondering the *Narodnik* thesis about Russian renewal, Marx came to the conclusion that history is open to hitherto unknown potentialities. Addressing the question of whether Russia could avoid capitalism in its developmental path, he struck a nondeterministic note by confirming the feasibility of a direct transition to communism of the village *mir*, which seemed to have inherited a dualism of communal property and all the social relations springing from it on the one hand and some development of individuality from sideline private house, cultivation, and consumption on the other, while retaining a historical element of collectivism on a national scale. Being the contemporary of Western capitalist production, the Russian commune could "appropriate its fruits without subjecting itself to its *modus operandi*" ([1881]1989: 352–356). The conditions would be a Russian revolution in synchrony with revolutionary movements in the capitalist world, to secure the needed working class dominance and internationalist aid to Russia based on European industrialism to provide material goods and enable technological transfer (Shanin 1983: part II). This new vista allowed Marx to disclaim any "master key" in historical understanding. Instead of a dogma of an unavoidable capitalist stage, he came to endorse a multilinear notion of societal development.

Less noted, however, is that Marx also underscored the role of revolutionary agency in such a transition against complacency and opportunism. "The finest chance ever offered by history to a people" to bypass "all the fatal vicissitudes of the capitalist regime," he warned, could be lost quickly ([1877]1942: 352–353). The historical opportunity of utilizing existing collectivist arrangements to skip capitalism had to be seized in Russia or any other part of the capitalist periphery. This conception of political determination, echoing his earlier remarks on an emerging "Chinese socialism" as discussed in Chapter 2, is a theoretical break-through in the Marxist conception of history. Searching for universality in Western and non-Western evolution and in capitalist and noncapitalist innovations is a riveting and necessary project. It takes us back to Marx, to internationalism, to the minimum and maximum programs of the twentieth-century social revolutions and, in a handy axiom for trans-formative politics, to the "communist hypothesis" (Badiou 2010).

In peasant China, a communist revolution, being simultaneously national and social in nature, was possible because the young and small working class was still stronger than the scanty national bourgeoisie. This was so due to an intervening variable of powerful foreign capital, and also a worker-peasant alliance with the poor peasants including hired labor in agriculture being proportionally much more numerous and poorer than urban wage laborers, while suffering aggregate forces of exploitation and deprivation. Rural China was thus far from an unlikely soil for communist agitation and organization in a broadly defined land revolution. In the event the communist "base areas" were gained and lost and regained throughout an extremely hard, prolonged struggle, which sustained the unity of party, government, and masses, and nurtured a valiant red army that eventually turned the world upside down.

For the orthodox Marxists, the nature of the Chinese communist revolution as a peasant revolution with a socialist goal and prospect is a problem. But many of their critiques are theoretically unsound, and the level of articulation the Chinese have achieved, ever since Mao Zedong's *The Chinese Revolution and the Chinese Communist Party* (1939), has not been surpassed. The emblematic charge that without a large membership of workers "the CCP was a party of middle-class leaders and peasant followers" (Faulkner 2013: 256) is both factually false and analytically superficial. The industrial working class, however small, was a vital component in the revolution. And the daily popular struggle found its optimal expression in the party's mass line politics. More to the point, it was due to China's oppressed "class" position in global capitalism that the Chinese party emerged as an innovative proletarian organization, and that a "bourgeois democratic" revolution carried within itself a socialist ambition, as further elaborated in Mao's *On New Democracy* (1945). "Class" cannot be a positivist sociological category as its defining identities are rooted in the dominance of global capitalist political economy.

The vantage point for understanding China that historical materialism offers is that only by taking capitalism as a central reference to gauge the Chinese modern trajectory can issues of the fundamental historicity and justice of China's communist revolution, and hence of the legitimation of reform in partial repudiation of that revolution, be clarified. At stake is Chinese socialism, once enormously popular and unprecedented in ambition and scale, in its greatest ever crisis as a result of the present transformation, which has evidently departed from socialism. Yet most of the positive reformist developments are directly attributable to the foundational work painstakingly accomplished during decades of socialist modernization—from essential infrastructure to an exceptionally well educated and healthy workforce. Despite serious erosions in recent years, China continues to lead the developing world in the United Nations Development Program ranking by nearly all the key indicators relative to its per capita income.

Continuities between Chinese socialism and socialist reform would thus be crucial for the latter to succeed as judged by its avowed objectives. Severing the two projects so as to complete a capitalist transformation would be suicidal for the reformers—reform fails by definition as soon as it becomes "revolutionary." The very meaning of socialist "reform" entails opposition to a wholesale capitalist transition; and any "revolution" in the historically postrevolutionary context would logically denote counterrevolution. Missing this counterrevolutionary nature of a neoliberalized reform by underestimating or denying the extraordinary character of the Chinese communist revolution as a *"new democratic"* one leading to socialist rather than capitalist transformations in the first place, those who view the postsocialist reform as rather representing "the consolidation of the bourgeois revolution" of 1949 (Davidson 2012: 621, 252) are paying an unintended price. They have granted a capitalist integration a natural validity or historical justification.[1] This is fully in line with official Marxism in China arguing for an ultimately unskippable capitalist development (see next chapter).

Abandoning socialism in the name of reform, however, is precisely what has been happening and is openly advocated by an intellectual elite speaking for the wealthy and powerful who have advanced their positions by exploiting the loopholes of the system. The problem is that totally embracing capitalist integration cannot be socially desirable in China and has been resisted not least through mounting "mass incidents." The demands in such conflicts are often anticapitalist with regard to land loss, labor rights, abuses of power, and other forms of social injustice. In this context "socialism" makes more sense as protest than as official language. In the same vein, government countermeasures in the name of "maintaining stability," often physically or symbolically violent, are detested and ineffective, being perceived as morally wrong and offensive in a nominally retained "people's republic" and "workers' and peasants' state."

It is thus important to reconfirm that the communist revolution in China was an epic struggle for freedom and prosperity for the Chinese nation and people. The "people's war" was groundbreaking in surrounding the cities from the countryside to seize state power. New China then pursued its own brand of socialist industrialization. As far as modernization is concerned, socialism turned out to be a shortcut to popularly desirable socioeconomic results without capitalist tortures. Contradictions or missteps notwithstanding, the communists in power were everywhere effective modernizers and nation builders. Structural transformations of the economy and society enabled self-reliant development of the country based on its nationalized industries and cooperated agriculture. Thanks to this specific local path, China's nationalization and collectivization differed greatly in method and process from the earlier experiences of coercion and violence in the Soviet Union (Lin 2006: 65–81). Within a few decades, the country succeeded not only in laying an industrial foundation but also in creating a rudimentary social security system for the world's largest national population. And it did so without the typical costs of primitive accumulation ranging from rural deprivation and urban sweatshops to conquests, genocides, and slavery. In terms of raising food production and feeding its population, in particular, Chinese policies since 1949 have been very successful, "so much so that it is fair to say that China uses its available land far more productively than any other large-scale agricultural producer on the planet" (Bramall 2009: 226, 231). Against overwhelming odds, the Chinese communists achieved "the most massive—and perhaps the most heroic—revolution in world history." Its necessity and validity, as Maurice Meisner contends, lie in the simple and vast fact that "few events in world history have done more to better the lives of more people" (1999: 1, 12).

Socialist modernity in China entailed not only national development encompassing human and social development, but also a thoroughly participatory polity that engaged citizens in work units, residential communities, and mass campaigns for social change (reducing illiteracy, improving general health, and getting women into gainful work, for example). The revolution had thus transformed traditional China and thereby the country's position in the world. These transformations were simultaneously cultural in perceptions and aspirations. Chinese communism, after all, has creatively "Sinified" Marxism—Mao's "mountain valley Marxism" is exemplary of the Chinese ability to take advantage of diverse resources transcending national borders.[2] Internationally, revolutionary China set up a model in peripheral capitalism, showing how things could be turned around by the oppressed and exploited people locally and nationally (cf. Therborn 2012: 8–9).

The revolution had in particular solved China's age old land problem, addressing which was central not only to agricultural production and rural class relations, but also to the state and the grassroots from which it sprang. Apart from unequal land ownership, exploitative rent, and clan power, the revolution also eliminated a more "modern" element of bureaucratic-financial capital in the countryside. The latter expanded since the mid to late nineteenth century into entrenched nexuses of landlordism, warlordism, usury, local bureaucracy, and trading monopolies, relying on profit seeking brokers who had replaced the old gentry elite. This trend of "state involution" (Duara 2010) had political backing from corrupt central, local, and village autocracies. In dismantling these forces the land revolution was necessarily also a cultural process of education and socialization. It was through such a process that the poor peasants in China could begin to shake off their primordial subordinate status and mentality and attain a new social subjectivity through constructing a new social order.[3]

As is generally agreed among historical sociologists, the lack of thoroughgoing land reform is a major developmental obstacle in large parts of the postcolonial world. The fact that China has done a great deal better—in meeting basic needs, alleviating poverty, raising the general standard of living, and giving political recognition to the social standing of labor and the common people (as in the Maoist legacy)—is an awesome testimony. It carries a universal implication: By transforming "feudal" structures and relations, land reform, broadly defined to also include cooperative farming, eradicates backward and reactionary social power while empowering hitherto subjugated and marginalized classes. In so doing it can be a decisive promoter of economic growth and social development. Barrington Moore's axiom informed by his macrocomparative studies is prudent: modernization entails and requires "a revolutionary break with the past" (1966: 431). Even if this axiom should not be taken literally everywhere, historical evidence has amply vindicated the superiority of revolutionary paths in transforming large, poor, agrarian, illiterate, and patriarchal societies.[4] This affirmation is not confined to the communist conviction; it is a broader liberal consensus not bypassing even astute cold warriors (e.g., Huntington 1968: 266). Empirically, as Theda Skocpol explains, successful social revolutions have "given birth to nations whose power and autonomy markedly surpassed their own prerevolutionary pasts and outstripped other countries in similar circumstances" (1979: 3). More generally, as Condorcet puts it, the essence of revolution is freedom (Arendt 1963: 21). Transcending unavoidable sociopolitical upheavals, revolution "became a normative principle...as modernity's *techne* and the right to revolution as freedom's due" (Douzinas 2010: 92).

Socialist modernization, difficult and costly as it must be, not only is rationally conceived as faster and more just than the capitalist approaches, it is the only viable option in countries like China. The contrast between the options, revolutionary and colonial modernity, is instructive: those choosing the former strive to establish their places in the world through liberation struggles; those choosing the latter are brought into history "not as subjects but as objects of the transformative powers of capitalism" (Dirlik 1994: 22).[5] However "Asiatic" this contrast may sound in distinguishing between active historical subjects and passive historical objects, the point is that in breaking free from the "law" of capitalist development, the revolutionary and socialist movements can be more effective in overcoming the anguish of backwardness. China is thus not merely a part of but also apart from Asia, and, for that matter, from peripheral capitalism at large. Further still, if, historically speaking, the communist revolutions succeeded only where capitalism failed to develop a society, is there not a causal linkage between capitalism and *under*development and, by extension, between capitalist failures and the noncapitalist alternative? Conversely and conceptually, has not the revolutionary causation between "socialism and development" established itself in the cases of China and others through their surmounting the predicament of "socialism and backwardness"?

In this light the earlier achievements of the communist revolutions and socialist transformations, to which hundreds of millions of men and women devoted their lives, must be defended. In China, the collective endeavor to achieve national and social liberation, equality, and prosperity has conferred on the PRC an ultimate sense of pride and legitimacy. In particular, committed to meeting basic needs by developing an organizational capacity, the postrevolutionary state supported a "public good regime" for sustained public investment and management in physical infrastructure as much as in human capital. Rudimentary but free or inexpensive public services in housing, schooling, transportation, health care, and so on were inclusive. The medical system emphasized mass sanitation, universal immunization, antiepidemic works and preventive medicine. With respect to "women's liberation," "state feminism" was not without its own pitfalls, but new China's record of pursuing gender equality was outstanding, despite many problems such as in political representation.

On the other hand, the communist project in China has taken quite a few misguided and disastrous steps. It entailed enormous personal sacrifice, including internal purges prompted by fears of defeat or threats of subversion. It also involved catastrophic economic adventures. The Great Leap Forward and Cultural Revolution were meant to address such problems as sectoral inequalities and bureaucratic privileges, yet they failed badly. These mistakes are no doubt utterly indefensible. But it is still important that we view things in perspective. The communist endeavor has a dark side because the enemies along the way were extremely brutal and powerful, because the Chinese undertaking (which diverged from the Soviet path) was largely unprecedented, because the postrevolutionary state had to keep running a quasi-war economy while being confronted with formidable geopolitical adversities, and in the end also because the intrinsic contradictions of the new system undercut its formation and consolidation. In other words, China's relational position with capitalism in its historical and international contexts explains the country's limited policy options and their underlining rationality and coherence (Lin 2006: 62–74). Cooperatization and collectivization in the 1950s is an outstanding example of the difficult and original Chinese search, in the face of perilous international conditions, as a necessary move constitutive of China's self-repositioning to counter imperialist aggression and global strategy. It did involve open discussions and debates within and without the party over the phases, pace, and priorities during the "transition from new democracy to socialism" through semisocialist forms of organization (Ma 2012). Urban bias, a common developmental headache but especially salient in Chinese development, is another example. It was persistent under an extraordinary developmental state striving to finance industrialization deemed imperative for new China to survive and prosper. All considered, there was simply no assured peace or chance for the country to follow any path of "normal" development.

The practitioners of Chinese socialism were keenly aware of their errors and limitations long before smart revisionists and historical nihilist crusaders rose to attack everything communist, and the bold attempts at surmounting it are also part of the story. One of Mao's better-known explanations for launching a cultural revolution was precisely to allow "the dark side of our work to be exposed openly, completely, and from bottom up." The argument is thus not about revealing or concealing moral dilemmas or policy blunders associated with the Maoist strategy but about how they can be truthfully evaluated, as they have engendered intense feelings and emotions. For instance, at the peak of Great Leap, Mao actually tried to cool down an adventurist "communist infantilism" widespread also among the communist leaders.[6] The popular image at the time of new China advancing in defiance of capitalist blockage also had its own cogent appeal. As to the ideologically charged issue of death due to famine, it is necessary for objective criticisms of official census data and many frequently cited yet dubious figures derived mainly from those data be taken seriously (Wertheim 1995; Ball 2006; Jin 2009; Yang 2013).[7] Statistical manipulation features a growing "famine industry" racing for body counts (Benton and Lin 2009: Introduction; Vukovich 2012: ch.4). Carl Riskin, among an authoritative group of economists, economic historians, and demographers inside and outside China, cautions against inconclusive numbers. He also insists on a differentiation between "the indications of hunger and hardship" and "the kinds of *qualitative* evidence of mass famine that have accompanied other famines of comparable (if not equal) scale, including earlier famines in China" (1998). Such a comparative perspective is necessary for better analytical insight and accuracy, as exemplified in Mike Davis's documentation of "imperialist famines" including those in old China (2001: part IV). The responsibility of colonialism for tens of millions of deaths cannot be evaded, for example.[8]

Moreover, even a devastating famine cannot obliterate the larger fact about Chinese socialism: that the government had otherwise demonstrated its commitment to basic food security for the population, that China had achieved a much greater and faster reduction in infant mortality and increase in life expectancy than most other poor countries in the same period (Dreze and Sen 2002: chs 3 and 4; Sen 2000), and that the Great Leap was intended to attain national self-sufficiency while improving lives and life chances in rural and urban China. Looking at mortality trends in China throughout the twentieth century, researchers have also shown that rates had been regularly and consistently higher before 1949 than after, taking into account the worst years of famine, 1959–60.[9] On the basis of such horizontal as well as vertical comparisons, Utsa Patnaik asks why India did not experience a "famine" when its total food output per capita was actually less than that of China, where, moreover, the egalitarian rural structure should have mitigated any crisis of food supply (2002: 64–65). To be sure, output is not the same as availability, given destitution, pricing, entitlement, and other policy or market factors.[10] But a telling phenomenon is that a questionable computational procedure utilizing a calculation of "excess deaths" based on (pedantically yet unrealistically) estimated fertility rates (which allows "death" to happen without birth in the first place) "does not seem to have been ever applied by demographers and economists before, and never applied in contexts other than China" (Patnaik 2002: 53).

Likewise, the "verdict" characterizing the Cultural Revolution as Mao's "great purge" and a "ten-year national catastrophe" is one-sided. In hindsight, it seems quite clear to many in China, for little reason beyond a judgment after the fact that it was premature, that the movement was totally misconceived. Launched to rectify or remove from power "capitalist roaders" in a "new bourgeoisie" within the Communist Party, the Cultural Revolution in search of its yet-to-be-configured target was bound to fail, losing its way and the cause itself. It ended up persecuting the wrong people for wrong reasons, confusing contradictions between the people and their enemies with those among the people themselves, as articulated in Mao's own *Correctly Handling the Contradictions among the People* (1957). And the tragedy did not stop there. More ironic still is that the reaction to cultural revolutionary excesses had allowed or perhaps even accelerated the emergence of an evermore monstrous bureaucratic capitalist class. Counterfactual speculation about where China could have been today without the Cultural Revolution might be futile. But the daunting reality is that just as such a class is consolidating its power, another cultural revolution, now with a real target and urgency, is a sheer impossibility or already lost. "Revolution is dead." The radicals do still say "long live the revolution," but that no longer resounds. Such is the dialectic and irony of history.

The adventurous, ultramodern policies in Maoist China may have been defeated catastrophically. But judged with common sense by both intention and outcomes, they are still categorically distinguishable from anything like deliberate "starving" of people or "genocide," as represented in an influential literature. The intended goals of these campaigns also had a utopian, noble, egalitarian, and emancipatory character, which encouraged concrete practices in that direction with some important and positive results. It was in the Great Leap and Cultural Revolutionary years, for example, that China decisively improved its rural irrigation system and agricultural infrastructure in general, which directly enhanced the success of subsequent rural reforms in the early 1980s. It was during the same periods, as another example, that such urban privileges as medical expertise, educational reforms, and cultural entertainments were extended to benefit the peasants in remote villages (Gao 2008: 13–30). Bureaucracy was tackled with a genuinely democratic impulse for realizing the creativity and self-organization of the masses. The high degree of popular participation puzzled formal democracy theorists, promoting the political scientist Giovanni Sartori to complain that the concept of participation "is by now so ill-defined that it might even lead to the finding that (on a participation measure) the fullest democracy ever to exist was China at the time of its so-called cultural revolution" (1987: 183–184).

The Cultural Revolution was in truth an era of profound contradictions, "of both great successes and spectacular failures, and both in abundant measure" (Meisner 1989b: 352).[11] Beyond the debacles very extensively and often also highly ideologically recounted in academic works as well as personal memoirs, the other side of history is crying out to be honestly accounted for in equal measure—daring, idealistic, high minded collective movements, upsurges of productive capacity in the economy and society, democratic experiments in the political and managerial spheres. True defenders of the socialist legacies cannot be unprincipled apologists. The politics of debating Chinese socialism is not about restoring any past but about learning lessons for its rejuvenation.

If the cultural revolutionary stance was uncompromising toward capitalism, it was nevertheless Mao who took the strategic initiative to end China's international isolation by approaching the capitalist West. The PRC gained a seat on the UN Security Council in 1971, and Nixon's visit to Beijing and later the normalization of Sino-US diplomatic relations followed. Mao's move remains controversial among socialists inside and outside China, but the point here is simply that the actual alteration of China's traditional anticapitalist stance did not happen until so-called ultra leftism had been thoroughly discredited under the post-Mao regime. Before long, it became unambiguous that the monumental letdown of the Cultural Revolution was also a great irony due to a great revenge: The failure to eradicate the privileged "cadre lords" and bureaucratic apparatuses is nowhere better demonstrated than in the formation of a variant of capitalism or "national capitalism" in China (Anderson 2010)—"bureaucratic capitalism" (Meisner 1996: 300–345). The phrase brings in a feeling of *déjà vu,* as in the communist vocabulary it had referred only to the family monopolies of China's political economy under a Guomindang kleptocracy before 1949.

The erosion of socialism in China is undoubtedly also the work of a "peaceful evolution" through capitalist integration. The reformist plan, however, has in reality been overrun not so much by the logic of marketification as by a reform project itself hijacked in the absence of any effective political mechanism of checks and corrections. Even under a heavily disguised (capitalist) ideology of anti-ideology, one does not have to be "ideological" to see how a gross undoing of the revolution has taken place—typically through brutal capitalist accumulation and its predictable social and environmental consequences. The degradation of the "people" in general and workers (rural, urban, and migrant) in particular is unmistakably accompanied by their physical and social deprivation. Widely witnessed are not only income polarization and inhumane or unlawful working conditions, wage arrears, and corruption, but also hyperspeculation and consumption in the marketplace and pollution induced occupational diseases and public health hazards. Class, ethnic, gender, and sectoral inequalities are all on the rise.

With an expanding economy, China seems a more significant player in world affairs today. But it has also for some time become heavily dependent on external market and energy resources. China's accession to the World Trade Organization (WTO) in 2001 was based on the condition that the country "substantially open its market in banking, insurance, securities, fund management and other financial services" (Branstetter and Lardy 2008: 658). According to the leading US negotiator Charlene Barshefsky, China's commitment to liberalization and corresponding concessions were "broader actually than any World Trade Organization member has made" (quoted in Panitch and Gindin 2012: 293). More astonishingly, such an agreement was signed without public consultation and was not even immediately available in the Chinese language. The PRC Supreme Court also pledged that in case of any inconsistency, domestic laws would comply with WTO statutes. As China's trade surplus and foreign reserves, mainly in dollars, have continued to pile up (Nolan 2012: 4–5), it has in particular and in effect been financing American consumption and the US debt contrary to the interest of Chinese labor, markets, environment, financial security, and much else. In so doing "Chinese economic dynamism is held hostage to US fiscal and monetary policy" (Harvey 2005: 142).

Making deep concessions in negotiating WTO membership, China gave up a golden opportunity to use its size and weight to gain counterconcessions for itself, as for the developing world, in matters of trade barrier, market protection, capital account control, and international division of labor. Before it joined WTO, China's total trade as a share of GDP was 43 percent. By 2007, its 68 percent trade-to-GDP ratio was "well above the average of those other countries." On the other hand, its average tariffs on industrial products were under 9 percent, compared with 27 percent in Brazil, 31 percent in Argentina, 32 percent in India, and 37 percent in Indonesia (Panitch and Gindin 2012: 293). And these numbers have since only gotten worse. It is a telling comparison that "the US would retain extraordinary provisions for tariffs to defend its domestic market against...Chinese imports, whereas China would concede to a brutally swift dismantling of protection for local farmers and manufacturers and vastly

increased freedoms for foreign firms and financial services"
(Wade 2004:151). This extraordinary policy preference for
foreign over domestic firms was shown in "the tax system,
subsidies, trade regulations, and access to finance," to the
extent that "domestic and foreign capital effectively operated
within different legal parameters" with "the more favorable
laws applied to foreign, not domestic capital" (Panitch and
Gindin 2012: 296).

The results were astounding. According to authoritative
estimates, by 2005 more than 70 percent of the value-added
profits of China's electronics and information industry,
90 percent of the production and market of its motor industry, and 80 percent of the management of its machinery and
chemical industries had been controlled by foreign capital.[12]
The drift has not since halted. In 2010, the foreign sector
in the Chinese economy overwhelmed the state sector by
13 percent (Zhao, H. 2012). Also importing inflation from
the United States, China has been losing its economic and
financial sovereignty while witnessing a rapid expansion of
comprador capital. A distorted national economy then suffers mutually reinforcing dependencies on foreign markets
and technologies, as well as a deficiency of domestic demand
because of intense labor exploitation (Lu 2012).

In these circumstances public domination as the foundation of a socialist economy as required in the PRC constitution
is fading away. According to an official release by the State
Statistics Bureau, the proportion the public sector contributes
to China's national economy is less than one-third. Even the
industries in sectors where there is a natural monopoly are
being divided, corporationalized, or partially contracted out
in preparation for privatization. The rush in March 2013 to
dissolve the Rail Ministry, a remaining symbol of the socialist industrial stronghold, met with popular suspicion and
protest. People gathered to say goodbye to the soon-to-be-tak-
en-down sign on the building; many were in tears. The statistician Zhao Huaquan offers a thorough study of the trend
since 2004, when a mixed economy was still dominated by
public ownership. The pattern seemed to have broken down

by 2010—as the total economy doubled in size, its nonpublic components grew faster, at 2.3 times (in which private economy grew more than 2.8 times and foreign capital 2.1 times). In contrast, the proportion of the public sector went straight downhill from 57 percent in 2003 to 48.6 percent in 2006, 35.2 percent in 2008, and 26.9 percent in 2010, including state sector 22.2 percent and collective sector 4.7 percent. By 2010, except for agriculture (taking into account the formal public ownership of the land), transportation, and telecommunications, public domination appeared to exist nowhere in the Chinese economy. Of the growing nonpublic sector in the same period (from 43 percent to 73 percent) individual business took 2.2 percent, private enterprises 45.7 percent, and foreign/joint ventures 25.1 percent. Among the nation's workforce 60–70 percent were engaged in wage labor in the private and/or foreign sectors. Meanwhile, of the total assets of the 16 strategic industries considered to constitute the national economic lifeline, state capital made up only 35 percent, of which no more than 23 percent was under absolute state control (Zhao, H. 2012).

It should be noted that the strong development of private economy in China's reform has relied heavily on direct fostering by central and local governments as well as support from state-owned enterprises (SOEs). As privately owned enterprises (POEs) tend to be in short cycle businesses with lower investment and higher profits, SOEs by nature and function engage more in longer cycle production with larger investment and smaller or even negative or uncertain returns. SOEs are thus likely to be POEs' most reliable and economical suppliers of raw materials, fuel resources, and infrastructural services. The difficulty small businesses find accessing credit from state banks is a real problem, but in the fuller picture, as indicated above, preferential policies are in place favoring private and export sectors with tax breaks and other incentives. Without state facilitation, the private sector would not have developed so rapidly and predominantly.

In the course of such a paradigm change, China also missed the opportunity of demanding technological transfers from the advanced economies, making the earlier slogan "exchange market for technology" a mockery. Firm after firm and industry after industry, the Chinese forewent such demands, leaving their manufacturing at the low end of the global productive chain. Only very recently labor intensive sectors of China's export oriented industries have begun to decline. Multinationals are moving away, or will be, to cheaper places. Limited industrial upgrading is happening with the surge of capital intensive and high-value-added production (Du 2012). China exports heavy machinery and is now the largest exporter of electronics with technological components. But despite significant progresses in research and development (R&D) mostly made in SOEs, the country's high-technology exports are still entirely controlled by multinationals and foreign companies (Nolan 2012: 84–94). The more technology intensive manufacturers are either foreign invested or still dependent on foreign monopolized core technologies. Moreover, this slow movement up the value chain has been paid for by two generations of semi-sweatshop workers and severe degradation of the country's precious natural environment and resources. If China had leaned to more self-reliant development and innovation it could have negotiated fairer and more balanced terms of trade against capitalist financial and technological monopolies. It would perhaps also have boosted local patents—given its proud historical and socialist experiences of awesome achievements in science and technology. Some combination of both would have brought the Chinese economy to a more autonomous and advanced level, and also fostered a cleaner environment, than prevails today.

The Chinese political economy and its changing nature and direction can be appreciated only in the global context and epochal conditions, and in relation to the larger "southern question." To secure profits, capitalism keeps expanding while retaining its tendencies of concentration, centralization, and financialization. Further from the Braudelian distinction between competitive markets and monopoly capitalism, the latter's "imperialist rent" is sourced from the surplus value of mass production on the peripheries. Capital accumulation, which defines capitalism in all its successive historical forms, is driven by profit and rent maximization: capitalism has "depended from the beginning (European mercantilism) on the production and reproduction of global polarization." Thus imperialism is not so much the "highest stage" as a "permanent phase" of capitalism.[13] If the development of monopolies at the end of the nineteenth century transformed the fundamental structures of the capitalist mode of production, the new waves of globalization since the late twentieth century seem to have revived those structures by the timely transformation of China and other "emerging markets" in the south "into a new growth regime" (Aglietta 2008).

Conversely, as a weighty part of the global market and its game of "racing to the bottom," China's movement has far reaching international implications. Immediately, "China's dramatic capitalist development affected economic activity everywhere, forcing industrial restructuring not only at home but also abroad and determining global commodity prices" (Panitch and Gindin 2012: 293). If the Zhujiang Delta becomes one of the most dynamic centers of accumulation through manufacturing for the world, then "this sets base-line standards everywhere with respect to labor costs, acceptable conditions of work, technological mixes, union organizing, and the like." Moreover, "deindustrialization of the rest of the world (even in low-wage countries like Mexico and Brazil) occurs as the China powerhouse takes over" (Harvey 2006: 112–113). Not to mention China's controversial foreign direct investment in Africa or Latin America. The process could repeat itself elsewhere. But in a further perspective, if socialism still makes any sense inside China with respect to labor, land, and other social and environmental struggles, it could also do so transnationally. And the Chinese movement is only constitutive of a broader global one for an alternative world.

# 4

# The Politics of China's Self-Positioning

To position China in the current history of modern capitalism is to look into the relationship between the two as they converge or diverge in their macro socioeconomic and political movements. The self-positioning of China is ultimately a matter of political choice at a time when capitalism has become incorporated into or internal to Chinese development. Yet also relevant is the conception of capitalism's essential historicity, that it is only a very particular form with a relatively short history and presumably an end, "which leaves open the possibility of organizing human subsistence in more socially equitable and ecologically less destructive ways" (Wood 2009: 55). Only when capitalism is taken as neither globally irresistible (thus as localized) nor the only imaginable historical horizon (thus as involving our compliance) can the depth, complexities, and possibilities of national developments—continuing from postcolonial or socialist "new nation" building—be adequately appreciated.

However, alternatives—especially a socially desirable, feasible, and democratic alternative to the capitalist universe—seem far out of reach under an evermore globally penetrating ideology of capitalist superiority and inevitability. This is so in spite of the historical calamities of capitalism and its ongoing adventures and destructions in the global south and north alike and in spite of the anticapitalist social movements arising in a postcommunist era from locally mobilized resistance to transnational social forums and "occupy" protests. The survival of the Nordic social democracies (and a lingering ambition for a "European social model") in the face of neoliberal offensives could be an explanation, as it shows significant systemic flexibility of inclusion and self-readjustment. The vanishing of the Soviet bloc as a challenge, physically as much as ideologically, offers another reason-cum-manifestation. In the same vein, the resilience and arrogance of capitalism are nowhere better demonstrated than in its transformation of China—"neoliberalism with Chinese characteristic" (Harvey 2005: ch.5). As noted in Chapter 1, capitalism expands through, and depends on, a "spatial fix" in neglected or debarred outlying areas. China's contribution by shifting its position vis-à-vis the intervening geoeconomy and geopolitics of regional and global order is spectacular, and "in part an unintended consequence of the neoliberal turn in the advanced capitalist world" (Harvey 2005: 121).

The self-positioning of the PRC can then be tested by the disparities between its stated aims and purposes on the one hand and its actual policies and capabilities for adapting or transcending the capitalist paradigm of development on the other. Official China has after all not formally abandoned socialism in its self-identity, insisting instead that the reforms are in line with the country's present developmental stage of "primary socialism." The revenge of history, however, is widely felt. China entered the era of "reform and opening" on the promise of selective introduction of market mechanisms in a "shallow" globalization in exchange for capital, technologies, and managerial skills. The intention, endorsed by a broad consensus, was to break both the Cold War blockages externally and a closed political power internally. The key idea was "making use" of advanced economies for China's own ends. Before long, however, that promising phrase came to sound satirical. As China itself, by virtue of its skilled yet low paid workforce and its vast markets and foreign reserves (read "inverted subsidy"), has surely been made full use of, rather than the other way around.

The question for us here is thus not whether China as it stands defies capitalism as a developmental necessity or "end of history"; it does not. Reformist China has on the contrary played a big role in protracting the global system (and helped with its chaotic rescue operations to bail out troubled financial regimes). As a willing participant in globalization, China has not only acted as an alternately submissive or reluctant collaborator with the capitalist superpowers in international affairs, but also directly or indirectly aided them economically. The question is whether socialism nevertheless remains relevant to Chinese development with a global impact, or whether there is still any prospect of China's returning to a position from which capitalism can be resisted and eventually taken over. This question should be legitimately asked in both present and future tenses. Does not the retained goal of constructing a "socialist market economy" in the constitution and public rhetoric necessarily impose some limit on profit-driven bureaucratic and private capital? Can the Chinese people in their collective agency hold on to the socialist aspiration in the first place? In an opposite scenario, is not the threat of a Chinese variant of a capitalist dictatorship overpowering? (Historically, fascism based on state corporatism as much as repression was a shared European and Asian experience.) More generally, the question is whether "global modernity" has really eliminated any (potential of) space for local distinction and alternatives: Is it ultimately feasible to replace the monopolistic and destructive power of a capitalist (as opposed to Western) world order?

The current policies and conditions in China could not be farther from what a socialist position would require, even according to the party's own critically compromised promises. Above all, losing the ground of national self-determination is losing the precondition for any alternative to global standardization. As indicated in Chapter 3, China's essential autonomy since before and especially after its WTO accession has been eroded by swelling foreign control over the Chinese economy, including part of its strategic and banking sectors. Privatization of SOEs in the 1990s resulted in massive layoffs, interruption of production, embezzlement of state assets, and foreign acquisitions. Private and foreign shareholders have entered the state sector to partake in decision making while receiving dividends previously going to the state treasury and national public wealth. Quite a few policy makers advocate further reorganization of the remaining large SOEs into multinationals, which would change the nature of state industries altogether. The fact that, enjoying various sorts of preferential treatment, foreign capital has grown aggressively in China indicates a fundamental shift in the Chinese developmental approach from self-reliance to global dependency. Problems of national economic security and foreign trade balance indicate China's structural distortion, with an overrun export sector in which both supply and marketing are externally dependent.

Meanwhile, as an "absolute principle" in Deng Xiaoping's doctrine, growth continues to be prioritized at all costs, allowing developmentalism or, even more crudely, GDPism to dominate policy thinking and making in China. The damage due to insufficient national autonomy has also been laid bare, especially during the credit crunch in a troubled global economy with sluggish recovery of imports in the United States and financial meltdowns in Europe since 2008, which hit a deeply globalized Chinese economy hard. The structural quandaries have accumulated so intensely in China that, as is widely admitted, nothing less than a total reorientation could offer the national economy a chance of rebalancing. In other words, the pattern of Chinese development has to be changed and recentered on domestic production and consumption. This is also a moral imperative, in view of a Chinese scene hardly recognizable as socialist: segregation between wealthy gated residential compounds and ordinary buildings or shabby and crowded "urban villages" used to house migrant workers is one example; the designation of automobile manufacture as a "pillar industry" is another. The cars produced in and exported from China are mainly foreign brands assembled locally by the foreign controlled multinationals. The industry might have been good for short term GDP calculation and helped to fashion a growing "middle class" which separates itself in lifestyle and aspirations from blue labor and the common people. But Chinese cities are beset by traffic jams, unruly parking lots blocking sidewalks, heavy pollution, and rising prices for petroleum, over half of its surging consumption has to be imported.

In the realm of social policies, the first round of market driven health service reforms was officially and rightly declared a "total failure" (as concluded by the State Council's development research commission) because of its outcome of commonly unaffordable hospital bills. The second round has sought to repair the damage and achieve a mixed scheme of universal coverage for basic care. Yet its guideline remains to lean on market incentives. Similarly, in education, while nine-year compulsory schooling is being implemented, the "professionalization" of rural system by dissolving tens of thousands of village schools for larger, more uniform ones away from scattered villages makes school attendance a daily struggle in many places, especially those stranded by family difficulties and girls. Children of migrant workers are still frequently excluded from regular urban public schools. Universities tend to turn their backs on smart young people from poor families, offering only meager scholarships as compared with their lavish spending elsewhere. Fees can be doubled or raised even more in the third and lower tier colleges, whose students are likely to be rural and poorer. The government has done nothing so far to address this absurd disparity. The fact that education is no longer free for all is one of the biggest losses in the transformation of Chinese socialism. Even worse, none of these policy reforms that have directly affected the wellbeing of the nation and people were discussed or approved democratically through proper public consultations and popular input. The constitutionally and legally stipulated rights of citizens in China to information, participation, and supervision are ignored and wasted.

Popular resentment is strongest against the new elites who have combined economic and political fortunes: "As political families move into business, private tycoons are entering the political sphere."[1] A telling institutional factor, as deplored in China's massive Internet, is that "the 'people's deputies' [to the NPC] have nothing to do with the people." Apart from the mainly decorative members from cadres and the professional ranks, the legislature is filled with rich and well connected notables from business and other elite circles.[2] Likewise, the Communist Party's class basis has undergone an astounding change since its sixteenth congress in 2002, when private entrepreneurs, classified as "advanced elements in the new social strata," were welcomed into the party. According to the 2013 annual Blue Book published by the Chinese Academy of Social Sciences (CASS), one-third of China's quasi-capitalists are formally "communists." Of those who own more than 100 million *yuan* (about $16 million), 53 percent are party members, and many also assume the position of party branch secretary in their own companies.[3] Seven of the nation's richest men attended the eighteenth party congress in November 2012; each is a multibillionaire. Among China's super rich, with a collective family net worth of $221 billion, 160 are identified as party representatives, NPC deputies, or members of the People's Political Consultative Conference.[4]

That is, the rich and powerful not only enjoy a freewheeling "civil society" of private institutions and asymmetrical competition but also manipulate the supposedly public processes of decision making and resource allocation. Somewhere along the way of market reform, it has become commonplace that party, government, and army cadres make private gains, big or small, by abusing their offices. The exposed phenomenon of officials keeping bank accounts overseas or fleeing the country with bags of cash fuels popular indignation as much as political cynicism. Corruption tops China's social ills in public surveys. In early 2012 General Liu Yuan, the political commissar of the logistic department of the People's Liberation Army (PLA), found himself in a difficult fight, if not eventually a losing one, against networks of factions and patronage in bribery for promotion, business extortion, luxury personal spending, and broad violation of discipline within the army. He warned his colleagues that "our own corruption can smash us and cause our armed forces to be defeated without firing a shot."[5] The now crushed "Chongqing model" of "singing the red and cracking down on the black" once raised popular hope for a return of socialist morale and an end of corruption facilitated crimes. That hope is shattered not only because the local experiment fell through but also because of the extent of rot, involving local and central politicians and anticorruption agencies themselves, that the chain of events exposed. The problem is so entrenched that few are clean enough to dare to confront it or to disobey the "hidden rules" configured in the system. The fear of backfire is real, as corruption charges can be activated as a political weapon to bring down opponents.

The competing interpretations of China's relationship with capitalism are part of the ideological and discursive struggle. They represent conflicting interests and forces which push the country into different directions. To validate a capitalist transition within a nominally socialist state, theorists from official "think tanks" (notably the party's central research offices, the State Council's research center and departments, and provincial and municipal policy research bureaus and academies of social sciences) use "internal" and open publications, newspapers, and other media to propagandize a deformed Marxism. The phrase "socialism with Chinese characteristics," for instance, is popularly known in China as a "basket" in which anything goes. The Central Party School has rather successfully turned itself into a neoliberal stronghold notwithstanding disagreements within its faculty. Harvard's Kennedy School of Government is jokingly called China's "second party school," as senior officials are regularly dispatched there to be trained in proper modern thinking about globalization. Pseudo Marxist and other formulations are duly produced to "naturalize" the capitalist teleology and institutionalization as the party's monopoly power becomes an end in itself (Meisner 1989b: 343).

The expansive and expensive "project on Marxist theoretical research" was launched for regime relegitimation in the face of an ebbing socialist commitment at all levels of the establishment. Unambiguously, however, side by side with this loud rhetoric drive, anti-Marxist constitutional amendments had been approved to validate "inviolable private property" and the virtue of the power of capital. The only superficial constraint on such radical moves is that rather than verbally embracing "capitalism," an inventive euphemistic language referring to *buke* or "making up a missed lesson" has been adopted. The refashioned theories, concerned with a mistakenly skipped yet necessary "developmental stage" (of capitalism), promote a long period of "primary stage socialism" or "new democracy" (the label is borrowed from the party program of the 1940s on a mixed economy and accompanying policies before the transition to socialism). They argue that capitalism is either historically inevitable for laying the material foundation for the future transition to socialism or morally desirable for protecting individual rights and political democracy, which are of universal value, or for both. A system of "primary" socialism must accommodate these indispensable features. Not noted is a conspicuous logical barrier in the case of socialism remaining to be officially upheld: If capitalism in post-socialist China can be successful, how and why should it be expected to lead to its own demise? Conversely, if it is bound to fail, what could justify its necessity, let alone desirability? Moreover, corruption has not spared even a specifically designated Marxist project that involves fierce competition for a huge fund allocated by the party center. What a misuse of public money; and it dishonors Marxism, in whose name greed and fraud are rampant.

Not surprisingly, then, the language of class is sidelined or even tabooed in the "Marxist" interpretation of China. The denounced era of Maoist "continuing revolution" and "class struggle" without materially definable classes after nationalization and collectivization is dead but refuses to die. For, paradoxically, "class" is abandoned in the Chinese political vocabulary precisely at a time of the rebirth of a capitalist class and the making of a new working class in China's sunbelt "workshop of the world" (Lee 2007: chs 5 and 6), and consequently led to the emergence of horrendous class divisions and conflicts. The laboring classes, urban, rural, and migrant, are now called "vulnerable groups" in public and media specifications. The hegemonic "quest for globality" driven by the neoliberal ideologies needs the depoliticized Weberian terminology of "social stratification," which subsumes class discourse and obscures class relations (Pun and Chan 2008: 76). Salient in the background is the recently constitutionalized, legalized, and often also patronage based power of private capital. It is "one of the greatest ironies" in the PRC's political history, as Zhao Yuezhi remarks, that "the discourse of 'class struggle' was taken to its essentialized extreme when Chinese society was relatively egalitarian during the Cultural Revolution, and was totally suppressed during a process of rapid class polarization during the reform era" (2009: 97).

Within China's policy circles, powerful people are on behalf of private tycoons and compradors advocating withdrawal of public control over the national industries and capital accounts. Quite a few communist managers and Wall Street bankers have managed to enrich one another personally as awkward economic partners. Self-contradictory but influential market fundamentalists simultaneously condemn state intervention and demand that the government force further privatization and deeper financial liberalization. In consonance, some "Marxist" academics dismiss any conceptual distinction between socialism and capitalism. It is time to admit the political anachronism of such a distinction, they insist, as the identities themselves are purely ideological Cold War relics. Already blurred demarcations between the two models can now be discarded altogether, and convergence, considered in terms of varieties and management of capitalism, is the order of the day. The problem, of course, is that for those who have lived through the painful social consequences of the transition, the difference between the two is only too real.

As China is "rising" through hypergrowth, frenzied urbanization, and single minded global integration at grave moral, social, and environmental cost, its vulnerable feel the pain: the low waged or unpaid workers, land losing peasants, struggling migrants, separated couples, and the old and young left behind in impoverished villages and, unsurprisingly, angry strikers, petitioners, and protesters. The nation grows economically but is dwarfed culturally by abandoning the most valuable legacies in its revolutionary and socialist traditions. In particular, the widening gulf between the elites and ordinary citizens is a clear indicator that the PRC is moving away from its founding promises of equality and popular power and wellbeing. This poses a disturbing question about the legitimacy of radicalized "reforms." If China has fallen into a kind of "looters capitalism," as perceived by many, what was the point of the socialist revolution? What is the meaning of reform in negating socialism? Such questioning has so far not implied delegitimating the reform project on the whole, but it does demand a resumption of the socialist reform initiatives.

It was the crisis of Chinese socialism that brought about the reform. It is now the crisis of Chinese capitalism that has engendered debates over the reform's direction. The argument here is that what happened did not have to happen; China did not have to be where it is by any inescapable logic, economic, sociological, or cultural. If capitalism cannot be teleological, then where the transition leads is a matter of political struggle with a vital ideological dimension. Given that China's historical path would make the transaction cost too high, a total reversal of socialist achievements is unlikely. "Contradiction" remains a key word in depicting Chinese realities. A subtler observation drawn from the experience of capitalist transitions in Russia is that a previous systemic structure can provide a newly established order with a needed "social subsidy": "it is precisely the persistence of the old that has underwritten the stability of the new" (Wood 2012: 7, 33). Reforms in China have likewise benefited greatly from the Maoist structural groundwork. "Mao's invisible hand" is still in one way or another behind China's policy considerations, organizational style, and government responses to social demands, reminiscent of a socialist state (Heilmann and Perry 2011). Without such a state it would have been impossible for the country to survive typical postcommunist shocks, breakups, and devastations. Moreover, experimenting with a "socialist market," China's economic, industrial, and social policies are open to innovation. Driven by social crises and ruling quandaries, innovative proposals for improving governance have developed: in many cities electronic channels are being created for citizens' input and governmental transparency. Exercises of community polling and public budgeting are spreading. Central and local consultative-electoral politics is in one way or another democratizing. The quality of village elections is elevated in some localities. Public consultancy in policy and lawmaking is expanding, to the extent that at least one round of thorough consultation among experts and stakeholders is now required for major decisions. The "pro-people" guideline has encouraged governmental effort in reducing inequalities, defending labor rights, tackling corruption, strengthening market regulations, and achieving better conservation, carbon diminution and energy consumption controls. After "socialism in one village" (e.g., Nanjie, Huaxi, Zhoujiazhuang, and hundreds of other remaining collectives), the "socialist countryside" is promoted as enhancing benefits of growth for the rural population. This effort began with the removal of agricultural taxes and increased public investment in schemes of social security, medicine, and pension. Urban China has also witnessed more public housing projects for low incomers. A runaway real estate market fueled by a trend of land commodification has been halted in places with a more visionary leadership.[6]

In principle, a reverse course of anti-neoliberal deglobalization is not a vain wish. Weighty actors such as China could move to "overload" the global system by artificially raising wage levels and manipulating prices to protect sales domestically. This in turn would enable retention of surpluses and hence offset multinational profits and concentrate capital accumulation in the capitalist core regions (Harvey 2001). With its somewhat incomplete membership in the world economy, China might also be able to distance itself from the volatile international market of financial capital by maintaining sovereign control over its capital account and monetary policy. Even if radical reformers advised by the IMF and World Bank economists would like to have this last defense of national economic autonomy and security dismantled, there is really no "iron necessity" to justify their proposal. On the contrary, it is not impractical that the new "parameters established by political struggle" locally and accumulatively be activated to override existing conditions (Wallerstein 1991: 121–124, 168). Wages in China have already risen significantly, though disproportionately, with civil servants and state sector workers making the most gains. And the growing cost of labor in general has already affected the strategic movement of global capital. Autonomous and far sighted players in the world market should also be prepared for whatever it may take for the rules of the game to be remade. China in this view possesses a relatively flexible and favorable position.[7]

No such development, however, can materialize without a conscious social movement from below, which must gather momentum as in the case of a Polanyian double movement in rebuilding public medicine (Wang 2008). Capitalist domination, exploitation, and injustice have no appeal to China's working people, who have a collective memory of socialism as contrasted with the ongoing brutality of a primitive accumulation in which labor is considered and required to be "cheap." Controversies over class consciousness or patterns of labor activism notwithstanding, the politics of labor has "creatively drawn on Maoism, socialism, and liberal ideologies of legal justice and citizenship" (Lee 2007: x). More generally, socialism remains a major source of regime legitimation, insofar as it is alive in China's social commitment and public expectations. As the income gap rapidly widens and "class" returns to mourn a lost world of egalitarian pursuits, mass protests escalate in both frequency and scale. The authorities are compelled to respond to them.

Waves of strikes by Apple suppliers across China since 2010 were triggered by a shocking string of suicides of young migrant workers suffering the humiliation of low wages, restrained life, and constant verbal abuse by shop floor managers (Pun and Chan 2012).[8] The strikers forced concessions from the management. Foxconn, which produces 40 percent of the world's electronics goods in China, reached an agreement with Apple in late 2012 to improve labor conditions and relations for its 1.2 million Chinese workers. A similar course was followed by Flextronics International, another global electronics manufacturer, and a few other multinationals. In some SOEs, especially the privatizing ones, laidoff and current workers organized to defend their rights. Although repression involving police is not uncommon, workers at times also win sympathy and support from government. In December 2012, striking workers in a state owned Shaanxi oil firm demanded equal status and pay for their female spouses working as second class employees. The *Workers Daily* reported on the event and criticized unilateral decisions by management as a "blatant breach" of the labor law and union rules.[9]

As the labor NGOs and official trade unions contribute to the state's effort to individualize and institutionalize conflict arbitration in industrial relations (Friedman and Lee 2010), China's labor and social movements are caught in a remarkable post-socialist dilemma: To strive for independent unionization, collective bargaining, and legal protection would also be to legitimate relinquishing of the responsibilities of a "workers' state." Workers have to learn to fight for their legal rights precisely because they are losing the commitment to their political recognition and material security that is in the nature of a socialist state.[10] The Labor Contract Law of 2008 might be seen as a landmark in the PRC history for its ultimate legitimation of the avoidance of the governments, central and local, to side with the workers on the political and social ground. Capital-labor relations, in reflection of the fundamental relations of production, are transformed into an "objective" legal matter of "liberal neutrality" and "legal fairness." Leaning toward capital for investment and growth, the state and its corporatist arm, the All China Federation of Trade Unions, may still act on the workers' behalf intermittently under path dependent pressures. But the interests and voices of workers are in pressing need of adequate rearticulation at a time of confusion and disillusionment. The situation is just as acute in the countryside. The standoff between the villagers of Wukan and corrupt local officials over illegal sales of collective land in Guangdong in late 2011 ended in the hope of a fair settlement. The "social media" in their Chinese forms of cell phone and Internet have become a "weapon of the weak." But the problem persists. Lin Zulian, the leader of the protesting villagers who has been elected director of the village committee as well as party secretary in Wukan, convincingly argues that the state is responsible for protecting the land and farmers in any land dispute. None of the ways the provincial arbitrators suggest—dialogue, bargaining, or suing—will resolve the conflict. "This is the government responsibility. If the government acts as a mediator its role is mistaken."[11] The class position of the state is clearly a decisive factor in China's popular struggle for social justice, cohesion, and development.

In February 2012, right before the annual NPC convention, a "People's proposal" to be delivered to the Congress was circulated on the Internet. It includes such popular demands as that "the personal and family wealth of all officials be publicized and their source clarified" and that "a nation-wide anti-corruption online platform be established, where all PRC citizens may file reports or grievances about instances of corruption or abuse, and the state should investigate in an openly accountable manner and promptly publicize the result"; that in defending national economic security, "a self-reliant approach to economic development" should be pursued and "any policy that serves foreign capitalists at the cost of the interest of Chinese working class should be abolished"; that "the losses of public assets during the 'restructuring' be thoroughly traced" and retracted, and the wealth of current managerial personnel in the state owned enterprises be publicly determined and controlled; and that "sweatshops be thoroughly investigated" and "enterprises with arrears of wage, illegal use of labor, or detrimental working conditions" be closed down. The demands also addressed issues in public education, health care, and other areas of social discontent.[12] Predictably, the proposal went nowhere; none of the NPC branches has ever responded to it. It will be a critical test for China's newly installed leaders to tackle these popular concerns, beginning with investigating accusations of corruption at the top impartially according to the party discipline and laws.

Any optimism, however, will have to be grounded in China's political economy. So far the signs are not particularly promising. In February 2012 right before the eighteenth party congress, the central Developmental Research Center and the World Bank jointly issued a report overseen by Robert Zoellick, *China 2030*, in which the key word is "privatization."[13] Chapter 3 of the report, "structural reforms," specifies petroleum, chemicals, and electricity among the major industries to be privatized. Chapter 7 promotes a radical relaxation of government control over its fiscal and banking systems. The Bank's prediction of the desired percentage of state sector in the national economy in 2030 is 10 percent, almost a twofold plunge from an already dismal figure of 27 percent in 2010 (as compared with the capitalist social democracies dependent on a solid public sector). A highly recommended method in the report is broad securitization of state assets, including foreign acquisition, in the name of anti-monopoly. This would also entail liberalization of the capital market and the banking system as part of the "internationalization" of China's financial sector.

The collective land is also an imminent target of thorough privatization. In the December 2012 Asia-Pacific Economic Cooperation summit, the outgoing Party Secretary Hu Jintao reaffirmed China's commitment to further trade and financial liberalization. Since his assuming the office in March 2013, Premier Li Keqiang has repeatedly confirmed this commitment and acted swiftly on creating a free trade zone in Shanghai among other measures. The State Securities Regulatory Commission had earlier announced a tenfold increase in the quota of foreign investors in China's stock market as a step toward radically increasing liberalization of the country's capital control.[14] In the two-decade effort of privatizing the Chinese economy, the role of the State Council under the influence of powerful lobbying vested interests comes to the fore. In a typical directory (document number 13) it authorized in 2010, the areas singled out for entry of more private and foreign capital are infrastructure, finance, social projects, defense, and science and technology. The industries named include petrochemical, gas, nuclear, telecommunication, military, and banking. This unequivocal case exemplifies how effective a state led capitalist transformation can be.

In this context, calls for political reform without opposing privatization, or what is described in Chinese as "the capitalization of power and the empowerment of capital" (*quanli zibenhua*; *ziben quanlihua*), cannot be about democracy in any meaningful sense. Such a call in China's present reality is rather about securing and legitimizing what has already been illegitimately grabbed from public coffers by private hands.[15] Political options for China are therefore not superficially between protracted one party rule and a multiparty system based on interest group politics. The alignment of state and capital could instead perpetuate an authoritarian "free" market and unequal "civil society," in which political and economic elites control electoral politics and decisionmaking processes. Underlying a light weight and complacent democracy discourse there is the heavy dual power of "both a state and market logic to the trajectory of civil society" in China (Howell 2012: 281). A "democracy" in such a society would be useless for the common citizens if their popular preferences were not articulated and translated into state power. Any "political reform" premised on private property and capitalist transformation is thus deceitful. Meisner's intuition that in China, "any serious impetus for democratic change will more likely come from the victims, not the beneficiaries, of state-sponsored capitalism" (2007: 41) makes good sense. The point, as the theory of revolution always warns, is that the fundamental question is political power. For a hitherto enslaved people, losing the new regime resulting from their liberation struggle is losing everything. The importance of the state, or for that matter distinctions between states—socialist, reformist, variously capitalist, and so on—is measured by the gains and losses of different people under its power and by the violence surrounding the seizure of that power. It may generally be the case that globalization impinges on the autonomy and capacity of states and undermines national self-determination. But the changing nature of the PRC state is more directly due to the voluntary surrender, so to speak, of its own political class. From Deng's doctrine of "cat theory" and "no argument," which in effect banned any socialist criticism of the transition, to Jiang Zemin's "three represents," which depoliticized the Communist Party ideologically as much as organizationally, the political essence of pragmatism is to allow "capitalism with Chinese characteristics" to be legitimized. This, no doubt, would at the same time also delegitimize socialist resistance.

The leaders could have their way because public scrutiny and supervision were lacking, and this is where the compelling need for democracy really manifests itself. The ideology against ideology has been empirically "falsified" by the lost direction of development in China, and the negative lesson to be learned is that any undertaking with the magnitude of the Chinese reform must have its orientation and movement constantly and democratically scrutinized, evaluated, and adjusted in line with its intended objectives. Logically, if China is to retain its socialist positioning in the world and world history, the vital task for its socialist advocates would be to recapture the state and party by reinstituting their original constituencies. This could be a Gramscian "war of position" in which a new democratic bloc of counterhegemony against bureaucratic capital is constructed so as to reverse the course of a neoliberal authoritarianism with Chinese characteristics. This construction will rely on a renewal of the Communist Party by its communist constitution and on the popular classes across social cleavages centered in organized labor and united in the universal identity of direct producers (see Chapter 6).

The Chinese struggle will also ally itself with parallel movements in other countries and globally. But there could be an essentially "socialism in one country" hurdle inherited from Cold War anticommunism, as seen not only in a "China threat" discourse but also in actual constraints, sanctions, "anti-dumping," and other trade barriers against China along with direct military provocations. As the world's largest importer of energy and mineral resources and having joined the global competition for raw materials, the country faces a worsened external environment. This would force China to rethink and revise its "global strategy" from a socialist and internationalist position. The incompatibility between the two is not only a matter of principle but also a peril in *realpolitik*. Ideologically, the Chinese socialists have to be nationalist insofar as the PRC remains a site of socialist struggle and search. Their internationalist and universalist commitment, meanwhile, must be distinguished from the false "universal values" of liberal capitalism. How the (re)positioning of China at the crossroads will play out in these circumstances is a matter of politics, practice, and chance.

# 5

# Can There Be a Chinese Model?

Modern China's national development defied the teleological "master course" to follow an alternative trajectory. It was essentially a collective search for, successively, a revolutionary alternative to colonial modernity, a socialist alternative to Stalinist statism, and a reformist alternative to capitalist integration. This trajectory, never smooth and full of contradictions and setbacks, has nevertheless modified the typical periodization of the modern and "world time" of globalization (Lin 2006: 57). This unique historical experience distinguishes itself from other national paths or choices, typically Soviet communism, considered a betrayal of a socially centered socialism, and third world capitalism, which has mired much of the postcolonial world in poverty and conflict.

Complicating this historical overview, as discussed earlier, there are not only negative aspects of the construction of Chinese socialism, but also the realities of its destruction as the reform derailed into a capitalistic transition. In the context of continuities and discontinuities between socialist and reformist projects, to engage the question of a "Chinese model" is to create a space for rethinking the reformist project and its needed repair. Such an intellectual task is then far from legitimizing China's current ways of doing things. On the contrary, any existing element that contradicts the long term socialist commitment must be rectified according to the socialist representation of a "model." Missing in the mainstream arguments in the recent "China model" debate is precisely such a critical stance. On the one side there is blind idealization of how China manages growth by blending political authoritarianism and market liberalization. On the other this deceitful discrepancy is confirmed but seen as resolvable only by a political reordering in line with a "free market.". "Regime change" coincides with a wholesale capitalist transformation. Sidelined in the debate is the voice opposing both these versions of the domination of either bureaucratic or private capital. Instead, a socialist China model can draw on the best living resources in China's revolutionary and socialist traditions.[1]

In the background is the "rise of China" associated with economic globalization at one level and political threat to the world order at another. In truth, however, with a sense of history, it is unquestionable that China rose some six decades ago in 1949 when the "Chinese people have stood up," followed by new China's most valiant self-defense in the battleground in Korea. That was a true "Chinese moment" in world history. China might have become a weightier player in global affairs today, as its moves have instant impact on global markets and international relations. And domestically as well, it has certainly reduced poverty and lifted the general living standard significantly.[2] But nothing close to this would have been achieved in the world's largest developing country had it not been an independent, liberated, and proud modern nation in the first place. The fundamental national, social, and physical as well as human infrastructure had been transformed earlier, before *jiegui* (global integration) or reform and opening. Not to mention that every great gain in the reform era is paid for by great losses in the same measure. It is thus very tricky to speak of China's rise or a Chinese model ahistorically, without recognizing important historical and causal links.

A parallel assumption is that of the "Beijing consensus." As a descriptive rather than prescriptive construction, while it convincingly focuses on the importance of national autonomy and innovation, it overlooks obstacles and dissent. As is widely admitted inside China, a GDP-centered and expert-led growth pattern is socially and ecologically unsustainable.

Developmentalist distortions have also resulted in public policy deficiencies and, consequently, popular discontent. Internationally, the space in which China can maneuver is severely constrained not only by its geopolitical position but also by the generic boundaries of the global system. Tensions necessarily arise with China's FDI outflows, for example, regardless of any difference between the Chinese investment without political conditionality (except on the "one China principle" concerning Taiwan) and the Western practices of either old colonialism or newer aid programs.[3] The rich countries have also used the issue of labor rights to put China on the moral defensive. Where then is the alternative "consensus" to the "Washington consensus," which is globally fading yet remaining deeply influential in Beijing's policy circles? Can there really be any valid consensus on exploitation, pollution, or dependency?

By comparison with a nonconsensual "Beijing consensus," a normative Chinese model would stand by its socialist commitment, opposing any reforms that depart from that commitment rather than concealing or legitimizing the departure. The formulation of such a model would thus necessitate room for present as well as possible future rectifications. There are no doubt serious disagreements about a "China model" or "Chinese path," "Chinese experience," "Chinese advantages," and the like, as well as opposition to such formulations altogether. The debate, however, facilitates an escape from the ideological straitjacket of "no argument" that has shown the green light to capitalist development in China. The ultimate question is about a shared, postcapitalist vision—what kind of society could be commonly desirable and practically viable for China? To be critically scrutinized are the making, unmaking, and remaking of Chinese socialism and its world-historical positioning. Chinese socialism with its egalitarian and collectivist traditions and nonconventional development methods defies the standard models of modern transformation. If historically the Chinese experience, along with the Soviet endeavor, represents "an unrealized utopia; not necessarily an unrealizable one" (Jameson 2012: 127), it is all the more compelling today that we seek the renewal of the socialist project and take steps toward its realization.[4]

Prerequisite are a few ground rules for any rational conceptualization of a socialist Chinese model. The starting point is that such a model has been historically prepared for, and preconditioned by, China's twentieth-century revolutionary transformations. In other words, the model is premised on a collective appreciation of the historicity and fundamental justice of the Chinese communist revolution. For—to recapitulate—it was that revolution that has liberated an oppressed nation and its exploited classes and social groups from the old bondages, thereby politically and organizationally enabling China's modern development.[5] This development appears to have diverged from or leaped over several "normally" expected economic or political movements. The hindrances, slips, and uncertainties along the way would be predictably attributable to its experimental character. Any historical determination of Chinese socialism thus also simultaneously entails its developmental indeterminacy. Argument over this historically conceived positioning is at the heart of the "China model" debate, underlining the divides between pros and cons and among competing defining features of the model.

In terms of conceptual or cognitive prerequisites, to indicate the historical preconditions for the Chinese model is to reconfirm its socialist preoccupations. For one thing, capitalist development has created multiple models, and no Chinese addition can be really novel. An authoritarian state enjoying "embedded autonomy" (Evans 1995) while "governing the market" (Wade 1990), for example, is characteristic of the developmental state model, as differentiated from the models of predatory and "failed" states. It would be problematic if not worthless to treat the Chinese experience as just another example of the "East Asian miracle." Part of the scholarly consensus in the literature of "bringing the state back in" is that the lack of a developmentally functional state—whether communist, state capitalist, or national populist variant—is a symptom as well as an explanation of postcolonial under-development. And state function is the logic not only of a planned economy but also of advanced market economies whatever their self-deceptive ideologies might be. The PRC state is indeed developmental (not necessarily developmentalist) from the outset and shares a few characteristics with its neighbors, such as economic nationalism and state capacity. Yet, stereotypically speaking, China's distinctiveness in historical trajectory, political and ideological orientation, social embeddedness and extraordinary organizational power makes the PRC state a different species, precluding any superficial affinities. After all, the Chinese model cannot be just about state-led development; it is first and foremost about socialist development.

That is, a true Chinese model cannot emulate capitalist ones, and the uniqueness of China lies in its anticapitalist posture and the potential of an alternative it offers. Socialism is thus the first conceptual premise of any meaningful construction of a Chinese model not limited to methods of growth. The modern history of China's revolutionary struggles for national liberation and social reorganization, and for development and prosperity, is where the origins of its present or path dependency must be looked for. Meanwhile, history goes much farther and provides further sources for modern changes. "From Confucius to Sun Zhongshan," as Mao symbolizes it, China's great traditional treasures (much richer than mere Confucianism) also get continually reinvented. The diverse eco-natural and material-cultural worlds of an evolving "China" are contemporary with its everyday experience. The recognition of a needed "revolutionary break," however, keeps "1949" as the most foundational milestone in Chinese development.

Another necessary premise is a self-consciously "China-regarding stance". The capitalist parameters are severely constraining but not deterministic. This stance insists on the centrality of local desires, knowledge, and resources as an antidote to the *jiegui* fever anchored in a postsocialist self-demeaning worship of the capitalist West, especially the

United Sates. The problem with the West as a model is not just that the Western standards are often sought at the cost of local preferences, but that such standardization is a total illusion. China, or for that matter any other late developer, has no chance to proceed in the footsteps of historically privileged Euro-Americans (Chapters 2 and 8). Even "East Asia" is hardly replicable without the unique advantages it enjoyed from huge US market and economic-military aid as regional Cold War allies. Self-regard, however, is by no means autarkic protectionism. A confident China is open in its attitude and outlook. A potential Chinese alternative is, moreover, comprehensible only in its transformable and transformative relationship with capitalism.

The last premise, as already hinted, is the model's normative character. To define a Chinese model is to specify its normative scope and features, or what China has achieved and still ought to strive to achieve normatively. Again, such a model cannot be a descriptive affirmation of the existing order and is not a matter of articulating any "Chinese style" of development or governance. From historical capitalism to historical communism and anything in between, development has proved possible under different regime types, in different social-political systems, and through different economic approaches—autocratic or democratic, centralized or decentralized, planning or market, import substitution or export-oriented, and so on. If China is only one among the nations that manage rapid economic expansion without social explosion, a "model" based on that experience would be unremarkable.[6] An eloquent Chinese model should instead identify the most crucial factors about China's modern transformation and future prospects. Any quality indicator emerging from the model must unambiguously differ from all what is cynically permitted under the guise of "Chinese characteristics". Needless to add that even a normative model cannot be a closed one; it has to be open to scrutiny, correction, adaptation, and novelty.

Simply put, the contradictory Chinese realities cannot be fused and justified through a spurious model building. The persistence of sweatshops, the collusion of money and power, the dictatorship of capital, and the reign of developmentalism all violate socialist promises and are incompatible with the normative properties that a Chinese model incorporates. Conversely, such attributes as the communist morality of "relying on the masses" and "serving the people," the social organizational efficiency of government for public good, state promotion and protection of working men and women, the national commitment to independence, dignity, and international equality, and so forth would validate the model. In other words, a normative Chinese model is constrained by its socialist foundation, standards, and ambition. To live up to such a model, China will have to break course with a capitalist integration, as another battle after the communist revolution in a long march to eventually overtake capitalism. As far as capitalism is concerned, viewed in its unending crises—socioeconomic, ecological, financial, and political—and persistent poverty, wars, and other devastations, it is incapable of solving the world's or China's problems. Reforms in China have so far posed no challenge to the parameters of global capitalism, or, more accurately, have mightily contributed to that system's perpetuation. But the future a Chinese model embraces would demand a change from the present.

We can now proceed to consider what a plausible Chinese model, conditioned on its historical and conceptual requisites as specified above, might look like. With the aim of uniting logic and history and synchronizing realism and transcendence, a preliminary characterization should be permissible.

First, to articulate a Chinese model is to accentuate the socialist state. Such a state has the political power, moral confidence, and popular support, and organizational and policy capacities to mobilize human and material resources, to make China strong as an equal to the world's other nations.[7] Historically, with a purposeful and powerful state committed to socialist modernization, the PRC was able to seize a rare chance of actualizing a "privilege of backwardness" in uneven development (Chapter 1). It had avoided models of "colonial modernity" and "dependent development" or "development of underdevelopment" as elaborated in the dependency theory. In its external relations, socialist self-identity of the state also entailed internationalist foreign policies, despite distortions caused by the Sino-Soviet split, which led to a most unfortunate chain of intracommunist conflicts. By and large, new China found itself some precious space of autonomy in an extremely complicated and difficult geopolitical milieu. But if China today has emerged robust from autarkic closeness and isolation, its position in the world has become most ambiguous with respect to whether any of its socialist traits can survive globalization.

The founding of the People's Republic enabled a proud people (*renmin*) to aspire collectively to be the "master of society," as it is put in everyday Chinese, replacing a shapeless mass of "subordinate subjects" (*chenmin*) of the emperor or "conquered and stateless slaves" (*wangguonu*) of the imperialists and colonizers in the past. This groundbreaking modern foundation of China was of both substantive and symbolic significance. It has since normatively defined the ultimate source of state power and regime legitimacy in the PRC. The postrevolutionary state in its ideal type, as stipulated in its constitution, is then simultaneously empowered and constrained by the supreme power of a sovereign people. Consequently, popular preference and interests are fundamental criteria for legislation, policymaking, and government services. Without formally repudiating this overarching principle of a "people's democracy,"[8] post-socialist transitions have nevertheless in effect replaced the ideology of the people with a mythology of market and capital. Much of the civil society debate inside China over the conceptual soundness, utility, and priority between the languages of the "people" and "citizens" reflects this change.

From the PRC trajectory as a whole, two interconnected historical lessons stand out: On the one hand, a powerful socialist state committed to people's sovereignty, national development, and public welfare is a foremost condition for China to prosper. On the other hand, only under institutionalized supervision by autonomous social organizations within a constitutional and legal order can the state be kept on track and check. Socialism cannot be if freedom is suppressed and creativity stifled, because the social, intrinsic to socialism, would be hollowed out. Political persecution and personal mistreatment in the era of "class struggle" had inflicted deep wounds and disillusions, distorting socialism and catalyzing antisocialism from within the system. However, neither formalist legal reforms nor the pursuit of a "normal politics," electoral or otherwise, can substitute for democracy. A shared message from both pre- and postreform periods is then the imperative of a socially substantiated democracy centered in the people as collective subject as well as individual citizens. In other words, if the Maoist populism as an abstract idealization did not fulfill that grand desire, neither would post-Mao legalization and proceduralism. In a socialist China the state alienates the people and overwhelms the social, and hence loses its mandate, by either glorifying "the people" merely nominally or subjugating the population in an order of capital over labor, elites over masses, and the powerful over the vulnerable.

In light of the aspects of normativity identified so far, the socialist state should be capable of strategic guidance, agenda setting, and effective policies and policy implementation. These capacities can be categorized as follows: (1) national sovereignty and defense—globalization may weaken a nation as much as boost it, depending on local determination and maneuver; (2) public control over the nation's essential resources of land, mines, water, forest, and other natural endowments; over the commanding height industries and public utilities of electricity, transportation, telecommunications, social housing, and public education and health care; and macroplanning in major investments and resource allocations, market regulation, and policy instruments; (3) financial independence and fiscal security in the budgeting, monetary, and banking systems, and capital account control to deflect global market volatility; (4) industrial and social policies in the long term interests of the population, physically sustained by state and nonstate sectors alike; (5) freedom, legality, civility, and voluntary and institutionalized participation from citizens as voters, consultants, lawmakers, and autonomous social actors.

A few clarifications are in order. Contrary to a widespread impression that China is always a highly centralized despotic power (as in the concept of AMP), the Chinese state traditionally has a sturdy local dimension and decentralizing tendency. Because of its size, unevenness, and regional divisions according to coastal-inland, urban-rural, majority-minority, and other demarcations, the country's political authorities have customarily been at once centralized and decentralized. A most noteworthy implication is that local leadership quality varies greatly and makes for differences in governance from place to place. In addition to the prominent provincial power in the PRC involving interprovincial competition as well as a bargaining relationship with the center, subnational and grassroots power has expanded in the reform era. This expansion was anchored in the phenomenal thriving of township and village enterprises (TVEs) and has been captured in scholarship as "local state corporatism" (Oi 1992). As the private sector grows and cross-border economic ties and zones flourish (such as in the Sino-Siberian and Sino-Southeast Asian regions), the market has also refashioned a multidimensional configuration of China's central, local, and global interplays. Local forces intercepted by global ones routinely bypass the center and its rules, regulations, and policy instructions, eroding public functions and the state system. Runaway decentralization also unbridles corruption. Departmental officials taking shares of private mining companies, for example, explains why so many dangerous mines can keep operating illegally.[9]

To be sure, the Chinese communist state has never been monolithic. Old intraparty factions (known as "mountain strongholds") inherited from wartime regional and army divisions have faded away, but new factions have formed under the reform regime. Fragmentation can be a threat everywhere to state capacity and policy coherence. Apart from decentralization being tainted by privatization and corruption, a "floating population" (numbered over 250 million in 2012) that continues to blur sectoral and administrative boundaries is another factor, complicating government tasks of macromanagement. The political logic of pluralization and decentralization is such that while fragmenting, they could also generate pullbacks toward recentralization, in which obstructions to national policy processes might be countered by interdependence and cooperation. Cadres acting on particularistic interests could also force the formation of alliances between the center and provinces or grassroots to restore state capacities. State role and accountability at all levels in the Chinese model are therefore defined within a dynamic and coordinated national network of central-local and vertical-horizontal balances. Traditional socialist methods of reducing disparities and redeeming disintegration through direct resource allocation or binding "sister" cities/provinces for economic and technological assistance in the poor regions remain valuable. The point is that the institutional infrastructure of China's nerve center must be safeguarded.

A further complication of the Chinese state is its ethno-regional constitution. Many localities have a distinct nationality or ethnic-religious identity, or more often multiple and mixed identities. In two-thirds of China's territories "ethnicity" and "locality" overlap, geographically as much as sociologically. Regional inequalities could thus have an ethnic appearance and vice versa, which in turn could be politicized in a contentious identity politics to fuel conflicts. Exactly because of socialist egalitarian promises, perceived "internal peripheralization" or regional discrimination can be more damaging in the PRC than in most other multinational states. As is unmistakably manifested in the rising tensions in Tibet and Xinjiang, accumulated policy errors have blended paternalism, developmentalism, paranoia, and repression. They contradict the state's own commitment and policy objectives. A civic nationalist proposal of deethnicization, by phasing out China's quasi-federalism and preferential treatment of minority groups painstakingly established in the 1950s, is gaining currency in Beijing's policy circles (Leibold 2012). This would be a political mistake, however, as any such reversal would only cause more confusions and resentments. However artificial the earlier ethnic identification process might have been, and however counterproductive identity related entitlements may still be, they are instrumental for the socialist pledge of national liberation. The relentless state project of modernization, even if materially successful, cannot work if needs and feelings of the locals, religiously or otherwise based, are disregarded.

As noted in Chapter 1, the PRC unitary state presupposes cultural and institutional multiethnicity within a constitutional and policy framework of political unity and social cohesion. It is of paramount importance that the Chinese model stand by the socialist mandates of minority rights, ethnic autonomy, religious freedom, solidarity of all nationalities, and equal citizenship. The fact that these mandates, however diluted, have not been formally repudiated in China—in the context of a global tide of ethnic nationalism and related destruction—speaks volumes regarding the morality and strengths of its precious socialist legacies. A paternalistic overtone notwithstanding, such legacies are fruits of a distinguished tradition of revolutionary nationalism in internationalist sympathy for the oppressed peoples and their emancipation.

A final point of clarification has to do with state-market relations. Even if in principle socialism can be compatible with a market economy, in practice the situation is far more ambiguous, as is shown in China's transition. The faith in market dynamism of the first reformist leaders was derived from the premise that China had a socialist state along with its political, legal, ideological, and repressive apparatus. Theoretically, and beyond Lenin's defense of New Economic Policy in Soviet Russia viewing state capitalism as a temporary retreat, the market may function as a means toward socialist goals given an apposite political-legal order and public culture. Such an order relies on a secondary tier of regulatory-monitoring regimes and technical agencies of production, circulation, and distribution. Logically, then, if exploitation and any other market vices occur, they would be straightforwardly a product and responsibility of the state. Market failure indicates state failure. In this the dashed early hopes of China's reformers may not necessarily have been misplaced; the Chinese case is contingent on a derailed reform. In other words, the argument stands that the nature of state resolves the nature of the market—by the dialectic of counteractive functions of the "superstructure." To resume the project of a socialist market is therefore a matter of recapturing the state. Only with a socialist state as the guarantor against a capitalist transition can a "socialist market" be ever conceivable.

A vital qualification to the first feature of the Chinese model is thus not a powerful state but a socialist state. Without a socialist commitment the model collapses. There is certainly no guarantee of the viability of the socialist state, and the best way to achieve and uphold such a state is through the social power of a democratically organized citizenry—a social state, so to speak, of, by, and for the people; and only socialism can maximally actualize democracy. The PRC state today, however, is full of contradictions. There is no illusion that it could not slip into something even more estranged, rent seeking, repressive, or overgrown in the course of a capitalist transition. The more resistant the social forces, the more ferocious the "new order" could be (Wang 2012a). It must crush critics and pacify protests. Contrary to the false perception that there is opposition between economic neoliberalism and political repression, the real logic is that the market liberals depend on a repressive state; in some key areas, such as finance, they are the state. It is on this ground of popular demand inside China for a socially committed and accountable government, more than because of any parochial standards or condescending instruction pretending to be universal from abroad, that democracy makes concrete and pressing sense for the Chinese people. That is, with its unfinished project of democratization, China needs to explore its own relevant modern legacies: the revolutionary conception of history from below, the ideas of people's sovereignty and "mass line", and the experiments of labor participation in management. These indigenous traditions may well enjoy a moral and organizational advantage over global norms of electoral politics too often featuring plutocracy more than democracy.

The second component of the Chinese model, required also to fulfill designated state functions as specified earlier, is a strong and resourceful public sector. Such a sector secures the nation's economic and fiscal foundation. Much of what the People's Republic has managed to achieve in national development and public provision is accredible to its public sector. This sector has for decades enabled the country to sustain an independent and internally coherent economy, in which investment is concentrated in infrastructure and manufacturing rather than speculation, the mainstay industries are under public control, and the state's fiscal capacity and stability are protected from regional and global financial crises. These achievements, however lingering today, are important. And, against a backdrop of recurring global and regional financial crises, they show in particular that banks and bankers should belong to the public sector. Capital control is conditional for democratic control over the allocation of major resources, credit, and investments. The prominent place of the public sector, the state sector, and SOEs is therefore logical for the Chinese model in search of a "socialist market." The renewal of socialism depends on the renewal of its political economy. "Public sector" and "state sector" are conceptually different but can be partially overlapping in practice. In China, much broader than state sector, public sector embraces a traditionally large and outstanding collective sector. This sector contains collective land, farms, firms, and many other types of accumulation, allocation, circulation, and service processes.

According to the PRC constitution, amended in the 1990s to accommodate market transition, public ownership, including "ownership of the whole people" and "collective ownership of the laboring masses," must still dominate China's mixed economy (article 6). This is a crucial stipulation for the definition of the system as socialist. However, in reality public domination is being undermined. On the one hand, certain mechanisms of public control are still in place: "predominance of state ownership, oversight by the comprehensive economic commissions, continued inclusion of firms in the state planning process, and continued high-level governmental and, ultimately, party control of personnel appointments in regulatory bodies and state firms" (Pearson 2007: 725).[10] State protection, albeit being weakened, of the few key sectors and embryonic national industries still makes a "governed" market in one way or another visible. The government is still capable of mobilizing and concentrating resources to target priority projects. It is also observed that China has fused macroliberalization with a selective continuation of public discretion and sectoral regulation (Hsueh 2011: 3–4). Meanwhile, large state owned commercial banks remain "a crucial part of the state's arsenal for engineering and channeling its massive domestic investment," leaving China "considerably less integrated into the global financial system" (Panitch and Gindin 2012: 300).

On the other hand, promoted by both neoliberal ideologues and direct beneficiaries of "insider buyouts" (involving former SOE managers and their personal networks), an aggressive privatization campaign has been carried out for "rationality and efficiency." Since then, as discussed in Chapter 4, in a mere decade SOEs have shrunk to merely a quarter of the national economy in terms of GDP. The centrally supervised SOEs have been regrouped into large conglomerates believed necessary for global competitiveness. The old norm of a prioritized state sector has been demoralized, with SOEs being discriminated against often by government departments themselves. In the official and semiofficial media, remaining SOEs are routinely targeted as privileged monopolies. They are seen as a drag on growth and society under years of influence of neoliberal propaganda. The fact that giant SOE managers are treated like capitalist CEOs with combined incomes of salary, dividends, and bonuses (often paid without regard to performance) a hundred times more than those of their bottom-most workers, and that state sector employees measured by pay level and status resemble a labor aristocracy, only reinforces popular antipathy. These changes are so profound and confusing that defending the state sector now seems inordinate even in a "socialist" economy.

Whatever the contradictions on the ground, a dominant public sector has every reason to feature a socialist Chinese model. Theoretically accountable to the state on behalf of the whole people, SOEs, in particular, ought to bear responsibility for the nation's economic sustenance and security. Their capital returns should be paid into the state treasury with the national government acting as the sovereign owner, residual claimer, allocator, and distributor. The assurance of a constantly enhanced revenue stream, most reliably from state firms, is crucial for public policy objectives (Lin 2008a: 16–19). To be sure, the state cannot be the sole provider of general welfare even in a socialist arrangement. Socialized revenues anywhere from nonstate sectors would be just as necessary, and public utilities might well be provided from private sources. In the advanced economies, so long as their governments under democratic constraints have the policy and fiscal means to curtail market forces, public sector provisions may not be so imperative. But in many poor countries, POEs are either unable or unwilling to take far sighted corporate responsibility, and nonstate contributions cannot be nearly adequate anyway. Without a state-sector-based common pool of resources to tap, central and local authorities with a social commitment would be impeded from delivering public goods and policies.

It is also argued in a liberal socialist tradition by James Meade and others that while the revenues drawn from private bases can be put to public use, the tax and regulatory regimes enter a bureaucratically costly contractual agreement in one form or another with payers of tax, fees, and rent. The trick is that without substantial incomes from state capital and other earnings from publicly managed resources, the economy would be burdened by overtaxation relative to profit margins, resulting in swelling debts and diminishing incentives. The government would then have to keep issuing more bonds and consequently raise interest rates to control excessive borrowing. These would in turn impair productively optimal investment. In this exposition, a performing state sector of sufficient scale is both necessary and desirable for a market economy to operate healthily (Cui 2011: 654–656). In a deficiently socialized or transitional economy such as China's, moreover, the public sector remains resourceful and (if not entirely so) is far more dependable in the policy processes than the private sectors (Lin 2009: 39–44). This is clearly seen in the areas of education, health care, social security, and environmental protection, where insufficient public allocation and investment or inefficient public scrutiny and approval of major decisions have had large, disastrous results.

With comparative strength in its energy, heavy, and high-tech industries, China's reduced state sector still possesses an unmatchable advantage for supporting industrial upgrading and general economic growth. It is as well the ultimate institutional defense of the country's financial market and fiscal process against externally induced downturns. This sector thus counterweighs POE monopolies and the concentration of private wealth and power, providing the government and its policy priorities with a secured economic base. The SOEs are by design instrumental for needed infrastructural work in the remote regions, redistributive social programs, risk-taking or low-return yet publicly desirable R&D projects, and many other needs for investment and service without the lure of profitability. Lacking market incentives such needs are likely to be neglected by short term, profit driven investors. In other words, SOEs by definition may not be profitable, while making critical contributions to development, employment, and structural balancing. Subsidies from state banks in such cases would be completely justifiable. Precisely because of their duties to remedy market failures or waste or exploitative behavior, SOEs, while subject to standard budgeting and accounting, cannot be evaluated by the market criterion of augmenting profits.

Serious reforms of SOEs, not further privation, are required by China's strategic adjustment and industrial integration toward a refocus on the domestic market and stronger technological autonomy. By current company law, for example, the power of shareholders and managers overwhelms any input from the workers' assembly about major managerial and appointment decisions. SOE returns, as another example, are not adequately paid into state coffers. State firms and conglomerates may have to be "modernized" further to become globally competitive, but they must aim at technological independence. For meeting the expectations of a Chinese model, the state sector must also resume the full range and depth of its public functions under effective public control. This could be achieved through a variety of inventive institutions in addition to the familiar ones (e.g., proposals in Guo 2006: ch.6; Shi and Liu 2012). While it assumes a leading role, if not necessarily a large share once a socialist market matures, in production in a uniquely configured economy, the underlying condition is that China's state sector now operates in a market economy and employs market tools. Open privatization is only one threat; another is hidden encroachment from within the sector itself. Throughout the former communist world, hijacking of the public by the private interests of a nomenklatura-oligarch-comprador class is commonplace. The Chinese variant of such a class has not only embezzled hugely in private accumulation but has also mediated massive outward transfers of wealth from China to foreign companies, banks, and governments. Interconversion of political and economic capital has allowed such a class to keep or take important positions in the state sector and government regulatory bodies themselves. "Stealing what is entrusted to one's care" is never culturally specific, but it is most tragic that it could have happened in a postrevolutionary society where not very long ago it took a bloody revolution to remove such predators and thieves.

The challenge of market integration to this insistence on a robust public sector as a component of the model is formidable. There seems to be no effective firewall to isolate the social national from the market global and public interest from private profit. Even with its capital account control not relinquished, China has witnessed its foreign reserves dwindling as the global financial turmoil is unfolding. The looming phasing out of transitional flexibilities regarding the WTO rules will squeeze the space for maneuver harder. The question is then whether and how a socialist state and public sector can make a difference. Given China's size, it can retain a maximal degree of autonomy by a maximal degree of reliance on its domestic market. Even if "delinking" is not literally a realistic option in an age of the global rules being nationally internalized, a least export dependent strategy should be achievable. Dependency theory's pessimism is not irrefutable, as is shown by socialist modernization if not also the more ambiguous cases of the developmental state. A country as big as China, and as committed as it can be, should have the will, preparation, and ability to pursue self-determination in development by way of remolding globalization itself. With its immense internal demands and market, China can certainly develop independently. After all, the reforms began with a smart strategy of "selective," not wholesale, integration. A public sector with sufficient reach and productive and accumulative capacities, a central ingredient of that strategy, should also define the Chinese model.

A third building block of the model, parallel with the discussions above, is the priority of popular wellbeing or *minsheng* in development. The fact that new China has managed to feed nearly one-fifth of the earth's population and continued to seek improvement in their living conditions is nothing less than world-historical. Using internationally applied social indicators, from human development in general to poverty alleviation in particular, one does not need to look beyond India for a telling comparison. While China has eliminated old exploitative and parasitic classes, India omitted a comparable "revolutionary break with the past." Although features of an overturned class society have returned in China's marketplace, there remains a huge pressure for legitimacy on the regime insofar as it retains socialism in its official identity. Indian democracy, which by holding free elections excuses its political class from needed social reforms and adequate welfare provision for the poor, the lower castes and classes, women and children, and a functioning citizenship in general, by contrast, has yet to be socially substantiated. Amartya Sen's argument for "development as freedom" (2000; 2011) centered on individual and human entitlements and capabilities captures the essence of *minsheng* in its universal signification.

*Minsheng* is an ancient idea. In modern times, it was taken by the republican revolutionaries as one of the "three people's principles": nationalism, democracy, and livelihood. To reach that goal of people's livelihood, China needed a social revolution, transcending a mere political one. *Minsheng* has been at the core of the communist programs from the outset to be materialized, and developed under a "public good regime" of Chinese socialism and subsequently a *xiaokang* (moderate prosperity) project of reform. The socialist workfare is now considerably dismantled, and gone with it is the nurturing of socialist workplace and work related identities. Rural communes used to take care of their needy, not only in an old manner of the moral economy with collectively accumulated funds but also with state schemes targeting most vulnerable categories (households of revolutionary martyrs and servicepersons, handicapped, and old and young without family support, etc.). The post-commune disorder and precipitous decline of physical and human infrastructures have eventually prompted the government to repeal agricultural tax, increase investment and subsidies in the rural sector, and take up its financial responsibilities for major social programs. While over 100 million people still live under the official poverty line,[11] the rebuilding of a comprehensive, urban-rural integrated social security system is underway. In terms of popular demands, throughout the years of hardship and affluence, state advance and retreat, the government has always been expected to meet basic needs as a matter of ruling mandate. This is a contrast with government seen as largely irrelevant to daily suppot in many countries of peripheral capitalism, and, again, explainable by the fundamental tenets established by a people's revolution in China.

Rarely noted are similarities in the commitment to (if not level of provision for) public welfare between states of historical communism and social democracy. The former in fact offer a stronger case in their concern with the labor process itself, and with primary distribution, whereas secondary distribution is the sole consideration of typical capitalist welfare states. The neoliberal assaults, however, hit China harder, where egalitarianism is directly denounced in the reform discourse; and such hallmarks of Chinese socialism as the "big pot" and "iron rice bowl" or collectivist organizations and provisions are largely abandoned. Dismantling many of its hard-won achievements, China has become one of the world's most unequal societies, in which, for one thing, the rich do not pay progressive and inheritance taxes. According to the National Bureau of Statistics, the Gini coefficient was near 0.50 throughout years in the new century and 0.474 in 2012.[12] These official figures could also be seriously underestimated.[13] As documented in the Chinese Academy of Social Sciences (CASS) annual blue books, which are also likely to be conservative, income inequalities between urban and rural households, coastal and inland regions, residents and migrants, officials and commoners, and other forms of social polarization are astounding.

With respect to the wellbeing of labor, China has since the Mao era nurtured a largely educated/skilled and dedicated workforce that rivals workforces elsewhere in quantity, quality, and discipline. By a dialectic twist, abundant high quality labor underlay the reform's bid for China's integration into the capitalist global market. As soon as that "comparative advantage" in neoclassic economics is misread to equate "cheap labor," it turns out to be a real disadvantage for workers. "Cheap labor" in these circumstances is a symbol of exploitation and contempt, and should not be acceptable. In conception and in practice, it is this superior workforce itself rather than any "cheapness" of labor that is the genuine comparative advantage underlying the spectacular "Chinese speed" of growth. In crystal clarity, labor cannot be "cheap" in either cost or esteem in a socialist political economy. Exploitation, degradation (as in the label "vulnerable groups"), and management controlled industrial relations all depress wages and welfare. Labor needs to be more "expensive," insofar as a labor market exists, not only as a moral matter but also as a demand of economic rationality with respect to right incentives, purchasing power, and sustainable growth based on domestic consumption. Instead of the Chinese currency *renminbi,* which continues to appreciate under US pressure, as the more perceptive economists argue, what needs to appreciate is Chinese wages. Raising wages artificially not only would help rebalance China's economy of export dependency but would also lessen competitive tensions in the global job market. China would strengthen its economic capacities and retain profits for its workers—surplus retention should not be a problem in a socialist state.

*Minsheng* is not the same issue as growth. Growth as such may or may not benefit society uniformly. Likewise, growth is not the same as development, especially human and social development. Indeed, developmentalism as an ideology disregarding the human-social and environmental costs of growth is adverse to development itself. Public welfarism as a social responsibility also entirely differs from market consumerism. Polarization in Chinese society today between frantic luxury spending at one end and poverty induced underconsumption at another is a sheer policy failure. Other pressing problems affecting people's livelihood—jobs and wages, hospital bills and university fees, housing prices and food security, and so on—only negatively reaffirm the essential morality and materiality of the commitment to universal wellbeing. *Minsheng* does not require abundance; it is about the satisfaction of needs. It is also a measure of unity between the social and natural worlds, and of overproduction and overconsumption.

It would be a perversion of human desire and an insult to human decency to make everything for sale. Moreover, the market by itself does not lead to common prosperity; critical, rather, is a decommodification of labor and basic public goods. Marx's critique of commodified labor is continually refreshing: "The worker becomes an ever cheaper commodity the more commodities he creates. The *devaluation* of the world of men is in direct proportion to the *increasing value* of the world of things" (1844: 69). The language of intrinsic human values and their market alienation in Marx's early writings may not be perfect from a "mature" historical materialist point of view. But this insight, and consequently that "in transforming our environment we necessarily transform ourselves," constitutes Marx's "most fundamental theoretical point concerning the dialectics of our metabolic relation to nature" (Harvey 2006: 88–89) and also our social relations. The accumulation of capital works through the ecosystemic processes, the physical, chemical, and biological processes, and the social, political, and cultural processes, in which resistance also takes place. These processes transform both the subjective and the objective and may open up unprecedented possibilities of development as well. In the end, only when working men and women are liberated from tedious daily pursuits for survival and from fear for their livelihood can they be rounded (as opposed to Marcusean "one-dimensional") individuals and active citizens. *Minsheng* therefore carries with it a political and transcendental ambition as well.

Inside China, the boundaries of the market in terms of such protected zones as health care, education, and pensions have been heatedly debated over. Also on the policy agenda is a computational scheme for "green GDP," as the nominal growth rate can be discounted by various costs and externalities—bubbles, speculative transactions, repeated construction and demolition, energy consumption and emission generation, and so on. Investing in green technologies is more emphasized in China than in some advanced economies.

A related proposal is to use a more comprehensive system for assessing economic and cadre performances that would incorporate social and environmental indicators. Energy saving, emission reduction, and resource-extraction restrictions are among such indicators of sustainability and an enhanced quality of life. So far China's developmental pattern has proved to be extremely obstinate because of vested interests entrenched at every level of management. The latest demonstrations against pollution and polluting constructions have blocked a few projects, and the government has imposed more stringent standards on industrial expansion. But other considerations, such as local revenue or job loss from shutdown factories, are still difficult to tackle within the existing order. Relocating problematic enterprises in the less affluent regions is to merely transfer or disperse, not reduce, pollution, about which urban middle class protesters do not necessarily care. *Minsheng*, however, is not achievable without political leadership, economic coordination, and social solidarity, and must be duly articulated in the Chinese model.

The final aspect of the model, conditioned on and ingrained in the previous three, is social organization, participation, and power. Public provision for universal security and well-being is the immediately necessary material basis for the activated agency of popular participants. Only such provision can gain people freedom to self-realization and freedom from fear. Democracy in its Athenian origin is seen "as a political system in which the members regard one another as political equals, are collectively sovereign, and possess all the capacities, resources, and institutions they need in order to govern themselves" (Dahl 1989: 1). "Capacities" and "resources" for autonomy and organization are, however, often overlooked in more superficial but also more prevalent elaborations of democracy.

One of the greatest achievements of the communist revolution was thoroughgoing social organization, which can be appropriately appreciated only in the historical context of people in China being like "a plate of loose sand" (in Sun's lament). Effective revolutionary mobilization and organization are a hallmark of communist politics and an indispensable source and bulwark of Chinese modernity. The "mass line," or the articulation of popular interests and preference through a continuing spiral of "from the masses (solicitation and inputs) and to the masses (aggregation and outputs)," was a novel method and rational choice by the party for bringing the revolution to victory. The method was retained in subsequent movements of socialist mobilization and transformation until "normal politics" prevailed after the Mao era. In a broad sketch of the vicissitudes of China's social organization, most notable is a bifurcated system of organizing urban and rural work and life. State and collective work units (*danwei*) in cities and in county towns and communes in the countryside were both set within a structure of central planning and full employment, though differently managed with an "urban bias." Collectivization and decollectivization twice transformed rural China, where new forms of organization have also emerged (Chapter 7). Despite systematic acts of self-destruction, including the distortion of its ideology, the party's organizational capacity remains formidable.

The idea of a participatory society and politics is indigenous to China, having been greatly fostered in the communist revolution. The revolution set itself the aim of creating a new kind of politics to enable the previously oppressed and marginalized people to acquire historical subjectivity. Maoist populism thus claimed a "grand democracy" of participation from below, which culminated in the cultural revolutionary attacks on the perceived bureaucratization and degeneration of the party-state itself. Throughout, the PRC has displayed complex qualities in both engaging and manipulating popular aspirations. The more participatory political processes do not seem particularly compatible with the presumed "progress" of economic and political liberalization, and "normal politics'" can be socially arrogant and repressive. Atomized individuals as market actors nevertheless make leeway for a holy alliance of the managerial, financial, intellectual, and media elites—known as an "iron quadric" in China's popular perception. Collective spirit and popular participation are especially wanting at a time of social fragmentation and erosion. Tocqueville has a good reason to see political apathy and material greed as "despotism's safeguard because they divert men's attention from public affairs."[14]

Normatively, the combination of social organization and popular participation is integral to social power and democracy. And the empowerment of people and society is in the nature of self-government, in which free development of both individuality and collectivity is attainable. If socialism is by definition centered in the social, then it is destined to be socially democratic. These normative propositions are useful for a critical examination of the Chinese experience, past and present. But they cannot be taken as an ahistorical condemnation of historical communism. Honest critiques must be leveled and lessons drawn. The epic episodes of China's popular movements have to be historicized, and their democratic values deserve recognition. Even the statist and undemocratic tendencies at the time should be situated in their internal and external circumstances. For one thing, the communist regimes were generally under acute security pressure and had to seek self-defense through fast industrialization and effective social control. For another, the Maoist response was still unique in that it was anti-statist in its ideology and policy experiments. Strong party commitment to "activating society" in the Chinese experience intensified the paradox between socialism and statism common to the communist enterprises.[15]

Nor should the social be conceptualized as opposed to the state; an antistate social would be antithetical to both state and society itself. Indeed, a participatory society coextensive with a socialist state should feature the Chinese model in both respects. These two reciprocal components sustain each other in terms of democracy based on social power. The contemporary conception of "civil society" differs from the Hegelian and Marxian usage but follows the Tocquevillean emphasis on social mobility and equality. While promoting autonomous social activism, it can also be fallacious if trapped in a presupposition of antagonism between state and society. The ideological preoccupations of this and similar benchmark concepts of social science cause confusion when such concepts are uncritically applied beyond the liberal capitalist states that provided their initial empirical basis. The CCP, for example, as an enormous mass party with a compelling ideology and far reaching social roots at the peak of its hegemony, has penetrated society through its grassroots organizational reach and foot soldiers. It thus becomes conceivable in a Gramscian reading that "the party *is* civil society," while its propaganda department operates in a "directed public sphere" (Cheek 1998: 237). Predictably, this understanding is unappreciated by mainstream scholarship and not accepted in an overgrown discourse about civil society. However, the overlapping spheres of state and society and social organization from above and below, as especially in Chinese socialism, forestalls their mutual exclusion as needed in the standard language.

As elements of state power in China have gradually yielded to market forces in a muddled process of devolution, Chinese society may have indeed developed into something more distinctive in scope and identity. Yet if "civil society" colludes with "market society," it cannot be free of exploitative and antidemocratic propensities. The self-deceptive liberal antistate doctrine ignores unchecked private power resisting state regulation, concealing the ties—open and hidden, legal and illegal—between public office and private profit. In such cases, the accumulation of both political and economic capital in some "associative actions" of "civic privatism" is a world away from social participation, depriving society of its latent power and self-corrective facilities (Offe and Preuss 1991: 152). A democratic public standing for social defense is therefore obliged to check not only state but also private concentration of power, wealth, and resources in a "civil society". Democracy in China, again, is then a matter of returning socialism to the social and recapturing the state from within. It is not about fighting a socialist dictatorship to win a capitalist democracy but about mobilizing the resources of socialism to overcome its contradictions and achieve its own democratization.

For a socialist Chinese model aspiring to social power of organization and participation, forms and channels of institutional support should be multifarious: the democratically stimulated people's congress at central and local levels; labor unions and farmers' associations; community and neighborhood self-managing committees; professional networks, consultative roundtables, and public forums; civic advocacy and protest campaigns; noncommercial communication outlets, the Internet and other social media; voluntary and other social initiatives and social movements involving young people (Fiskin et al 2010; Ma J. 2012). Unlike societies with a long and entrenched individualistic and money culture, China may tend to develop more collectivist strengths among its common citizens. Elections may have become the most regular and extensively employed means of participation, but there are and can be many others. The ancient method of sortition and its modern remodeling into the jury system, for instance, is based on an egalitarian and democratic conviction that everyone serves in the run for office or shoulders responsibility in state affairs.[16] As depicted in Marx's model of the Paris Commune in *The Civil War in France*, officials are not professional politicians and are selected randomly and subject to instant recall. Regardless of whether theoretically the state should begin to "wither away" in a socialist democracy, to democratize China here and now is to reject "institutional fetishism" (Unger 1997). There can be multiple—old and new, alternative, indigenous, and yet to be invented—approaches to achieving representation and accountability.

An important dimension of social empowerment is "economic democracy" in the sense that a democracy will be shallow or crippled unless its workplace is democratically managed (Dahl 1985). A Chinese example, short of calling for workers' control because of the presupposed assurance of a socialist state and public sector, is the Maoist "Angang constitution," a projected mass line style managerial revolution against Soviet "one man bossism" and Taylorism (Cui 1996; Lin 2006: 143–148). Endorsing participation of workers in management and of cadres and technicians in shop floor labor, the short lived experiments pioneered a model of combining industrial democracy and post-Fordism: flexible teaming, liquid hierarchy, multiskills and cooperative competition in production; participatory planning, collective budgeting, equal pay for equal work, and profit-sharing in management (Unger and Cui 1994: 82–86). This experiment is one of the more radical and imaginative legacies of Chinese socialism—new modes of work and life had been envisioned and implemented.

In the larger political and intellectual background, the Maoist idea of "walking on two legs" and liberating popular energy in all sectors at all levels is so deeply humanist (even though Mao was an uncompromising critic of "bourgeois humanism") that it turns into the extreme of idealism or voluntarism (Meisner 1982: 94–117). The idea is also fundamentally democratic. The usual charges of utopianism or adventurism notwithstanding, this emphasis—on the centrality of the people and human agency, the vitality of localities, the creativity of ordinary folks and equality and flexibility instead of rigid divisions of labor—contrasts with various contemporary "democratic deficits" identified in a self-critical literature of capitalist liberal democracy. A central tenet of the Chinese proposal is popular participation in government and governance, which places it in a qualitatively more advanced category than mere electoral politics. Transcending "bourgeois rights" as depicted in *The German Ideology*, Mao accentuates labor's and citizens' "right to management" of government, enterprises, communities, educational and cultural institutions and the like, which is "in truth their biggest and most fundamental right in a socialist system."[17] An explanation for the "revisionist" degeneration of the USSR, in Mao's critique of the Soviet economy ([1959]1977), is precisely the absence of such a right.

The social power should be not only foundational for regime legitimacy in the People's Republic but also an ultimate source of its developmental efficacy and cultural pride. The reverse course of transition from socialism in China may have fueled growth, but it also entails "widespread commodification of life processes and resources, including labor, land, nature, and bodies," catalyzing slips and shifts in society's normative infrastructure, moral values, and knowledge system along the way (Lee 2007: xii). Neither a strong economy nor a healthy politics, however, can really develop within the new fetters of a polarized and commodfied lifeworld. The rising social forces will have to bring the social and public back in while seeking their reconceptualization.[18]

The validity and viability of a socialist Chinese model are dependent on its moral and institutional prerequisites as identified in this chapter. Without the historically forged fundamentals including the revolutionary and socialist socialization of new China, little of what can be acclaimed in China's development today would have occurred. The defining political, economic, social, and cultural components of the model as delineated above should be defensible normatively but experimental and endlessly debatable in their actual, dynamic processes (e.g., Leonard 2012; Dallmayr and Zhao 2012). To sum up, these components are a popularly mandated sovereign state possessing governing and policymaking capacities; a substantial public sector (in search of a socialist market) as a secured basis for the nation's prosperity and economic-financial security; an institutional arrangement for taking government and societal responsibility for public welfare and popular wellbeing; and the rising social power to fulfill socialism through broad political and socioeconomic participation and transformative social movements. The contentions or dangers in each of these can be depicted, respectively, as further political distortion and policy capacity fragmentation of the state; deeper privatization of SOEs and other public assets and institutions; persistence of inequalities and deficient public provision; and destruction and decay of social commitment, power, and citizenship.

Insofar as a socialist project cannot be a teleological impossibility, it is worth articulation and debate. Finally to be noted is China's great advantage in its geographic scope and revolutionary tradition. Its policy autonomy remains broad enough to challenge the ideologically established superiority and universality of capitalism, global and Chinese alike. Whether the people of China will defeat adversaries and win time and space for a new navigation is a matter of politics, albeit within their specific historical and international conditions. Even if globalization is the order of the day, downplaying the primary position of the national and local, especially in the cases of geographically and demographically huge and historically and uniquely resourceful countries like China, would be a mistake. State roles and responsibilities cannot yet be evaded anywhere, nor should the power of the people as agents of history be ever forgotten.

# 6

# Class, Direct Producers, and the Impasse of Modernization

I have been using generic terms such as "the people" and "social," which are at the same time candid class terms in Chinese political discourse for a threefold reason. First, their actual referents and symbolic signification are historically derived from the Chinese revolution, which was both national and class liberating in nature. Second, while creating a common constituency, the revolution was predominantly based on and powered by the laboring classes with an elaborated self-identity of "worker-peasant alliance." Third, due to uneven development conditioned by global capitalism, oppressed and especially revolutionary nations necessarily acquire a "class" position. In formulating the revolutionary strategy, the opening passage of a 1927 article by Mao is classic: "Who are our enemies? Who are our friends? This is the foremost question of the revolution." Mao went on to delineate class identifications and relations of Chinese society in the immediate context of China's great revolutionary mobilization of 1924–27.[1] This primacy of the friend-enemy antithesis is a political sine qua non in the concept of an oppressed people in uprising, typified by "we the people" declared in the wars and struggles for democracy.[2] Later, on the eve of the founding of the People's Republic, Mao specified the class structure and basis for the new regime: "Who are the people? At the present stage in China, they are the working class, the peasantry, the urban petty bourgeoisie and the national bourgeoisie."[3] The "people" in the Chinese communist vocabulary (as in that of the East European people's republics) signalled a wider, popular front style politics distinguishable from the Soviet model of "proletarian" revolution and dictatorship. Class and class relations and their ideological construction and destruction have undergone a sea change in China since around 1949,[4] through a sequence of socioeconomic and political upheavals and transformations. The economic reform in particular has involved restoration of certain prerevolutionary class and social relations as well as creation of new ones in response to the global capitalist integration—the emergence of a bureaucratic bourgeoisie from within the party ranks (Chapter 3), for instance. However, as noted, class identities cannot be fixed at the points of production or distribution but are formed and transformed also through political, ideological, and cultural processes. Class is not a positivist category about sociological stratification, and class consciousness develops only through intensified politics. The largely abandoned language of "class" and "the people" in public discourse under a reform regime that denounced ideology is ironically only a sign of the severity of class exploitation and social polarization. The degradation of workers, peasants, and the common people, who had been glorified in the socialist tradition, is too threatening to the nominally communist state. The fact that these two notions have been up and down side by side throughout the history of the PRC is a confirmation of their shared connotation.

In the reformed social structure, most notable is the drastic decline of the state-sector working class caused by deindustrialization in the "rust belt" of old industrial centers and, especially, by privatization of SOEs. This has been paralleled by the development of a new private-sector working class during industrialization in the "sun belt" of the coastal south (Lee 2007). Catalyzing these changes in social contract is the sweeping commodification of labor, along with the "informalization" and "casualization" of employment followed by loss of job security and fringe benefits for workers (Kuruvilla et al. 2011). From 1991 to 2006, there was an increase in China's urban workforce of 260 million, of which 85 percent was due to migration from rural areas. An estimated 120 to 150 million workers—almost two-thirds of the industrial workforce and one-third of the service sector—worked long hours for meager pay without formal status in the cities. *Dagong,* literally meaning "selling labor," is how they describe their work life. They then joined laid-off SOE workers to swell the ranks of the 270 million Chinese known as "dispatch workers," or the world's largest "precariat" (Friedman and Lee 2010: 510–516). Also notable is a worldwide increasing "feminization of the proletariat" as part of the continuing destruction of non- or less commercialized rural production. "Capital now had access to the whole world's low-cost labor supplies. To top it all, the collapse of communism, dramatically in the ex-Soviet Bloc and gradually in China, added some two billion people to the global wage labor force" (Harvey 2010: 15–16). China has in this way critically aided global capitalism by presenting itself as a vast and badly needed outlet for the latter's surplus capital and indeed by turning the Chinese state itself into a rule-binding player in the world market.

Meanwhile, the rise of a middle class in China, fuzzily defined,[5] has entailed the decline of the traditionally protected industrial working-class (state workers belonged to a socialist "middle class," so to speak) and the (semi-) proletarianization of peasant migrants. The process then also involves fading solidarity or public commitment to class liberation and social equality. On the other hand, current and prospective young middle-incomers increasingly have difficulty finding affordable housing and stable employment. The white-collar, hightech sectors have also been feeling the pain of the global financial crises. Moreover, given the obvious ecological constraints alone it is seriously questionable whether China could ever achieve an "olive-shaped" "social middling" by the standard image of a family ownership of a house and a car. Ultimately, would not a leveled society be both morally more desirable and developmentally more feasible? Conceptually, just as the rhetoric of middle class appears all too blind or wishful, a seemingly apolitical, by and large dependent middle class compromises the politically charged notion of class itself. A more critical discourse in the field is needed without pretensions and illusions.

If the middle class is a cosmopolitan concept in a still substantially rural society—there are still 600 to 700 million broadly identifiable peasants in China—it does not follow that class redifferentiation is insignificant or that the new rich are not powerful in the Chinese countryside. The concept of "peasantry" must be taken with its own class composition: large- and small-household farmers, petty commodity producers, landless rural workers, tenant or agrarian wage laborers, and so on. Divisions according to income level and source of income are certainly indicative. However, such general terms as "peasants" or "farmers" remain useful in their specific identification of mostly small-holding agricultural producers. And in such usages the terms represent a category of class. This category, however, is plastic in a transitional political economy. Although over 50 percent of the Chinese population is now "urban," a large portion of it is unsettled. Many are temporary city dwellers traveling to work the land during the harvest and other busy seasons. Likewise, among the remaining rural residents some no longer farm but variously engage themselves in local factories, for example, and occasionally also join out-migration. It is not always clear whether the reference of "peasant" is narrow or broad, as the term is connected with a phenomenal "floating population" that is vigorously, if not exactly rootlessly, mobile. For convenience and without invoking a theoretical elaboration (cf. Cohen 1993), I use the terms "peasants" and "peasantry" wherever class is at issue and "farmers" as a mere occupational identity, covering also people in branches of the agricultural sector other than or mixed with farming, such as forestry, husbandry, or food processing.

A major intervening variable here is globalized circuits of production, trade, and financing. To be sure, the agrarian question is inescapably global in an age of capital that has subordinated the country to the city, peasant nations to industrial ones, and East to West (as depicted in *The Communist Manifesto*). But the socialist projects had for decades variously blocked those trends in a vast scale across Eurasia and in some other areas until they collapsed in one way or another to allow annexation by the world market, also increasingly in China. Global integration, however, remains a dual process of both capitalist expansion and anticapitalist resistance. The dynamic mobilization of the landless in Brazil, Mexico, or India is one example (Rousset 2009); the global peasant movement of La Via Campesina is another (Masioli and Nicholson 2011); the antiglobalization networking through the World and Third World Social Forums is yet another. In Goran Therborn's "plebeian prospects," even if Latin America is at present the only region where socialism is on the agenda, its popular and diverse social bases anticipate future transformations to be accomplished by a plurally constituted subject: class becomes a "compass of orientation—towards the classes of the people, the exploited, oppressed and disadvantaged in all their variety," and class alliance more than a single identity to be filled with proletarian consciousness. This is a controversial position in an ongoing debate on the left, but a more interesting observation in Therborn's prospect is that looking beyond Latin America, "for a new left to have true global significance, deeper roots will have to be dug in Asia" (2012: 26, 29).

Notwithstanding technologically advanced family farmers in the global north and assertions that "the figure of the peasant has throughout the world faded" (Hardt and Negri 2005: 120), that global modernity implies the world-historical "death of the peasantry," cutting us off "forever from the world of the past" (Hobsbawm 1994: 289) is unconvincing. From the point of view of a global south, the concept of peasantry cannot be merely a "great (if dwindling) residual of earlier historical epochs and modes of production". The "inherited notions of 'the peasantry' as anachronism or as 'backward' in material, cultural or political terms" have to be rejected (Bernstein 2001: 25–26, 46). This is so not only because small farming still dominates the lives of nearly half of humanity, or 3 billion people, but also because the phenomenon is not purely economic and sociological, but has important political ramifications as well (Watts 2009). The "peasant", backward and dependent in China's liberal narratives that dismiss a whole history of revolutionary peasant agency (Day 2013: ch.2), has been, and can still be, a politically inflected concept of class for regional or national movements and power.

A most relevant and also the largest case is the triumphant revolutionary socialization of rural China through the successive "new democratic" and "socialist" revolutions before and after 1949. Especially notable is the fact that the cooperative and communal movements in the 1950s proceeded largely on a voluntary basis "with neither the violence nor the massive sabotage characteristic of Soviet collectivization" (Selden 1982: 85; Nolan 1976). This was attributable to the peasants having already been engaged in the preceding land revolution, even if the communists were keenly aware of the continuing need to "educate the peasantry," including the massive peasant elements in their own ranks, in order to achieve a socialized agriculture.[6] As the agrarian question had been central to the communist program almost from the outset, a major upshot was the formation of a new rural historical subject. Collectively, in a recent historical and current constitutional alliance with the working class in the PRC, the peasantry cannot be regarded as "pre-capitalist" but rather is postcapitalist in its subjective identification and objective positioning. Unique to China's twentieth-century trajectory, then, is the paradox of the victory of a peasant revolution signaling also a political transformation of traditional agrarian categories. This transformation, along with the rise of a new rural agency, was so profound that even a sweeping decollectivization begun in the late 1970s could not overturn everything.

In this decollectivization, the household contract system was introduced to replace the people's communes. This led to a "triple crisis" (*sannong wenji*), peaking in the 1990s, for agriculture (land, production, and marketing), the farmers (displacement and urban-rural income disparity), and the villages (poverty, dilapidation, and collapse of public infrastructures) (Wen 2005). As the collective level of "double-level management" designed in the early 1980s to mitigate vulnerabilities of petty production collapsed in most places, individual households were left to fend for themselves. Later, land seizure also became rife, letting the push for land privatization seem rational. In the background the target of capital seeking "spatial fix" is now precisely the collective land and the remaining peasants, to be driven away from the land in order to sustain the supply of extraordinarily cheap labor.[7] The immediate paradox here is the dependence of a low wage level on the land's functioning as a source of security for migrant workers. In other words, land right accounts for a large share of the cost of labor reproduction in China and ultimately explains the country's "competitive advantage" in the global labor market. China's agricultural sector has so far not itself been conquered by the capitalist relations of production but is all too evidently part of that global order and on the defensive.

Defining "direct producers," a broader category than rural producers, is a conceptual challenge in the language of class. This Marxian notion signals a relation of production in which labor and its required conditions are in a natural unity. Literally, then, the proletarian wage laborer is excluded while the traditional peasant is included. But if the category is viewed as both descriptive and prescriptive, as in Marx's work, the direct producer would be either a member of a free collective or an independent petty property holder; in either case she has direct access to her means (and fruits) of production and her labor is not an exploitable commodity in the market. The productive and circulation processes directly engaging her are dictated neither by the power of capital for profit nor by the power of bureaucracy for rent. These processes are primarily of use value articulated by labor locally and coordinatively across localities. Such a realm in different forms is constantly present in capitalism and can be found everywhere, on the poor and neglected margins of the system as well as in the loopholes of its centers. Local networks of an informal, green "solidarity economy" of voluntary work paid for or rewarded in nonmoney exchanges (such as time or value vouchers banked in cooperatives) are not sporadic in Europe and North America.[8] But especially noteworthy are the still partially autonomous transitional economies wary of capitalist penetration. The identity of the direct producer in different situations is likely to be in flux and mixed with other identities in formal or informal employment and many forms of work.

Customarily and sometimes misleadingly, direct producers are taken as implying small peasants and analyzed in the class category of a petty bourgeoisie. Notably, despite the fact that the social basis of the Communist League and the 1848 revolution was constituted not by industrial factory workers but mostly by independent artisans and skilled laborers in corporate guilds for manufacture, Marx radically underestimates the sociological and political roles of petty producers. He also pays little attention to their anticipated historical agency in the intellectual thinking before the industrial revolution, from Rousseau's radical egalitarianism and popular sovereignty anchored in the freedom of a plebeian citizenship to Thomas Paine's "common sense" of the (revolutionary) right of the poor. Marx's bitter polemics against a "philistine" and "reactionary" socialism—"petty bourgeois socialism," "feudal socialism," "true socialism," and so on as half echo of the past and half menace of the future—set up a lasting "scientific" impact on the Marxist tradition of exclusively counting on the industrial working class for transforming capitalism.[9]

Marx did not attack decentralized labor associations or cooperatives as such, as advocated by the Proudhonists and anarchists. He also stressed that for workers to have any chance of victory they must work with and change the peasants. But his conditions were nothing short of a proletarian state power and socialized modern production. In his contempt for "rural idiocy," Marx treated the peasants as generally obsolete and prepolitical, awaiting either capitalist destruction or socialist transformation. After all, the revolutionary energy of subalterns in the peripheries was not yet on the horizon in his time. It is here that the singularity of the Chinese communist revolution must be appreciated—that it has transcended the Marxian law of industrial proletarianization by embracing the lowly and middle peasants, making them an organic builder of the new social order.

The petty bourgeoisie and direct producers may overlap in various social formations (some of which may accommodate multiple modes of production), but they are not conceptually identical. "Postindustrial" complexities in conceptualizing a petty bourgeoisie are notorious, such as differences between traditional small proprietors/producers and new science and technology professionals (and their bureaucratization), the issue of whether mental wage labor should be seen as an element of the working class, or how values of abstract labor might be calculated in terms of labor time (Mills 1951: ch.13; Poulantzas 2008). Regardless, the category of petty bourgeoisie is definitively narrower than the potentially all-inclusive conception of direct producers. The latter would be the primary protagonists in the new story of an ecosocialism. In fact the question of the future of direct producers can be the question of the future of socialism. And it is realistically raised in response to the ultimate challenge of our time and its alarming developmentalist impasse: land and water pollution, food and energy crises, rural decay and urban slums, toxic industries and inimical technologies, resource depletion and global warming, and, sociologically and politically, poverty, conflict, and the plight of the "last peasantry." Perhaps only a different civilization centered on the direct producers can in due course redress human and environmental devastations consequent to capitalism's predicaments of unsustainable growth and perpetual crisis of overproduction. Accompanying overproduction there is also the problem of overconsumption or, more precisely, a physical segregation between those who lavishly overconsume and those living in miserable underconsumption.

The limit of any petty bourgeois solution in the Marxist perspective is obvious. Concerning productivity, if the productive forces must be freed from the blockages of premodernity to create a surplus sufficient to meet needs, is there a valid place for petty production in an age of highly socialized modern economy? Where is the linkage or compatibility between the small and the large? Concerning the political identity of such an intermediate, vaguely defined class, can it attain any distinctive historical subjectivity through collective actions in class and social struggles? Commenting on Roberto Unger's "petty bourgeois radicalism" and its politics of empowerment, Perry Anderson points out that "the structural heterogeneity and ambiguity of the petty bourgeoisie alone militated against anything like seeing it as a force to remake the world" (1992: 139–140). Similar critiques have been channeled to contest conceptualizations in the same direction elsewhere to "modernize" class analysis so as to accommodate post-Marx social changes and recognize wider transformative social forces. The "popular bloc" for new hegemony (Laclau and Mouffe 1985) is one attempt, the "multitude" engaging also bio- and cyberpolitics against capitalist rent (Hardt and Negri 2005) is another. The latest, untheorized discursive tag of "99%" is popularized by the occupy movement.

These concerns might well be responded to positively at least in societies of less capitalist advance and more populist inclination. Marx focuses too narrowly on European workers' revolution but his case specific method is sound. He is sensitive to different preparations in different places for different strategies: "A radical social revolution is bound up with definite historical conditions of economic development; these are its premises." Bakhunin is wide off the mark not because of his idea about the liberation of all the "slaves" but because the idea is misapplied in his wanting "the European social revolution, whose economic basis is capitalist production, to be carried out on the level of the Russian or Slav agricultural and pastoral peoples." Confusing political tasks at various developmental levels, "willpower, not economic conditions, is the basis of his social revolution" (Marx [1874]1989: 518). That is, the agricultural and pastoral peoples should follow or be engaged by the working class and its political parties in struggles other than a single-handed proletarian revolution.

Cui Zhiyuan, who edited Unger's *Politics* (1997) as a political and analytical synthesis of Proudhonism, Lasellism, and Marxism, depicts an alternative in a "petty bourgeois manifesto" (2005). He defends small property holding, arguing that instead of perpetuating the proletarian status of workers, the point of socialism is to deproletarianize or enrich them. Together with the peasants and other small producers, the popular right-holders can achieve both developmental dynamism and political and economic democracy in a socialist market. This version of "liberal socialism," in competition "with Marxist, social democratic and neoliberal visions in China and the world" (2005: 157, 172), might be overtly charitable toward private property as a social formation,[10] but it does resonate locally and tangibly. Similarly, Philip Huang applies the notion of "middle class" broadly to include both "old" and "new" petty bourgeoisie standing between the capitalists and the proletariat. In that case, together with those doing well among migrant workers, they will account for 80 percent of China's workforce. Moreover, they constitute not only an economic but also a political middle class identifying itself with "agrarian cooperatism" (2012a). In these perceptions, heterogeneity of social groups encompassed in a "petty bourgeoisie" is a positive historical given, as in Unger's native Brazil or Cui's and Huang's China and the other countries in the global south.

Different from the traditional petty bourgeoisie and even more inclusive than a broadened middle class, both "transitional" in the Marxist outlook of ultimate class struggle, the notion of "direct producers" can be defined in line with Marx's original dialectic of the negation of negation in societal evolution toward a higher order. Such an order demands a socialized sphere that is free of an exploitative labor market, in which there is transparency not only of material and cultural production but also of extraction and allocation of the surplus, and in which use value and social values prevail. In such a sphere the direct producers are the precursors of unalienated labor, which will nurture individual capabilities as well as collective prosperity and rational management. This is in accordance with the Marxist fundamentals about surmounting the contradictions between capital and labor and between private ownership and socialized production. If the direct producers can be made a most inclusive class in a participatory and transformative politics, their conceptual and political construction would be far from a depoliticized "retreat from class," as in the case of post-structuralist revisions (Wood 1999).

Joao Pedro Stedile, the leader of the Brazilian landless workers' movement, offers a clarification of the movement's goal that concurs on this point: It is "an agrarian practice that transforms farmers into guardians of the land, and a different way of farming, that ensures an ecological equilibrium and also guarantee that land is not seen as private property" (quoted in McMichael 2010: 298). This resistance to the "machinations of the state system in converting agriculture to a world industry for profit" is then surely "a class politics," one that also shows "an ethical, historical and ecological sensibility" (McMichael 2010: 307–308). Moreover, the rise of an international peasant movement is a challenge to the notion of exclusive working class internationalism. The capitalist commercialization of agriculture and destruction of autonomous rural lives is a global project to compel global response. The peasant masses in the global South are shown to be capable of political mobilization and consciousness as a transnational class force fighting not for the past but for the future.

In China, having broken free from the chimera and practical confines of a capitalist modernization, the rural direct producers occupy a unique position with a unique historical experience. The fact that they have gone through a thorough-going land reform and a socialist transformation, that they still share the land even after decollectivization, that they are no longer in immobile or self-containing subsistence production and existence, and that their worldviews are shaped in modern mass communication using new information technologies, and so forth, makes all the difference (see Chapter 7). For whatever remains in their traditionally informed identities reinforced by the resumption of household farming, they are no old style petty peasants, and their anticapitalism beneath the surface of either some ambiguous urban aspiration or marketplace wisdom is, so to speak, not pre- but postcapitalist. With this picture of class in mind, the rest of this chapter will focus on whether the ideology and pathology of growth, productivity, industrialism, and urbanism can be questioned.

China's present agrarian crisis can be duly appreciated only in its political-historical context. If the communist revolution has paved the way for China's modern alternative to capitalist predicaments, it is above all because it has fundamentally changed class structure and land relations. Notwithstanding the tides of collectivization and decollectivization, the revolutionary principle of "land to the tiller" has been unrelenting and the land in the PRC is constitutionally designated as public and is legally owned by the state and collectives. The agricultural households have enjoyed use right over collective and (now resumed) individually allocated land on long term lease. This two-tiered arrangement of public ownership/control and household management is an innovative and decisive factor in national development.[11] To be sure, the republican revolutionary program had already combined the goals of land reform and nationalization to ensure that funds due to added land value from industrial or urban construction would go into the state treasury for public use.[12]

Scholars trace this specific structure further to the imperial tradition of duality of state and landlord, tax and rent (a focal point in the AMP debate). They also find it analogous in the separation, widespread for centuries in *jiangnan* and other relatively rich areas between so-called land bottom right (*tiandi quan* or ownership) held by the landlords (residential or not) and land surface right (*tianmian quan* or use right) held by the farmers. The peasants were supposedly protected by a customary "permanent tenancy right" (*yong dian quan;* emphyteusis) along with a locally favorable ecology of binding by clanship and village boundaries. The categorical difference between the new system and the old should be plain: the removal of a landed class and its structural networks is a precondition for socialist modernization; and members of the rural communities should have equal rights and shared stake.

It was the collective organization in the Mao era that enabled fundamental infrastructural improvement of agriculture as well as five small-scale rural industries—iron tools, cement, fertilizer, water and electricity, and light machinery—producing for local needs. Both depended on a land system without private metes and bounds. Communal factories also prepared for the TVEs to flourish in the early reform period, allowing absorption of a massive surplus labor in the countryside before what became the largest outflow of rural migration in human history. Indeed the start up of the whole state-led market transition banked on this crucial advantage of land being largely "free" to use for entrepreneurial initiatives. TVEs, for instance, enjoyed extraordinarily cheap productive factors: direct possession of land and easy supply of low cost labor as well as credit from previous collective accumulation and friendly financial cooperatives (Wen 2011: 19).[13] The retaining of public and communal land in the reform era also explains the outstanding phenomenon that China has so far avoided the worst scenario of slums, poverty, and a "lumpen-prolitarianized" underclass typical of an industrializing society the world over since the eighteenth century. Likewise, by contrast with postcommunist transitions in Russia and quite a few other Eastern-bloc countries, resistance to land privatization must be part of the Chinese story in which a similar plight of economic contractions or plunges in living standards was avoided.

China's existing land management, however, has suffered inconsistencies and is fragile in the face of growing difficulties and threats. Based on the 2003 "farmland contract law" after the 1986 "land management law," the system had undergone several more revisions to accommodate new property laws. The current law was designed to stabilize farmers' land right, yet its implementation disregarded demographic changes on the ground and resulted in a "landless" generation—many grew up to share family land without a title of their own. But rapid urbanization is an ever greater strain. The government is concerned about the diminution of arable land and has decided on a minimum "red line" of 1.8 billion *mu* (120 million hectares) to be guarded. This baseline is calculated according to the goal of 95 percent national self-sufficiency in grain supply. Official data show that China's per capita arable land has been reduced from 5.2 *mu* in 1950 to only 1.4 *mu* in 2008 owing to population growth and land loss to industrialization and urbanization.[14] To incentivize land conservation, the government has also set up local markets where collective farmland that has been rehabilitated (by replacing individual houses with land-saving collective housing construction, for example) can be sold in the form of land vouchers for cash and counted toward the "quotas of building land" purchased by the developers, public and private alike.

Strides in land market liberalization, especially policies of "land circulation," have given rise to de facto privatization. The "red line," as many people fear, could have already been crossed. Instead of an urgent corrective, the latest policy statement (number one document 2013) confirms the direction of more land concentration and urban expansion. It requires the ongoing registration of rural land to be completed for land right security and augmentation of farmers' income, including compensation for their land loss. However, despite stricter acquisition procedures, the stipulation stresses that the land market is to be boosted even further to "free up more rural labor" by transferring the land to larger holdings—"specialized agribusiness, family farms of scaled agriculture, concentrated and commercialized production and management."[15] It is unclear how the other standing policies of either the minimal arable land or the farmers' access to land can thus be upheld.

As China is a manufacturing power built on migrant labor from the countryside, the land has been rearranged or internally circulated without legal ownership transfers for years. It has mostly changed hands among the villagers, relatives, friends, and coops, as well as between villages and developers or governments. The latter two players in the (nominal) land market often act in consonance for shared returns. The formal land-use right remains a crucial source of security for migrant workers. While many of them have been absorbed into urban production and distribution systems and should in that case withdraw their land right, many others still cannot settle in the cities and have indeed returned to farming, as has happened during the recent global economic downturn, which hit China's export-dependent sectors with factory redundancies and closures.

This last expedient of subsistence, however, is under mounting threat of privatization, which cannot really secure land right but is misconceived as a solution to the problems of land grabbing and "land financing." It is not. Urbanization and the enormous real estate profits are what have created wrong incentives. The municipal and township officials have discretion over the land under national ownership through taxation, licensing, zoning and construction permits, and they can also convert originally nontradable collective land in highly profitable land dealings in a runaway market (Hsing 2010: 33–38). Rising land values and a growing GDP—to which frantically repetitive demolitions and constructions make a notable contribution—encourage land trade and housing market speculation, altering managerial, financial, and territorial orders throughout the country. This chain of reactions in turn intensifies the "triple crisis" as well as various problems of urban living, such as unaffordable housing, *hukou* (residential status) or migrants being treated as second-class citizens (Han 1999), and ever heavier pollution in the cities—a vicious circle. The role played by corrupt village cadres was highlighted in the Wukan confrontation (Chapter 4). Such cadres may sell or let village land without any democratic decision making process. Although village leaders are usually elected, such leaders, because of enduring or reviving traditional kinship, patriarchal or other "feudal" relations in a strange coalition with market forces in many places, not to mention vote rigging, are not necessarily representative or public serving. The problem of grassroots governance in the Chinese countryside that extended since the dissolution of communes has never been so penetrating. The organizational strength that the revolution painstakingly fostered is vanishing. As "urbanization is swallowing up villages" and capitalist agribusinesses are expanding, "already more than forty million peasants have been displaced, and every year three to four million more lose their land" (Andreas 2012: 134). The present struggle over collective land and household land rights is thus not only about the peasants' self-preservation but also about the collective and the whole socialist tradition behind it.

Because rural and urban problems intertwine and both are manifestations of China's developmentalist predicament situated in the global context of market integration, only an integral approach can address them. There are essentially two strategic responses on the table. One is short term but standard, and advocated in the prevailing policy discourse: urbanization, modernization, and privatization as the only way to stop land grabs, real estate bubbles, and forced eviction, and also to convert rural surplus labor into urban workforce so as to improve rural labor productivity. The other rejects such a threefold "solution," seeing it as a cause of the very problems it claims to solve. The alternative has to be a long term strategy that seeks to achieve *minsheng* while putting an end to the violence of modern standardization. Much of the debate may have wider implications, but wherever the Chinese quest appears singular, it is only because of its class positioning inherited from the revolution, which nevertheless may still convey universally important messages.

Consider the question of urbanization first. Half of the Chinese population is rural, and tens of millions of migrant casual job takers in cities still work the land from time to time. The breakneck "China speed" brought the country's nominal urbanization rate from 18 percent in 1978 to over 50 percent in 2011.[16] This might be celebrated if one chooses to ignore the immediate as well as lasting destruction and its victims. China has become part of a globally evermore exploitative and explosive imposition on the rural world and has been trapped in the myth that the only future of the developing countries is urban and that is what development means. But the effects of continuing urbanization as we know it would be overwhelmingly negative in at least three respects: ecological, demographic, and social. Such effects, in turn, would hinder development itself.

China's current energy consumption in terms of GDP per capita is 2.2 times the global average, and its trend of energy and mineral dependency has been sharply upward. Industrial growth aside, urbanization (not necessarily connected with productive industries) is a foremost contributor. For, by global average "the switch from rural to urban life roughly doubles energy use and carbon emissions per person."[17] Worse still, China's land-to-population ratio is one of the lowest on earth. Its rate of soil erosion is also one of the highest owing to desertification and other forms of water and soil loss. Pollution in the Chinese urban centers and industrial zones is hardly contained because of a combination of profit consideration, employment, and other pressures on growth, lack of far-sighted commitment, and poor regulation.[18] The Global Environmental Performance Index 2012 ranked China 116 out of 132 countries.[19] The question of environmental and health costs of growth is all time pressing and has to be addressed.

Meanwhile, whatever its urbanization rate might ever be, China will have to keep a substantial portion of its population occupied in producing food to feed itself. The straight-forward determination here is that given its size the country must maintain minimal food self-sufficiency. If, for instance, it is only 60 percent self-sufficient, Chinese demand would so exceed the current world market capacity as to immediately exhaust its grain supply.[20] "Who feeds China?" is a classic question. Socialist China has addressed it heroically and remarkably successfully despite extraordinary episodes. The point is that nobody can afford to unsettle the situation even in post-socialism. Urbanization as part of a capitalist transformation, however, is exacerbating the issue by the potentially irreversible threats of food insecurity and dependency.[21] An innovative and more holistic approach has to be sought in policy thinking and the green social movements.

New "enclosures" in China and other countries amount to a global offensive against the agrarian direct producers by corporate power of actual as well as speculative capital. It has led to the forced conversion of massively displaced peasants into labor commodities. This process destroys the common bonds and social tissues of past communities or collectives, often of a less polluted and wasteful character. Without spectacular catastrophes, an urbanization built on the backs of migrant workers in China has gone wrong, as is evidenced by everyday personal and social sacrifices as well as shocking waste, and by desolated villages and broken families. In many areas only the old and sick tend to the fields, and children are left behind by parents working hundreds or thousands miles away. In the evermore crowded and bifurcated cities, the newcomers struggle without strong support from either the governments or any labor union. The domestic workers, of a very large number and predominantly female, are the least protected. The familiar scenes are disturbing: there are on the one end lavish but unoccupied buildings, exclusive golf courts and entertainment clubs, deserted tourist parks, airports and luxury shopping centers; and on the other underfunded public housing projects, visible urban and rural poverty, cramped trains carrying "floating" workers, and overloaded school buses running dangerously on country roads.[22] A deep sense of alienation and unfairness is widespread.

Even among those better off many are compelled to rethink modernization and consider that something precious might have been lost in the process. Calling themselves "mortgage slaves" (*fangnu*) or otherwise "snails" (*woju*) unable to afford more decent living, educated young urbanites begin to reflect on the contradictions of growth: What if the ruthless amassing of (virtual) wealth is not rational and not a true measure of wellbeing? Has not an urban-centered development already been delegitimized by its developmentalist logic and impairments?

These questions are especially acute in China's most contentious minority regions, where escalating ethnic tensions are directly related to this alien impulse of growth. Manifestations of this impulse include Beijing's "go-west" campaign launched in the 1990s without due spatial-cultural, environmental, and political sensitivities concerning ethnicity, religion, and locality. The inflow of Han settlers in Tibet and Xinjiang (where it began much earlier but was concentrated in state farms on what had been wasteland), in particular, has redrawn the regional demographic and economic landscape, causing fear and resentment among the locals. If there was never a deliberate state intention to undermine Tibetan and Muslim dominance and heritages in the two regions, respectively, an invasive market transition is doing the job all too efficiently. For many minority people this transition signals a horrifying threat of commercial homogenization or cultural extinction. It has also produced new class inequalities in addition to, or in the guise of, ethnic ones. Corrupt officials and money driven developers of Han origin with a chauvinistic attitude are a combination likely to inflame deadly riots (Pai 2012: 283–290). It would thus be fair to see the present impasse as the result of state-sponsored capitalist development and departure from the socialist commitment to equality and regional autonomy.[23] The spread of religious movements in China's largely secular zones in the past two decades, beyond the issue of constitutionally settled religious freedom for traditionally religious nationalities, has a similar origin in the moral crisis and ideological disorientation brought about by the market relations. The lesson should be plain that human and social development cannot be the same as urban, industrial, and commercial expansion. The Chinese government will have no choice but to resume its policy of the 1980s of prioritizing small cities and towns over big metropolises, in line with local preference and knowledge about what the sociologist Fei Xiaotong has characterized as an "earthbound China."[24] This notion, antithetical to large scale rural-to-urban migration, is about transforming the rural on the spot through incorporated productive chains of agriculture, sideline occupations, processing, and other locally sourcing and serving industries. The earlier experience has had its problems, such as polluted and unsafe TVEs under deficient regulation. But implemented right, a nonconventional and more sustainable method should induce more rational and desirable eco-social gains. The formal policy is, after all, about *cheng zhen hua* or urban- *and* township-ization as well as "urban-rural integrated development." It is intended to embrace in-place "industrialization of townships and villages" all along the urban-rural continuum or hybridity, enabled by public land and collective management (Li, Chen, and Liu 2012: 28; Day 2008: 69–70). The idea of an "eco-civilization" and its "efficient, hightech, green and low carbon" pathway is also being taken seriously as the Ministry of Finance has at long last announced the introduction of a tax on carbon dioxide emissions.[25]

The second layer of the neoliberal prescription is capital intensive, scaled agriculture run by the "new managerial subjects" in a "new agricultural management system" officially promoted for modernization. Encouraged by policies of preferential treatment, capitalistic agribusinesses, local and multinational, have been gaining ground on the ruins of a collective agriculture. As land is being aggressively put into their possession, the old feeding-China question again comes to the fore. The problem is that China's agricultural sector provides the basic livelihood of the Chinese population, not only through its commodity products but above all through the self-subsistence of peasants themselves. And, as noted, the sector includes also those tens of millions of migrant workers who remain only temporary residents in the cities and can reclaim their piece of land on returning home. This existing arrangement, imperfect as it is, has optimally worked as a "two-tiered structure of urban-rural generational division of labor" in He Xuefeng's depiction: Insofar as the older people can stay in the villages and the younger ones who fail or no longer desire to settle in stable urban jobs can return and live on farming, the model secures both an industrial labor supply and a self-sustaining as well as surplus-producing agriculture, both basic social stability and continual growth (He 2010).

The secret of a "Chinese miracle" so far without the tribulations of landlessness and a massive "reserve army" of labor should be found in this extraordinarily "low-cost" arrangement of labor production and reproduction. The issue of human costs aside, to be emphatically recognized is the fundamental and gigantic economic responsibility as well as the sociopolitical function of rural China for popular subsistence and security. Any ideologically motivated "scaling" of farming or modernization would be a grave error, if only because nowhere else can the nearly 200 million rural households resettle without ruining their own basis of living.

In addition, agribusiness capital is invested mostly in cash crops and livestock, because grain production other than fodder for direct human consumption is less profitable. One form of this investment is direct land enclosure along with the conversion of a small proportion of affected peasants into wage laborers in the new mechanized farms. A softer and fast spreading model, which involves similar land concentration but less peasant displacement, is known as "dragon head enterprise plus household" (Zhang and Donaldson 2008). Together, these methods lead a dangerous trend of "degrainization" or even "deagrarianization" in a sector tasked with feeding a country of China's size.

In the end, the severe population pressure on land makes it straightforwardly irrational to let big business in either form "compete" with or, rather, crush small producers by seizing their land, taking away their profit margin, and destroying their valued way of life. For the greater the investment allowed from big business, the larger the section of nongrain production becomes, and the lesser the sideline returns left for peasant households. Capital inevitably extracts most surpluses. In other words, negatively affected would be not only the state's capacity for food supply, but also the already squeezed, meager market income of the farmers, since agriculture as a whole only makes up 10 percent of GDP (He 2010).

Rural labor productivity is a wrong concern in this context. For one thing, the "proletarianization" or partial proletarianization of small landholders implies the invasion of capitalist exploitative relations in the preexisting commons (which in China are modern collectives rather than traditional petty economies). For another, the throwing out of people who must then seek work and livelihood somewhere else is to "transfer" rather than transform low productivity, along with the accompanying personal and social problems. That is, if higher productivity is preconditioned on dispossession and displacement, that productivity is diminished from a macroeconomic point of view. With respect to mainstay agriculture, historians and economists tend to agree that family management can be most suitable given the sector's crop cycles and eco-climate dependence. In the long-enduring agricultural civilizations, it seems also historically the case that household intensive farming can be most productive with regard to unit yield. A petty peasant economy may not be efficient in terms of labor productivity but can well be efficient in terms of land productivity. This point, however, cannot be pushed too far to negate the pivotal role of cooperation in agricultural organization, of which the scholarly and policy debates are highly relevant.

In the same vein, there are also geological and ecological constraints, especially given China's low arable land per capita ratio. For all its celebrated accomplishment, the green revolution has also had some dire consequences. The deterioration of land fertility owes to chemicalization in a vicious circle of requiring evermore chemical input to keep the soil fertile. Nutritional and taste value of agricultural produce has diminished, so has toxic contamination of land, water, and food itself in an increasingly industrialized agriculture. For China, most alarming is the country's reduced degree of food sovereignty[26]—even though it has retained a self-sufficiency rate above 90 percent, imports have been growing substantially.[27] China's WTO accession has bankrupted its numerous soybean producers and weakened the market position of many others (Wang 2013). Foreign food and seed corporations led by powerful multinationals such as Monsanto and DuPont have found most receptive investment opportunities in China and entered almost every key stage of its agricultural production and supply. The rising share by transnational agricapital in China's corn, wheat, rice, soybean, and vegetable markets has been warned against by expert critics but ignored by the government. Similarly, unscrutinized introduction and conversion of generically modified products are tolerated as the State Council and Ministry of Agriculture do not seem to care whether such development has any long term negative impact on domestic production and consumption.

In his critiques of industrial capitalism "robbing the worker" and "ruining the more long-lasting sources" of the land, Marx sees "the rational cultivation of the soil as eternal communal property." He condemns factory wastes, toxic disposals, pollutions of rivers and air, deforestation, and other costs of capitalist "progress." For him, the history of human society is part of natural history, and communism is a "fully developed naturalism." Only cooperative associations of free producers can sustain that synchrony of the social and natural, preserving the earth's finite resources and reversing the commodification of labor, land, and life in general (Bensaid

2002: 313–324; Eagleton 2011: 220–230). It would be in line with this Marxist perspective—contrary to those scientific Marxists who dismiss any "antimodern" or "romanticist"' thinking about small producers or the petty bourgeoisie— that the direct rural producers be taken as the rightful counterforce to capitalist integration.

This can be argued for at least in the case of China with such crucial conditions as collective organization and state support (Chapter 7). A new rural economy centered on these producers would halt the destruction by managing the finite land to sustain the population, following more energy- and water-saving approaches, preserving organic and biodiverse seeds, nurturing the soil using green and animal manures as well as systems of fallow and crop rotation, avoiding monoculture and its heavy application of fertilizers and pesticides, and ending the misuse or abuse of land and food. The validity of the contention that monoculture is economically more rational because of its higher labor productivity is a matter of choice between different cost-and-benefit calculations. In the long run, however, especially in the Chinese conditions, a compelling case can be made that only relatively small, flexible, and highly intensive farming can be both productively and environmentally optimal, provided that it is well organized in cooperative networks based on collective land. The goal is to conserve the eco-biosphere through healthy agrosystems of switches and linkages and inputs and outputs in a "closed-loop," achieving locally the best possible economies of scope if not scale.

Philip Huang's "new-age agriculture" is an example of a modern, forward-looking vision of petty farming in which the family is the basic labor unit. It, as he argues, could set China on a path of "de-involution" (referring to his notion of China's historical "involutionary growth without development," discussed in Chapter 2), not by scaled and extensively mechanized production but by both capital- and labor-intensification on small farms and horticultural cooperation among them. It is again premised on the acknowledgment of the "special logic of family economy under population pressure" (2012b: 86), a logic that also follows from China's specific property structure of land rights for the household-responsibility system (2011: 110–114). Additional reasons for seeing "small capital-labor dual intensifying family farms" as the future of Chinese agriculture are changing food consumption patterns in the country (which though requires a critical consideration) and a corresponding structural transformation in rural production. Small family management is better suited because of the intensive, incremental, and variegated hand labor required in livestock-poultry-fish raising and hothouse or garden vegetable-fruit growing (2011: 107ff). But even staple crops involve hand labor in multicrops, intercropping, cultivation of edges and corners, and so on. In comparison with a land-rich agriculture, greater intensity in capital and labor inputs per unit land is a shared East Asian experience, with China being the hardest pressed in that direction. This, however, must not involve intensified energy consumption and be pursued with due attention to conserving natural biodiversity and use value of wild plants.

Yet fragmented and atomized petty production by itself would inescapably suffer myriad risks and bankruptcy threats in the face of natural disaster, market volatility, or other individually insurmountable obstacles. This vulnerability was among the rationale for rural China to collectivize in the 1950s in the first place. In the present situation of fragmented and weakened rural communities, for any "new age" small farming to succeed in enjoying both the security of a moral economy and benefits of the market, three institutional conditions are imperative. One is self-organization, that the peasant households must organize themselves into multilayered and multifunctional varieties of cooperatives. This may also involve a desirable degree of land concentration wherever it can benefit from mechanization or other productive advantages. Another is government support from central policies and subsidies to local infrastructure and services through the public means and socialized agents. The third is public ownership and management of land, to be discussed next. The first two institutional measures should both cover operations throughout—upstream (manufacturers of agricultural inputs; credit; and banks), midstream (machines and technologies for cultivation), and downstream (food processing and other agroindustries, transportation, and retail chains) —wherever the job is impossible for individual households or when they can be better handled collectively or governmentally.

This would in turn curtail agribusiness "dragon heads" acquisition, apart from a few limited areas where they could engage certain infrastructural projects or explore idle resources, under strict land, environmental, and labor regulations. Small farmers would not then become lowest-level subcontractors subject to monopoly control by big capital. Instead, while pursuing "vertical integration" of all streams they could form self-owned (by joining land, labor, or money shares, etc.) or self-managed (by democratic decisionmaking) coops and connect members at different ends of the operation "in contractual terms based on cooperative principles." Such a system could be "superior to a wage-based firm in terms of incentives and stability" (Huang 2011: 124–128). "Associated labor," in the Marxian vocabulary, would also effectively help the farmers to attain more advanced methods of production while developing themselves as free and rounded individuals and as self-governing citizens. Moreover, only a household based yet collectively organized rural economy can be organically integrated into the socialized national economy, achieving desirable exchanges of urban-rural mutual nurturing. The purpose, as Chen Xiwen, director of the office of the central leading group on rural work, rightly clarifies, is the strengthening and consolidation of the managerial subject position of farmers themselves.[28]

The last component of neoliberal "solution" to China's rural crisis is to privatize the land while deepening market reform, claimed to be fulfilling a fundamental peasant demand. While the third condition for the viability of advanced small farming (following the other conditions of cooperatization and state backing) is precisely the collective land to which farmers enjoy equally distributed use right. Without this condition, not only would the cooperatives be far more difficult to form and funds and aid from government and industries far less effectively materializeable, but the collective protection and support of individuals and families, including any land issue, would also be lost. If the land could be traded freely, no legal ownership would prevent people from selling it in need or crisis. Ignoring these objections, the threat of privatization, however, is growing, as land "circulation" had already involved up to 20 percent of the contracted land by 2012. Large scale and long term "enclosures" often by private capital with or without government shares of farmland, agropasture meadows, and forests happen wherever local leaders prioritize cash returns in the name of "modernization."[29] Degrainization and the shrinking of arable land would be a direct consequence. In the end, if the farmers and pastoralists as direct producers were to be separated from their means of production and subsistence, there would then be no security or subjective position for them in rural China, conditions deemed vital also for the whole nation's basic grain self-sufficiency and stability.

The current project of "clarifying rights" (que quan) to recertify collective ownership and individual use right has yet to be completed. As a double edged measure it could also be a step closer to land privatization. The existing system of land tenure does appear ambiguous enough to enable local officials and private developers alike to reach lucrative deals. But such ambiguities, despised in professional economics, also serve an essential function of blocking a wholesale privatization. This delicate yet principled distinction between owning and using, or "possession" and lease right, is meaningful in a socialized and publicly regulated market, in which rights might be tradable without transfer of legal ownership itself. Wen Tiejun explains why China's traditional duality of common and private rights in land has an enduring validity, showing that the tighter the land supply, the higher the cost of privatization would be (1999; Day 2013: ch.6). In particular, this necessary two-tiered system must not be undermined by overemphasizing the solidity of use right as de facto private property.[30] The trading of land rights must be strictly limited and regulated. To be safeguarded is government monopoly over the primary land market based on a state land reserve system of increased land value that is not due to private owners' labor going to the public coffers (Cui 2011: 651–652).[31]

Those in China's policy and academic circles who advocate abandonment of the system in favor of a "mature" capitalist clarification of property rights have a few superficial arguments for their proposal. But they are either naïve or deliberately deceptive in asserting that privatization is about curbing land grabbing and protecting farmers' fair share of urban development. In truth, as is profusely shown by China's history of landlessness and peasant revolts as well as by the recent trends of displacement, privatization would only quickly lead to land concentration in the hands of real estate gamblers, domestic and foreign agroindustrial capitalists, and new landlords created from private accumulation. The rebirth of a landed class would take China all the way back to the "old society," which after all compelled and justified one of the greatest and most violent social revolutions in world history. The land's ultimate functions of security and stability in China make it all the more imperative that privatization be opposed as a radically irresponsible move. It would only worsen the existing problems and cause spreading unrests if not immediate social breakdown. It could also push rural China deeper into becoming just another and surely the largest victim of the most exploitative global productive chains and relations.[32] Rather than any of the classical Prussian or American paths compared by Lenin and more recently debated among concerned Chinese intellectuals (Qin and Su 1996; Lv 2012b: ch.1),[33] China could, as Li Changping warns, end up taking a Philippine direction.[34]

Much of what China has achieved in development, including the market transition, is due to its public land system—state sovereignty over the nation's territories and mainstay natural resources, government control of urban land and prerogative to requisition collective land for policy priorities, collective management of communal and village land, and the right to equal use of collective land in the countryside. This system has enabled substantial infrastructural transformations across rural and urban China since 1949, including a degree of rural industrialization. This industrial development has in turn enabled higher household income as well as absorption of a surplus agricultural labor. Public land is thus also a major factor that explains the lack in China of typical third world urban diseases. The fact that public ownership, control, and management of land is a fundamental condition for China's national wellbeing and development is in itself a sufficient reason that the system, having so far withstood erosions of informal privatization in farming, mining, and forestry, should be rigorously defended.

Moreover, security in collective land is behind personal incentives as well as the organizational logic of maximizing unit yield in agriculture. Further still, it is where the reverse flow of migrated labor and its decommodification might be encouraged. The state-owned land, meanwhile, is essential for industrial development, urban planning, and infrastructure. Affordable housing for new workers and newcomers, for example, depends on public land and funds. With state ownership, central and local governments should have the power to limit land depletion—land lost to legal and illegal seizures for urban expansion, wasteful construction, deagrarianization, and idled (excluding fallow) farmland. In particular, if a socialized land market is to exist at all, it must be run directly by professional state agencies in the public discretion. Chen Xiwen is sensible in noting that rural homesteads might be circulated within the village collectives but not "sold" to outside buyers. No land under use right should have to be mortgaged. Policies need to be geared toward supporting cooperative financing and microcredit for the household economy and small business in addition to agricultural subsidies.[35]

To insist that the land be publicly owned and managed is to seek an optimal reordering of the relationships between state, capital, and labor, between the nation and the global system, market and community, and city and country. China is at a developmental crossroad. It faces choices between buttressing direct producers and welcoming (multinational) agrocapital domination, between organization and atomization of petty production, between rebuilding the collective level of "double management" and privatization, between revitalizing rural society and continuing to sacrifice it for urbanization that is in any case unsustainable, between securing food sovereignty and relying on a risky and ultimately insufficient global market, and between a capitalist transformation of rural China and a socialist transformation of it into a modern moral economy. The choices China makes will determine its own future as much as the world's.

The politically charged agrarian question of land, food, peasant politics, and rural organization is also an ideological one. Taking industrialization, urbanization, and commercialized agriculture as measures of development is an ideology; so is understanding modernization in terms of market, industrialism, and urbanism. If the rise of capitalism featured industrial and urban transformations, that path is both humanly undesirable and ecologically unrepeatable in the twenty-first century. Not only has the earlier interconnection between the processes of industrialization and urbanization more or less broken in "postindustrialism," capitalism's promise of integrated global modernity has also shattered, as is attested to by the deep gulfs and calamities the system as "a scheme of destruction" keeps reproducing (Polanyi 1957: 163). Capitalism survives "by destroying the two main sources of its own wealth: the land and the laborer" (Harvey 2006: 114). As overextraction, pollution, and a "planet of slums" (Davis 2001) corrupt growth and its claims, the fetish of wealth accumulation is bankrupt.

The justice of poor people exercising their socioeconomic right to development is indisputable. It is only when developmentalism is allowed to reign that "development" derails. Locally adapted modernization is possible, as is seen in new China among the historically socialist and developmental states. At issue is thus not whether economic nationalism is justifiable, given the past and present conditions of global polarization and injustice. It is rather an issue of what kind of development is entailed—one that is independently pursued to alter an underprivileged national position, one that is benefitting a previously impoverished population at large, and one wherein the organic social tissues of local communities and their natural environment are protected in the process. In the end, human flourishing cannot be measured by GDP, urbanization rates, or market values and cannot be about standardization and homogenization. Indeed, the standard methods of modernization have come to negate socially desirable development. Likewise, it is time to decouple the ideologically paired notions of modernity and capitalism.

The formidable objections to modern standardization for the predicaments identified in this chapter include both "hard" and "soft ones." Economic, ecosystemic, and geopolitical logics are hard, counting as well diminishing returns of land as one of the finalities human society faces.[36] Such constraints can be even harder in China's adverse ecological and demographical conditions. Geopolitically, moreover, despite its "low-profile" diplomatic stance and collaborative contributions to the world economy, China keeps confronting international misgiving in a Cold War mentality. The United States has reaffirmed its "strategic dominance" in Asia in a post–Cold War era. The unending campaign of "China bashing" has spread to some of China's neighbors. In contrast with the large extent of foreign business in China, Chinese companies often fail in their acquisition bids in the West, where protectionism is especially strong against China. Meanwhile, unlike the old colonial powers and morally distant from their practices, China after all cannot pursue overseas expansion for ecological relief or resource extraction and its "go out" policy is self-contradictory. Even if it is an error for historical and ideological reasons to liken the Chinese energy quest to old imperialist exploration, China (and India, etc.) is "certainly in the game" of capitalist global accumulation (Issa Sivji in Patnaik and Moyo 2011: 3) and out of the lost world of internationalism.

Yet, precisely because the hard determinants make the global developmental impasse unsustainable, deep seated social-moral preferences would play a "soft" but no less decisive role in forging alternatives. Such preferences are evident in class consciousness, social commitment, political movements, and communal ethos in various parts of the world. Breakthroughs somewhere could involve material, cultural, and political preparation for a new moral economy. Hence the contours of the agrarian question—state-facilitated land grabbing by rich counties for outsourcing and by private investors for profits—which "in its scale, generalized nature affecting all the peasantry and its depth is quite unprecedented." While hightech genetically modified seed and plants are taking over agriculture and its biodiversity and giant transnational corporations are acquiring extraction rights over minerals, precious metals, and water in the south, there is "a deep theoretical failure" in understanding the links between the agenda of international finance capital and the destruction of people, their livelihoods, and resources outside the capitalist core (Patnaik 2011: 51–52, 59). Since China is only one case, albeit a giant and relatively new one, of such links, the Chinese search for an alternative could be globally resonant. It is also inevitably political as a project of direct producers (re)gaining subjectivity, organization, and power.

# 7

# The Rise of the Social: For a Communist Moral Economy

The most creative thinking emerged from China regarding the invigoration of Chinese socialism rejects conventional modernization and globalization in their prevailing forms. The new vision is "local," local national, local social, and local communal, in the sense of locally desirable and feasible, as a negation of the standard modern markers of relentless industrialization, urbanization, commodification, and homogenization. In line with a normative Chinese model outlined in Chapter 5, this project toward satisfying needs, common pursuits, and free development of individuals and communities must be measured according to its own goals. It could be a long and difficult yet confident process in which the direct producers assume their rightful place in crafting an unparalleled political economy as an advanced social formation born out of China's indigenous, revolutionary, and socialist traditions. Such a formation is to be based on thorough socialization as opposed not only to isolated petty production but also to private control over the market, thus paving the way for a future global postindustrial and postcapitalist reorientation. The ongoing struggles in China to undo privatization of land and strategic industries are intrinsic to the reinvention of local and national moral economies, a project that breaks the monopolistic yet false equation of capitalism and the modern.

The label "postindustrial" is deliberately and emphatically used here to indicate the level of socioeconomic development of the new age moral economy. For one thing, many observations in the classic works by E. P. Thompson (1971) or James Scott (1976) about the rationality and justice of rioting peasants, subsistence ethic, and reciprocal security or patronage in preindustrial societies would not readily apply. The new model is set in a very different historical context with a very different national political economy of developed and socialized relations of production. For another, the creation of the model is dependent on a solid industrial foundation. Moreover, the remaking of the "last peasantry" in these circumstances is also a postcapitalist ambition. It has nothing to do with the familiar romanticism of preindustrial or precapitalist fantasies but everything to do with socialist renewal and novelties.

In China, an industrial foundation has been laid since the early 1950s through a massive, tortuous, and yet successful undertaking of socialist industrialization. It has in turn enabled the country to achieve a degree of agricultural mechanization and a grand "green revolution," for better or worse.[1] Above all, China's feat of managing in due course to eradicate hunger among its vast population would not have been possible without a strong urban sector—the support of agriculture from the governments, cities, and industries is the other side of the coin of a socialist primitive accumulation.[2] More generally, adequate industrial inputs and infusion—to be distinguished from a total industrialization of agriculture—serve two important purposes: in combination with labor-intensive farming, it helps increase land yield; and in the process it lessens labor intensity so as to liberate the peasants from backbreaking toil as well as poverty. None of these gains is adequately appreciated in the notion of "labor productivity." Industrialization is then not something a socialist moral economy can dismiss or escape; it forms the very basis of such an economy of agrarian development and rural organization. The latter, in turn, would boost industrial growth.

The capitalist accumulation and industrialization of creative destruction are a different story, although they now become a contradictory part of the Chinese story as well. To gauge the nature and extent of industrial and urban transformation in China, as anywhere, is to assess to whose costs and benefits and by which optimality the construction or destruction involved is determined and calculated. At stake is then the desirability and practicability of a different mode of modernized production, in which new moral economies can flourish, as in China with half of its population in one way or another remaining on the land. The sketches below focus on its defining features and rationality, along with its historical premises and contemporary conditions.[3]

In his critique of the primitive accumulation in which the capitalist class formed through epoch-making revolutions,[4] Marx stresses "those moments when great masses of men are suddenly and forcibly torn from their means of subsistence and hurled as free and 'attached' proletarians on the labor market." As "the expropriation of the agricultural producer, of the peasant, from the soil, is the basis of the whole process," "the so-called primitive accumulation... is nothing else than the historical process of divorcing the producer from the means of production" ([1867]1971: 738–739 and part 8). "Accumulation by dispossession," as David Harvey puts it, is about the massively dispossessed peasants being turned into commodities in the labor market. Accelerated destruction on the land itself, meanwhile, is due primarily to the two systemic agents of state and capital: "Uneven geographical development is not a mere sidebar to how capitalism works, but fundamental to its reproduction" (2010: 58–60, 213). These processes continue to commodify land, convert shared property into exclusive private property, suppress the commons and public welfare, and wipe out indigenous or alternative forms of production and consumption. There has also been a military expansionist impulse; British imperialism, typically, was "built on the foundation of agrarian capitalism" (Wood 2009: 55). "Colonial, neo-colonial and imperial processes of appropriation," of exploiting natural resources, are historical as much as current (Harvey 2006: 43).

As Marx notes, capitalist primitive accumulation assumes different aspects, phases, and orders of succession in different countries and different historical epochs ([1867]1971: 738). What remains questionable is whether the pillaging of resources and accumulation at one end based on pauperization at the other can be altered, along with the seemingly inexorable modern ideology of industrial and urban superiority; and whether what Polanyi among many others sees as "organic forms of existence" can still exist outside that overwhelming process or even develop independently and compete with it.[5]

The socialist experiences, including those of historical communism, however limited, are a foremost case in point. Opposing the capitalist system, which "presupposes the complete separation of the laborers from all property in the means by which they can realize their labor" (Marx [1867]1971: 737–738), Chinese socialism is an attempt at validating that integrity of the producer and her means of production— "the natural unity of labor with its material prerequisites" (Hobsbawm 2012: 67). By the same token, official China's claim for a "socialist market" today cannot be substantiated insofar as the access to the means of production by direct producers is not defended. As noted, despite the country's formal commitment to public ownership, privatization of SOEs and excessive urbanization have turned old and new workers into exploited wage laborers. Involving private land dealers and driving away of members of a hitherto collective rural economy from the land, rapid urban expansion also relies on low-paid jobs and often unsafe or abusive working conditions. Insofar as defending and prizing direct producers is to defend and prize socialism, this stance coincides with the recognition of the subjective position of direct producers as the "masters of society". A once penetrating popular notion in China, it needs to be revitalized for reinventing socialism itself. Such a position, to be reified through the rise of the social and social power after state socialism, is defined negatively as freedom from market exploitation and alienation on the one hand and from wasteful and repressive bureaucratic imposition on the other. But it is also defined positively, as freedom to utilize and benefit from both market dynamism and state provision and protection, in a coordinated framework of socialist moral economies. This dual subtext is where "the social" must be demarcated and defended from its right wing rhetoric and abuses, which confuse the social with the market, deny class conflicts or asymmetrical power relations in society, and attack a regulatory and redistributive state.

Logically implied in the commitment to labor's retaining direct access to the means of production is the idea of "surplus retention"—to borrow from dependency theory's critiques of capitalist international trade relations, in which the core countries take the lion's share of any profit created on the periphery, depriving the peripheral countries of any opportunity to "catch up." Domestically, it opposes "cheap labor" and cycles of dispossession and (semi-) proletarianization. That is, does not only the direct producer produce, she produces in the (local) commons. Two aspects of the idea are then expected: One is that to various extents direct consumption of one's own products in the modern, developed eco-economies is of a natural value and entirely possible. This is not confined to traditional economies but is also extensively demonstrated in contemporary advanced societies. Examples are many, such as collective architectural design of, and voluntarily sustained facilities for, residential communities, or neighborhood schemes of demand and supply in locally produced food, folk handicrafts, home care, and other services.[6] The other is that labor would share control over the allocation of surpluses as an ultimate measure against exploitation. The nature of a mode of production and social formation is ultimately determined by the outcome of perpetual contention over what to produce, why, and under which conditions and how the surplus is utilized and distributed. This is where struggles to overcome capitalism are fiercest, further requiring institutionalized monitoring, supervision, and direct participation from labor in management to stimulate incentives and rewards for production. The dual offense of commodifying and degrading labor in China's market reform is thus criticized on not only moral but also rational grounds (Meisner 1989a). In a nutshell, the model of new moral economy is centered on the direct producers most broadly conceived. They are constitutive of the common social at all levels across all cleavages—urban and rural, coastal and inland, Han and minority origins, and so on. And they are voluntarily organized in all possible forms of united labor, in which their economic and political power lies. This social organization is premised on equality and citizenship in terms of class alliance, reciprocal solidarity, communal associations, and productive cooperation in open, interactive, and coordinated national and subnational settings. The model thus negates autarky while featuring autonomy, direct democracy, and a degree of communal self-reliance at the unit level. The local need oriented and environmentally minded ways of production and consumption would support organic and collective webs of life of a fresher, greener, simpler, and more economical and energy efficient character. Concerning economic rationality, for example, because of urban and industrial expansion, large areas of agricultural land have been lost in southern China, necessitating transportation of grain from the north; but then water shortage is most acute in northern China, in turn pressing for gigantic hydraulic projects to transport water from the south (and the west). Modern economics may see all these movements as normal or even good in terms of growth or economy of scale (in e.g. urban concentration and rural monoculture) as well as in creating jobs. But the obvious irrationality of resource mobilization with serious social and eco-environmental implications must be confronted in policy considerations.

Transcending the modern superstitions of both a market centered in private property, pathological consumerism, and money/wealth maximization and bureaucratic statism in either conventional socialist or capitalist variants, the new vision of a national moral economy constituted of numerous local commons can be defined by its communist ambition.

This depiction is commonsense, simply denoting shared access to common resources by the commoners in public communications based on the fundamental social nature of human existence. The direct producers in their (re)assumed subjective position will find themselves in social relations categorically different from traditional ones, whether in the confined mutuality of closed societies or in the coexistence of competition and monopoly in the modern marketplace. Individual and collective contributions or achievements are recognized by their use value over exchange value. The Marxist axiom of "from each according to ability, to each according to needs" applies without regard to the often misconceived notion of "abundance." The social rises to manage its own affairs at all levels rationally and democratically.

To further clarify how the new and old moral economies differ, two factors should be accentuated. Above all, as indicated, unlike any pre-capitalist mode of production, the new model is postcapitalist and fully modern. It is not an echo of the past but forward looking and conditioned on a socialized political economy sustained by industrial development. It relies on the socially beneficial progress of science and technology as well as on selected market mechanisms. Rural communities in the new model are sustained by a modernized or modernizing eco-agriculture receptive to locally suitable modern machines and green technologies. Far beyond self-subsistence, they produce substantial surplus for the industrial and urban sectors. The old dilemma of resisting mechanization and maintaining a degree of "technological conservatism" in the face of surplus rural labor should diminish as the new model gains ground.

This would be a continuation of the historical socialist process of modernization, in which industry and agriculture were meant to be synchronic, only at a higher level of forces and relations of production. The purpose of the "socialist upsurge in the countryside," as Mao sees it, was not only a revolution in ownership structure, but also a revolution in machinery production and technology ([1955]1991). For the first time in China's very long agrarian history, cooperatives and communes were formed for gains in factor productivity, for rural industries that could absorb agricultural surplus labor on the spot, and for deployment of heavy machines and advanced farming technologies while supporting urban development.[7] The national economy must now achieve both further, independent industrial upgrading and modern, capital-labor dual intensive agriculture (Chapter 6).

The other factor is that the new moral economy is not merely spontaneous but is highly organized as well on a voluntary and cooperative basis. Rural China must organize to secure itself a future because, as has been argued, urbanization in its present form is at a dead end. A developed economy does not have to be prevailingly urban in either theory or reality. A socialist urban-rural relationship should be mutually nurturing and, apparently, the less the disparities between these sectors, the weaker the push for migration from rural areas would be. That is, a collectively autonomous rural sphere can be constructed upon peasant networks with government support through grassroots party and mass organizations, along with state investment, subsidies, welfare provision, and price manipulation in favor of rural income. Only through cooperation can small producers make full use of the modern means of production, gain beneficial terms in marketing and trade, and find security in situations of emergency and natural disasters.[8] And only through reorganization after the dissolution of people's communes can they overcome the fragmentation of land and vulnerability of isolated petty farming at odds with an advanced and socialized national economy. This point is immediately practical: the scattered households must attain a sufficient level of organization to possess a material linkage with the state and other sectors for transmitting inputs and outputs. In addition, and no less important, given the patriarchal remnants of the old society, public intervention remains critical for protecting and promoting women in China's unfinished project of gender and general equality.

That peasants need state backing should not be controversial. The agrarian question is always a matter of national policy and rural transformation a state project in the PRC, a tradition rooted in the Chinese revolution. Economically, even the classical anarchists recognize that the supply of social capital must be "protected and encouraged by public authorities" if independent petty production is to be viable (Hobsbawm 1998: 46). The influential antistate stance defending the "precious autonomy" of the petty bourgeoisie (e.g., Scott 1985) overlooks continuing miseries of the nonproletarianized poor and the decisive difference a social state, or for that matter a socialist state beyond "primitive accumulation," could make. The fact that the present PRC state has abandoned many of its socialist policies or become more predatory cannot in itself invalidate the argument. To recapture the Chinese state (Chapter 5), however, is precisely to see the rise of the social as an actual historical trend as much as a necessary political and institutional project. Unorganized producers would be subjectless and powerless. As the reorganization of rural China is underway and tailored to foster a collective ethos and social cohesion, worth remembering are those resounding rationalities behind the earlier communization movements—empowering poor peasants, curbing class polarization, and raising productive capacities (Mao [1955]1991). These goals are all just as pressing today.

There are several explanations or favorable conditions relevant for the Chinese undertaking. Above all, given China's long experience with developed markets without typically capitalist accumulation, it is clear that the Chinese economic ability should be appreciated in its own right. As discussed in Chapter 2, the pattern according to which "men plough and women weave," at least in *jiangnan*, was a feature not of a natural economy but of a highly commercialized one. It differs categorically from Marx's sealed-off and stagnant "self-sustaining community of manufacture and agriculture" as a central element of AMP. The Chinese market in relatively rich regions, accordingly, was based not on a social division of labor required by the capitalist mode but on sophisticated "technical divisions of labor" within the productive unit. As described in William Skinner's classic *The City in Late Imperial China* (1977), China as a stable agrarian civilization was founded on autonomous rural societies rather than independent towns as in Europe (Lv 2012a). Such a rurally rooted and family centered economy also contrasts with those of either feudal manorialism or large scale factories of hired labor. Salaried employment has always been marginal in China's agricultural sector, where certain traditional forms of organizing work persist. This model of "capitalization without proletarianization," in Philip Huang's characterization, is different from the economies not only of Western Europe but also of India and elsewhere in East Asia (2012b: 85).

Another major deviation, also noted in Chapter 2, is that rather than being concerned with overseas expansion, the Chinese empire was mostly a domestic market. Arrighi uses Smith to compare these two distinct paths of growth: the foreign trade based and the home trade based (2007: 69; chs. 2 and 3). China was an exemplar of the "Smithian path to economic maturity" or what Smith calls "the natural progress of opulence," as opposed to the "unnatural and retrograde" European path featuring interstate competition within Europe as much as colonial conquest. Not a bearer of capitalist dynamics, the Chinese economy lacked either endless accumulation of capital or expansionist movements. Nor did it follow the pattern of financialization. In the end, if it was Western military power that sustained an unnatural path, it is also the case that "the synergy between capitalism, industrialism, and militarism" eventually engendered European descent in view of the Asian "resurgence" (Arrighi 2007: 57–59; 93–95; Arrighi et al. 2003). Revising his analysis in *The Long Twentieth Century* (1994) in light of the formation of an "East Asian-centered world-market society," Arrighi picks up the controversial concept of "industri*ous* revolution" (*qinlao geming*) as a comparison with industri*al* revolution, although both are market oriented.[9]

The making of the case for an "industrious revolution" in the long sixteenth century begins with a challenge to the Malthusian doctrine of population hindrance. Kaoru Sugihara (1996; 2003) argues that abundant human capital and proficient allocation of quality labor can confer an advantage over the concentration of industrial and financial capital. A labor- and animal-power intensive production along with its specific methods of managing resources has offered an escape from Malthusian checks and provided a sustainable alternative to capital- and energy-intensive growth. The first "East Asian miracle" occurred before the European takeover of Asia. Pomeranz and others illustrate that an industrious advantage did account for Asia's once remarkably advanced position in the world economy. Apart from intensive agricultural cultivation and sidelines (Li 2003), the economic backbone in the Yangzi Delta was also representative of a type of rural industry managed through family, partnership, or guild. This type featured flexible, resource-saving, and low cost production, as well as skilled labor and niche markets. The flourishing industries and soaring exports depended not so much on mechanical technologies as on sophisticated artisanship and specialization (or technical division of labor) between and among petty producers and traders (Pomeranz 2008: 91–95).

Notable here is also an Asian contribution to the useful idea of "human capital." If Theodore Schultz is right that in place of the notions of "surplus labor" or "inefficient allocation" of resources, rational peasant and traditional agriculture have their own criteria of optimality in terms of marginal cost and returns (Schultz 1964), then an industrious revolution can be seen as superior to forced imitation of the methods prevailing in industrialized countries. This has contemporary relevance, as in the sweep of global south, the needed agrarian transformation based on internal inclinations is still preferably achievable through local enhancement of human skills and capabilities. It would involve a critical state role in line with Schultz's original theoretical formulation, from policy support to capital investment, but it also entails peasant initiatives and self-organization.

This mostly positive story of an industrious revolution, however, is apparently also a limited one, as "industrious revolution" can be a contradiction in terms. For it has no way to be really revolutionary as compared with the industrial revolution in terms of propelling the forces of production and all that follows. "Revolution" could be the wrong word for a gradual spread of quantitative changes different not only from European industrialization but also from qualitative economic transformations in parts of twentieth-century Asia. Is not the term "industrious" itself an unambiguous indicator of the limitations of the economy so described? Critics also point out that the notion, once applied to China past and present, overlooks the country's severe demographic and echological constraints. There land pressure is so great (worse than in the other Asian economies and among the worst on earth) that even a really successful green revolution accomplished during the Mao years could not bring a permanent relief (Huang 2012b: 86). Moreover, China's age old reliance on fossil fuels such as coal has been far from resource saving (Elvin 2008: 99). In a necessary global perspective of history, it is also worth noting that the Chinese economy cannot be viewed as being shielded from industrial developments elsewhere and their international impact on the division of labor. By the same token, industrious facets can also be identified in the European path.[10] And, above all, even if an industrious revolution can be positively recognized as an economic model, politically there would be nothing lamentable in any subordinate social relationship preserved in the old modes of household production and reproduction vulnerable to all kinds of premodern pitfalls. It is a ruling-class fantasy that elevating the past can legitimize the present.

The observation that China has for many centuries followed a noncapitalist, nonindustrial developmental path, however, is empirically sound. Moreover, even in the heydays of socialist planning and industrialization, the government was never the only organizer of production or the only provider of public goods. Many traditional mechanisms remained functional, especially in the rural collective sector with a considerable level of autonomy. The Chinese economy and society past and present have also always included a substantial section of small units and networks, not only in agriculture but also in large segments of urban life. Boosted by market reform, petty production grows throughout regions and sectors, taking various forms of management—individual, family, partnering, cooperative, collective, and so on—that militate against monopoly. Collective economy, in particular, has also formed the basis of grassroots democracy. Election of unit and team leaders have been a routine practice across rural China long before the NPC introduced village electoral laws in 1987.

This unique experience is also represented in a living intellectual tradition in local thinking of a deep suspicion of capitalist modern cruelty and arrogance. Liang Shuming, not a communist, shared with the communist party a vision of the need for a "great social transformation." In *A Theory of Rural Construction* (1927) he argues that a backward China could never catch up with advanced nations by copying urban centered industrialization, whether by Western style competition or Soviet state power. Only an integral movement of peasants and concerned scholars like himself could succeed, since a new society would have to be built from the bottom up through an expanding network of local coops (Lv 2007; Lynch 2011). Liang was aware of how immensely difficult the task could be in the midst of chaos and wars, but believed that "it is exactly necessary to head straight for the distant, great ideal in order to resolve the immediate problems." That is, "what ordinarily might seem merely 'utopian' was also, at this juncture in China's history, the only practical option" (Lynch 2011: 36). The popular educators Tao Xingzhi and Yan Yangchu and the sociologist Fei Xiaotong were among the influential spokesmen in the same tradition. Fei most rigorously advocated "moderate townships" over grand cities for a distinct developmental strategy to fit the Chinese conditions.

Given the weight of history and locality, the pressing question is obviously whether China has not already buried its legacies by entering into the global system, however reluctantly or incompletely. Are we witnessing in the country an inexorable capitalist integration, or only further hybridization of an interstitial system, or something else? What is the likely future trend, and can intellectual interventions and social movements reshape it? As far as this conception of dichotomized historical paths between China and Europe is concerned, it is fair to note that the Chinese experiences have remarkably blended social, industrious, and industrial revolutions. The idea of an industr*ious* revitalization is thus contemporaneous as China has never entirely deserted its historical patterns of development.

If China's history of noncapitalist economy can be a source of present search for an alternative to capitalist integration, a prerequisite is still the Chinese revolution and what it has achieved in the country's political, social, and organizational foundation. The revolution, both a nationalist revolt and a class war, has also transformed land and sectoral relations. The public land system, in particular, has enabled China to avoid a wholesale capitalist primitive accumulation. The "Chinese specificity" of defending public land is, in this view, a single most important factor that prevents contemporary China from being characterized as "capitalist". For "the capitalist road is based on the transformation of land into a commodity" (Amin 2013). If the argument that China will thus be able to resist further capitalist transition is plausible, then its rural sector can be seen as the new base area for socialist renewal. The fact that even the displaced are not necessarily dispossessed, given that migrant workers are either resettled or retaining their right of land use, makes reorientation uniquely possible. The separation of dispossession and displacement is a singular Chinese phenomenon.

Meanwhile, having carried out one of the greatest social revolutions in world history, the category of "Chinese peasantry" cannot be taken as a generic premodern identity. Residuals from old society or petty bourgeois tendencies notwithstanding, this class in China (see the qualification of the usage of "class" in the Chinese context in Chapter 6) is not premodern or pre-capitalist waiting to be integrated into capitalism and modernity. Participating in revolutionary modern transformations that partially destroyed their own traditions and outlooks, these peasants have undergone a socialist socialization to gain a new subjectivity. Their alliance with workers in multiple ways, especially through the Communist Party and its politics of recognition—political-moral glorification of the working class as much as the poor and later socialist peasants (in defiance of the Marxist doctrine)—has further shaken off their old structural position and mentality, enabling them to become a transformative agency of social change.[11] The distinguished class character of peasants in China due to a peasant revolution, meanwhile, also makes China's agrarian question different from those posed in other agricultural nations.

The contrast here between postrevolutionary China and the postcolonial third world where the peasants are not broadly treated as a political subject is instructive. But this distinctive subjective category of a socialist peasantry in alliance with workers can be lost in the marketplace, along with the dual process of political decay of the PRC state and ideological erosion of the party. The question is then whether direct producers can regain the political and organizational means needed to (re)build a communist moral economy, or how the party and state might be recaptured and democratized as a matter of commitment and politics. If history is any guide, only the communists have successfully organized the peasantry in China on a national scale; and only rural mobilization has sustained revolution as well as a socialist modernization. To reinstate direct producers in the rise of the new rural social will similarly conjoin forces from above and below. Incidentally, the experience of new China has yet to be incorporated into an important moral economy literature that has so far passed it by.

Contrary to the antistate thread in traditional moral economy, a socialist state as the foremost outcome of revolution is preconditional for the creation of a new moral economy. The socioeconomic and political power of labor, like that of capital, is rooted in the economic system and relations legitimated and protected by the political, legal, repressive, and ideological apparatus of a given state. It is state rules that secure or crush initiatives in society or within the state institutions themselves. A socialist state, especially in the environment of an open market and global integration, is requisite to constrain the reach of capital and private property. As was noted in Chapter 5 with respect to the state-market relationship, property rights, like any other institutionalized economic relations, are meaningless if detached from the context of political, cultural, and customary norms in which they must be embedded. Only with a postrevolutionary state as the guarantor of socialist development against capitalist transformation can a "socialist market" and a new moral economy based on such a market be conceivable. The future is thus premised on the nature of the state, or the popular struggle engendering powerful pressures on that state. Likewise, fragmentation of the state in the reform era and divisions within its policy circles can be indications of a possible change in the same direction.

In the same vein, most directly pertinent for rural reorganization are the collective knowledge and memories, positive or negative, of a collectivist past. Even if the people's commune eventually failed, collective agriculture by and large succeeded in a substantial degree of mechanization, irrigation and other infrastructural construction, and public-good management. Advantages of collective farming should be obvious and have been vindicated, however tentatively or incompletely, in the Chinese experience. Economically, for one thing, it leads to the creation of large fields by avoiding unnecessary hedgerows, boundaries, paths, and water channels. This in turn makes easier use of machines. Second, it allows the mobilization of labor, male and female, for carrying out essential soil and water works as well as developing rural industry, beyond the ability of individual households. Third, it facilitates diffusion of high-yield seed varieties and farm technologies for a modern agriculture. Finally, it pushes for sectoral trades to be more protective and beneficial for rural living, enabling also effective government regulation and price mechanism for the entire national economy. As such, "collectivization in China in the mid-1950s was not premature but instead a necessary precondition for the development of a modern agricultural sector" (Bramall: 214–219, 225–226). Socially and politically, the organized peasants attain institutional support, basic security and general equality. Collective and gainful labor also liberates women from the confines of family and housework.

To sing praises for collective agriculture in today's intellectual climate is held in contempt. But honest historical assessment is unavoidable for any serious thinking about the future, in China as elsewhere. The continuing debates over land reform, collectivization, and decollectivization are therefore important.[12] The fact that collective ownership of China's agricultural land is upheld even after decollectivization speaks volumes of the staying power of Chinese socialism. In the end, it would be fair to say that the Maoist economic strategy in general involved profound contradictions, but nevertheless laid the industrial foundation for China's modern development. This is also negatively demonstrated by decollectivization, which left in its aftermath fragmented land, defenseless households, inefficient allocation of productive factors, decreased machine use, and declining social services, hence hindering rural development (Bramall 2009: chs. 8 and 9). Without the benefits of cooperative, coordinated capacities that the "double management" design attempted yet failed to preserve, farmers and villages have suffered worsening conditions and run-down communities—typical of the "tragedy of uncommons" in spite of public land in legal terms (He 2010). This supports the argument that petty production in rural China must reorganize in multiple and inventive forms to endure, renew, develop, and thrive.

There are valuable legacies of Maoist developmental thinking. Critical of the Stalinist model, Mao elaborates sectoral interactions and corresponding social relations, as in *On the Ten Great Relationships* (1956), with great originality. He stresses, for example, the primacy of balance among heavy industry (dominant), light industry (priority), and agriculture (foundational) and explains why light industry, central to people's livelihood along with agriculture, is also where accumulation can most efficiently occur to fund industrialization. Specifically, Mao calls for decentralized industrial expansion in the rural settings—with small factories producing to supply local demands the countryside could be turned into an even more attractive place than the cities. In his vision, each commune could have its own farms, factories, nurseries, schools, hospitals, research institutions, shops, clubs, dining halls, and other service providers, and also transportation networks and militia. Such a multifunctional organization would nurture agriculture as much as peasants themselves, who farm but might also engage in politics, culture, technical invention, science, or other activities. Agricultural laborers should be liberated from narrow divisions of labor, so will not forever stay who they are. At the same time, to reduce urban-rural disparities, urban students and professionals should periodically serve in the countryside; doctors and musicians are among Mao's examples. Above all, bureaucrats at all levels need to be "re-educated" by direct producers on the ground. Mao welcomed the "cadre schools" created during the Cultural Revolution in which state functionaries were "sent down" to work in the communes ([1958, 1959]1999).[13]

These ideas are materially premised on collective land as both the means of production for direct producers and a source of their organization in communal work and life. The commune can be the institutional building block of a socialist society. The realities no doubt are a hundred times more complicated, but the experiences and experiments of not treating rural and urban labor as a commodity and of workers sharing managerial responsibilities or cadres and intellectuals "learning from the masses" were real and can be a precious asset for the present cause. An egalitarian, cooperative, and participatory culture in collectivist traditions remains appealing, especially in reaction to the appalling social consequences of a market transition. The new moral economy must accommodate and tame the market by developing a socialist market economy. As such, even a recollectivization is unlikely to take any old forms; cooperation has become a new concept with new meanings and possibilities.

In this context, it is worth revisiting Marx's breakthrough in his conception of history with the Russian question (Chapter 3). He is after all not inimical to the cooperative movement (in which workers are "their own capitalists") or to the market as such (Jossa 2005: 3). In a famous letter to Vera Zasulich in 1881, he explains why the rural commune should be able to escape the fate of annihilation in Russia and "become a *direct point of departure* for the economic system towards which modern society tends": collective production on a nationwide scale, and transfer to the commune of modern productive conditions. For him, given the crisis in the West, the future lies in "the return of modern societies to the 'archaic' type of communal property" —in L. H. Morgan's word, "the new system will be *a revival in a superior form* of an archaic social type" ([1881]1989). There is of course no comparison between the pre-capitalist Russian *mir* and the experimenting socialist Chinese collective; they are a world apart. But Marx has a point that common ownership of land plus simultaneous positive acquisitions of materials and technologies devised by advanced economies can lead to a new mode of production. Making a huge difference still, in China such acquisitions can now be provided domestically.

The third enabling condition for the new moral economy is therefore the socialist market itself. That is, this new moral economy project in China is a matter of transforming the entire national economy into an integrated national commons. The socialization of labor, capital, property, technology, information, land, and other basic physical endowments, in large measure also a matter of public finance, amounts to a program of socializing the market itself into a "social market."[14] Socialization is thus neither marketification nor metropolitanism. The conceptual questions concerning (in)compatibility between market and socialism require separate treatment.

Suffice it here to stress that petty production can be fully socialized; rural cooperatives operating in national and local markets can bring capital under communal management and control. As common resources are then fairly, rationally, and efficiently pooled for public use, social gains, and individual benefits, a complex "knowledge-commons ecosystem" will also arise (Hess and Ostrom 2007: 3, 10–12). Improved seeds, among many farming techniques, for example, should be a constituent of knowledge commons. Indeed, without any historically formed obsession with patents and copyrights, China can also be a relatively easy place to promote open source, open access, and free information as a public good.[15] The experimental project of Chinese socialism has the potential to encompass the intrinsically interconnected ideas of the commons, community, communism, communication, and common culture. The movement inspired by these ideas of communal self-governance, beautifully dubbed "creative commons," is intrinsically appealing and democratic. Democracy is, after all, transparent, collective, deliberative, and conversational.

Concerning the capitalist mode of production, Michael Hardt shows its new contradiction internal to capital: the more the common is corralled as property, the more its productivity is reduced—"capital remains generally external to the processes of the production of the common." As it happens, the more developed the forces of production, the more dependent the economy is on electronic media and the less possible it is to contain it to private ownership (2010: 136–139). In a digital age of biotech and bio- and cyberpolitics, the upshot of self-employing, flexible, and autonomous work, often associated with direct producers in the hight-ech sectors, is that "cognitive capitalism" can be subverted by such producers. They can appropriate not only the "relative rent" of capital—read "profit" (patents and copyrights guarantee an income based on the ownership of material or immaterial property)—but also its power of cognition and knowledge production (2010: 137). Any rigid conception of private property that neglects social capital and socialized market has long collapsed in the advanced economies anyway (Rifkin 2013: 218–221).

In this perspective, the communist moral economy cannot be an echo of anything lost in history but is forward looking with an ambition of seeking release from the fetters of capitalism and state socialism alike. It aspires to a truly participatory society, in which every participant is regarded as virtually a direct producer owing to her contribution to social labor (past, future, or latent contributions; understood as encompassing a broadest possible range of socially positive activities). An unconditionally guaranteed basic income is then her due reward.[16] A universal social wage across bounded communities (and eventually national citizenship as well) is materially within our reach for a long time, with human economic-technological development having amply passed the threshold of general scarcity.[17] As has been argued since the utopian socialists and French and American revolutionaries (e.g., Marquis de Condorcet and Thomas Paine), it makes not only moral but also economic sense to end poverty and insecurity. If liberty is a birthright, so is security (Stedman Jones 2004). Natural disasters excepted, any barrier to this promise of a world beyond want is only social and political. It cannot be an economic matter of absolute shortage anywhere but a political matter of government commitment and policies, domestic and international.[18]

In China, given the ongoing construction of "three-line" provisions (minimal living allowance, pension, and unemployment insurance) and eventually an urban-rural integrated, comprehensive social security system,[19] the management of social dividends toward a basic income might be institutionalized democratically under the NPC (e.g., proposed in Cui

2005). Many technical details have yet to be worked out, but a unified basic income—a "rubble rice bowl" if not iron rice bowl—can hugely simplify the bureaucracy of redistribution and welfare. Calculation and statistics are again a matter of politics more than economics. Without further discussion, the point here is simply that a social wage that secures baseline equality and minimizes risks in individual lives is in the nature of the new moral economy. It is also both necessary and practical in line with *minsheng* required by a socialist China model (Chapter 5).

In a labor surplus (and land scarce, resource poor) economy, a guaranteed scheme of basic income would also be a solution to the obstinate hindrance of unemployment. Despite recent "labor shortage" in the manufacturing sector in southern China due to a combination of harsh labor conditions, improved rural situations, rising wages, and militancy of migrant workers, the apparent "end of surplus labor" is not real (Chan 2012 197–199). It is essentially about "cheap labor" being refuted by workers themselves. Scholars have been debating whether China has reached the Lewis turning point when the dualistic rural-urban labor market begins to break down and a labor-surplus economy is transformed into a "normal" one of full employment. The one sure thing is that China has no way to absorb its labor supply within the old framework.

In the revolutionary new framework of participatory society and basic income such market problems as "oversupply" of labor or job loss will cease; and in that light both sweatshops and nominal, inactive positions become not only morally reprehensible but also economically irrational.[20] Work should not be equated with gainful employment or tied to a statistically countable performing workforce. A classic example is the value of unpaid housework, for recognition of which women's movements everywhere have fought a hard battle. Until we can discard the notion and practice of formal employment as the primary means of both household income and social participation, and until we can replace the utopian goal of full employment with the realistic idea of full participation, there is no chance that the anguish and stigma of joblessness or job insecurity will ever be surmounted. Nothing less than a society that prizes its producers with a social wage and social power can make people autonomous and free. Meanwhile, the time gained from reduced workdays or flexible schedules can be translated into personal development as well as civic and associational engagement and political activism on the part of a participatory citizenry. Democracy is inevitably also a matter of the politics of time or of liberation from imposed occupation in a realm of necessity. As is compellingly shown in the "future of work" debate, work should be personally or collectively gratifying; and the human desire to eradicate dirty, dreary, or repetitive tasks so as to reconcile work and play is closer to realization than ever before in history.[21] The stifling and humiliation of humanity in capitalist wage labor could end in a higher plane of civilization.

Dispensing passivity and idleness, time is another word for freedom. "Once the narrow bourgeois form has been peeled away," as Marx asks, "what is wealth other than the universality of individual needs, capacities, pleasures, productive forces etc., created through universal exchange?" (quoted in Anderson, K. 2010: 159). In the *Grundrisse*, he explains why true wealth can be measured only by the release of creative powers for their own sake without dull compulsion (Eagleton 2011: 105). This is a towering order, but Keynes's famous 15-hour work week was proposed as early as around 1929 and, as he believed then in the midst of the Great Depression, the change had against all odds "already begun" ([1930]1972: 331). If he sounds wishful, it is only because transformation of the old social contracts rooted in modern wage labor as a mere historical artifact is bound to be not only an economic and political but also a "soul-touching" cultural revolution. Keynes predicted a "collective nervous breakdown" given our deeply entrenched and foreclosed cognitive *habitus*.[22]

It is possible to argue that China is a most receptive place for such a transformation because of its historical and socialist legacies. The existing conditions in China mingle "post industrial" transitions faced in the global north and nonindustrial "organic development" promoted in parts of the south. Under multifaceted pressures, China's rising social of direct producers/participants will in time take up its political mission of creating a new society, before private profit intervenes to dominate decisionmaking and to allow human worth to be measured by market values. Such an organic social order presupposes neither material abundance in the consumerist form of endless commodities nor expensively administered welfare provisions in the statist form of bureaucracy. Rejecting the old productive and social relations, it stands for unalienated labor and true quality of life. Although in the short term job creation and security must remain policy objectives, in the long run, a need-oriented, resource-efficient, eco-environmental friendly, and yet productively and technologically advanced social arrangement would be superior to the private systems of overproduction and overconsumption. It would also be vastly more humane and economical.

The distinctions of the communist moral economy as delineated above—its unique and splendid historical resources, its revolutionary and socialist preparation, and its prospective substances of national and local commons, participatory society, and socialist market—clearly rule out any parallel between it and a pre-capitalist community resisting its own "historical disintegration." It can embed in itself a higher form of political economy which reorders productive, class, and social relations. The model can thus be confidently defended in response to influential criticisms of "agrarian populism" (e.g., Bernstein 2009: 68–75), "communal romanticism," or what is known in the Chinese vocabulary as "agricultural socialism" (as opposed to "proletarian socialism").[23] History matters; the struggle and the conception of that struggle in China are acutely about which history—socialist, pre-socialist, or post-socialist?

A rather powerful trend in rural China today, for example, is a mixture of capitalist market forces and "feudal" customs and superstition. To counter it, a more politically and culturally conscious *xiangtu* (village and soil) movement is taking shape, and in resistance to privatization, atomization, and agricapital dominated marketification. The village commons, meanwhile, largely remain in place across the country. Without demeaning small production—as argued, there is no feasible and socially acceptable option for the Chinese but to embrace and recast an "earthbound China"—rural conditions can be seen as in general having been qualitatively eased. As small farming can be organized in various cooperatives, it must be combined with suitable application of advanced machines and technologies to move toward a modern eco-agriculture. Also notable is that rural China has developed considerably more industries. Stronger government support would help the farmers to also gain control over the retailing of farming inputs and other trades, and microfinancing and public services as well. The policy goal should be to maximize the margin of rural productive diversification and income while restricting the entry of urban and foreign capital into those more profitable linkages of the productive chain. In an open, organized, and eventually also socialist market economy, petty producers are not necessarily private property holders, and peasants are not exactly the "petty bourgeoisie." "Petty production" is no longer as we have known it.

For Lenin, small production "engenders capitalism and the bourgeoisie continuously, daily, hourly, spontaneously, and on a mass scale" ([1920]1964). His "proletarian socialism" negates the *Narodniks* who "cannot rid themselves of petty-bourgeois illusions" or "a reactionary petty-bourgeois utopia" ([1905]1972). This is in line with Marx's attack on the variants of "reactionary socialism" (Chapter 6). The criticisms, however, are not readily applicable to the Chinese peasant as a collective identity, who has been a communist revolutionary, socialist commune member, and also, perhaps more problematically, reformist modernizer. The market transition has indeed brought back some features of preliberation society, reminiscent of the spontaneous capitalist tendency among a "mighty ocean" of the petty bourgeoisie in the early days of collectivization (Mao 1955: 255–256). To overcome such tendencies, and to develop socialism, the communists have been committed to industrialization. Mao wrote as early as 1944 that scattered individual and family economy as the foundation of "feudal" society must be replaced by an industrial one, which is "where Marxism differs from populism." Envisioning the future task of economically transforming China, he told his colleagues that "we have not yet attained the machines, so we have not achieved victory. If we cannot ever attain the machines, we shall never achieve victory; we would be wiped out" [1944]1983: 239). Collective agriculture was an indispensable part of the same ambition, only reinforced by the conviction that the petty peasant masses would otherwise be trapped in permanent poverty, and that through organizing themselves they can generate greater productive capacity while gradually dismantling private domination and transforming their own outlooks. Characteristically unorthodox, Mao also insisted on cooperatization before mechanization, or changing productive relations first so as to promote productive forces ([1959]1977). More than half a century on, these discussions still resonate in China's new *xiangtu* movment.

Mao's visionary "May 7th directive" would be another source of constructing the new moral economy. It depicts a whole scheme of thought about what might be called "communal socialism":[24] from "educational revolution" to combating bureaucracy, from breaking up rigid division of labor to elimination of the "three great distinctions" between urban and rural regions, industrial and agricultural sectors, and mental and manual labor. Mao advocates integration of the roles of worker, farmer, trader, student, and soldier, and hence people from all walks of life, men and women, could learn to involve themselves simultaneously in different professional and occupational as well as political-theoretical engagements. Moreover, everybody should shoulder some responsibility in state affairs while retaining their regular work duties and identities (in this context it is notable that the deputies to the NPC are not institutionally designed as professional politicians). Mao sees the experiments in the Anshan Steel Works and elsewhere in the 1960s as the direction to be taken in reforming state institutions (Chapter 5). He also specifies the role model of the PLA that in peacetime "our army should be a big school," in which the troops learn politics, military skills, and culture, farm and work in factories, and take part in mass liaison and socialist education. People in commerce, service trades, and government offices should do likewise. Every commune and work unit could become a school where people take on multiple tasks including "criticizing the bourgeoisie." Inspired by the Paris Commune, Mao imagines that multifunctioning communes can be set up around each county and city and several such communes then form larger and more integrated communes across the nation. In the "January storm" of 1967, a gigantic "Shanghai Commune" declared formation. It was short lived but exemplified the Maoist preference.

Mao's communal socialist model may have an air of utopianism, but it is also a serious attempt at finding an alternative to the standard capitalist, urban notion of modernity. Continuing from this vision and the historical experiences inspired by it, the project of a socialist—or communist in the sense of the centrality of commons—moral economy is about giving rise to organized social power counting on enhanced individual and collective capabilities. Here the idea of the social embraces both direct producers as commoners and the social state, with class power embedded in both and their mutual dependence and compatibility. Likewise, the public and commons cohere in their shared opposition to private domination.

To reiterate, first, such a model cannot be realized in a premodern, self-sufficient, natural economy. It is based on advanced economic development and public control over land and other productive resources. It relies on decentralized horizontal networks of market and non-market activities within a centralized vertical system of microplanning, regulation and coordination. Second, the local communities are not insulated from one another or antagonistic to the state. The socialized national economy and socialist state provide the communities with economic-technological and financial support within a designated political-legal-policy framework. The government at all levels at the same time is subject to popular supervision with a long-term objective of democratic planning and self-management. Third, rejecting primitive, closed petty production, the farming population is transforming itself not by an industrial urban civilization but by rural changes in productive reorganization, trade and sectoral structures, and personal and cooperative relations. The peasant identity will become free from the traditional image of a physically and mentally confined occupation through unprecedented educational attainments and diverse opportunities beyond farming. Fourth, the construction of a new moral economy is the same process as creating a socialist market that will champion direct producers and pursue a socially and ecologically more desirable mode of production and way of life alternative to capitalist limitations and destruction.

At issue, then, is not reconciling the models of "community" and "modernity"; socialism must reinvent both by removing their pre-capitalist and capitalist prerequisites alike. This project is thus not about reviving any agrarian populist illusions, but about the urgent imperative of forging an ambitious yet practical response to the developmentalist predicaments of the present. Obvious tensions between an all-embracing notion of "direct producers" and the concepts of class and class struggle, or between small farming and the urgency of rural reorganization may not be solvable until conscious social experiments can tackle them in practice. Analytically, concerning direct producers, like the "people" being a class category in the Chinese political and discursive context (Chapter 6), they too, from all backgrounds but collectively in the same position in their direct access to the means of production, provided the feasibility of a socialist market and participatory society. This is so also because of the "class" nature of a socialist China to be rebuilt in a capitalist global system, and its ultimate aspiration of surmounting the contradictions of that system. As such the united labor of direct producers is international and can be in internationalist solidarity in shared struggles for a different world. Analogous is the communist peasant revolution assuming a proletarian character and socialist orientation, due to its party leadership and worker-peasant alliance. Intended to be a postcapitalist as well as poststatist social model, the new moral economy traverses China's pre- and postmodern conditions in a development destined to be uneven and compressed (Chapter 1). To be sure, by seeking a modern alternative to capitalism, modernity is reaffirmed against the anachronism of premodernity. Yet the search opens up new horizons. After all, the capitalist "monopoly" of the modern cannot, and has never been, valid, as is amply attested by socialist modern development, then and now.

Transcending paradigmatic modernity and creating a new moral economy, however, is not on the official agenda. It cannot even begin without a "war of position" waged in multifold channels, forms and movements on the part of the rising social to win hegemony. The fertile ground in China is due to its revolutionary and socialist traditions, from its land and strategic industries remaining in public hands to its living social commitment to equality and justice that keeps the government under popular pressure. But that ground has to be vigorously guarded and consolidated—the first task and condition for the project to be viable. This in turn implies both resumption of a socialist state and its radically more socially inclined redefinition. State power is indispensable also in countering the capitalist states and their commercial and military forces. The ideological identity and organizational capacity of the party are decisive. These requirements are still possible because, after all, not ever erasable from China's popular conscience even in a gilded age of dissipation is the immeasurable sacrifice made by generations of devoted lives for the noble cause of communism.

# Part III

# 8

# Toward a Historical Materialist Universalism

In light of the review of Marx's conception of Oriental society and the comparative economic history debate over imperial China's place in world history in Part I and the past, present, and potential future movement of modern China vis-à-vis global capitalism in Part II, some tentative reflections from a critical and self-reflexive Marxist standpoint are in order. Self-reflexivity is both an intrinsic mechanism and an open manifestation of the dynamics of historical materialism's enduring relevance and rejuvenation.

First, though historians date and explain the rise of Europe differently, they agree in common sense that the ascendancy of the capitalist West depended on direct and indirect contributions from other regions, peoples, economies, and cultures. The "Western core of modernity" had sources near and far and continued to be remolded by outside influences. In particular, "without the cumulative history of the whole Afro-Eurasian Oikoumene, of which the Occident had been an integral part, the Western Transmutation would be almost unthinkable" (Hodgson 1974: 198). For this reason alone, the Eurocentric claim that Europeans are more rational, more progressive, and more of the "historical subject" is a horrendous lie and "theft of history" (Goody 2006). That is, the Europeans were privileged to lead an industrial revolution and build up industrial metropolises. But those accomplishments depended on extracting resources on a far-reaching and colossal scale outside geographical Europe. They also enjoyed extensive borrowing from non-European achievements and inventions through intra-Eurasian and maritime trade and communications. Major European states also afforded various forms and degrees of ecological relief, from a population outlet to a source of land-intensive primary products. The variously colonized land thereby became a vital means of production for the empires, buttressing a division of labor allowing slave plantations, impoverished farms, and deadly mines oceans and continents away. The contrast between this situation and that of most late developers (with a few outstanding exceptions) without comparable intention or option of eco-substitution is that the latter would have to manage any pressure mainly domestically, which is a fundamental economic disadvantage.

At issue is not the mere multiplicity of the sources of Western civilization from the beginning ("black Athena" in Bernal 1987). Nor is it simply a matter of revealing and refuting the pretense of Euro-American "universality." It is not even enough to recognize "emergent universalism" in non-Western ideas and developments (Kaiwar 2009), which is important and will be discussed later. So much has been explored and explained in the literature about the Oriental-Occidental mutual construction of the "West" or the fallacy of dichotomizing West and East as homogeneous entities that the points are fairly uncontroversial. What does need to be emphatically restated is the indispensability of the colonialist and imperialist dimensions of capitalism. And this can be done without underplaying the internal dynamics of capitalist genesis and development, such as revolutionary productive forces, state facility, and class politics. The other side of the coin is then the crucial agency of anti-colonial and anti-imperialist struggles in the global history of capitalism.

To begin with, as noted, the fiscal hegemony of European powers was in part a result of their war economies, which mobilized resources for arms and other military supplies inside and outside Europe. The primitive accumulation of capitalism was also directly attributable to Europe's overseas expansion. Such expansion drew wealth in advanced markets of a "commercial capitalism" in the East as a precursor of industrial capitalism in the West. En route, European ocean vessels linked American cotton and mining products derived from slave labor and trade from Africa with the Indian-Chinese-Arab markets. Gunder Frank recounts this gigantic trading triangle in which the Europeans took out American silver to "buy themselves tickets on the Asian train" (1998: 30). The required balance of payments was such that the colonies were compelled to sacrifice for the demands of their metropolitan masters, often violently.

In Asia, the opium wars intensified the depletion of China's silver reserve and de-(proto)industrialization in its coastal regions, which in turn bankrupted Chinese and Indian textile producers along with their transcontinental trading networks. India found itself not only a net exporter of cotton, but also a standing supplier of opium grown and processed by its rural poor to China in exchange for British manufactured goods. The "modernization of poverty" in India was part of the "late Victorian holocausts," as Mike Davis puts it (2001: 311). Between 1875 and 1900, during which the worst famines in Indian history occurred, grain exports increased until, by the turn of the century, "India was supplying nearly a fifth of Britain's wheat consumption at the cost of its own food security" (Davis 2001: 59).[1] Marx unequivocally pinned down the exploitative and militarist model of imperial dependency: London at the time depended for fully one-seventh of its revenue on the opium trade as a source of the empire's "life blood." And he was appalled: "The profound hypocrisy and inherent barbarism of bourgeois civilization lies unveiled before our eyes, turning from its home, where it assumes respectable forms, to the colonies, where it goes naked" ([1853]1979b: 220). The sheer inhumanity of these episodes of imperial history has yet to be fully and honestly confronted by the present-day Western democracies.

As to just how much overseas markets, extraction, and slavery contributed to a sustained primitive accumulation of capital in general and the first industrial revolutions in particular, information is far from complete, not necessarily quantifiable and perhaps also inconsequential. Regardless, it is plain and hardly disputable that without such contributions "Western civilization" and its material culture would not have come into existence. The assertion that external inputs were structurally marginal compared to domestic causal factors in explaining the origins of capitalism is logically endorsed by touchstone Marxist analysis. One example is material endowments such as coal in England, the use of which also required social intervention, especially "extensive state protection and regulation" of coal mining and market (Parthasarathi 2011: 152–153). The transition from feudalism is another. Britain's industrialization and mercantilist policies had been preceded by import substitution, which, nevertheless, was also accompanied by hegemony building in the global market. The internal causes cannot overshadow the sheer scope of so called free trade, often brought about by force.

Methodologically, it is not always possible to distinguish clearly between the intrinsic and the extrinsic. For Marx, New World plantation slavery was an organic part of capitalism itself: while "the slavery of Negroes precludes free wage labor," "the business in which slaves are used is conducted by *capitalists*. The mode of production that they introduce has not arisen out of slavery but is grafted onto it" (Marx [1861]1989: 516). To the extent that the relations of production must not be trivialized vis-à-vis the forces of production in economic history, it should be clear that neither the American resources nor English coal were decisive in the conditions favorable for an industrial revolution. The explanation of the presence or absence of such a revolution can be found only in differences in class structure and property relations between societies (restated in Brenner and Isett 2002). The "rise of the West" was after all about the rise of the bourgeoisie. For capitalism to become dominant as a social system, it "required that the bourgeoisie emerge victorious over other class forces controlling surpluses" (Harvey 2006: 90–91; Stedman Jones 1975). Yet the cosmopolitan capitalist ruling class ruled not only at home but also over colonies, destroying or preserving local class structures and relations in the interest of colonial rulers. A related issue of a metropolitan "labor aristocracy" sharing a small portion of "imperialist rent" is also no small matter and has continued into the present contention over welfare capitalism and much else.

In search of the "prime mover" in the transition to capitalism,[2] Robert Brenner singles out the unique "process of self-sustaining economic development characterized by rising labour productivity in agriculture" in England, which evaded the Malthusian trap of population growth (2001: 171–172). This "internalist" interpretation focuses on class struggle in the countryside leading to the emergence of agrarian capitalism independent of any external dynamics. Missing in the picture is what Pomeranz and others have documented about colonial immigration as noted above: in the few hundred years prior to and during the European industrial transformations, one-third of the population of the British Isles alone moved to the Americas, Antipodes, and elsewhere. This relief from tightening resource constraints also entailed absorption of Europe's surplus labor in the colonies (Pomeranz 2000: 6–7, 20–23). As Perry Anderson remarks, "the idea of capitalism in one country, taken literally, is only a bit more plausible than that of socialism." Marx instead notes the distribution of different historical moments of the growth of capital in a cumulative sequence from the European cities to their overseas empires (2005: 251). Ultimately, Marx offers his clarification with a temporal sensibility: "The competition among the European nations for the seizure of Asiatic products and American treasures, the colonial system, all made a fundamental contribution towards shattering the feudal barriers to production." Yet, decisively and domestically, "the modern mode of production in its first period, that of manufacture, developed only where the conditions for it had been created in the Middle Ages" (Marx [1894]1993: 450). The class-centered perspective can thus be perfectly in line with that of imperialism as inherent to capitalist expansion, which, in the end, is also a matter of class and in which proletarian internationalism is grounded.

More specifically, the story must be told through different substories: The "social revolution of industrial capitalism" happened organically only in Britain. "When its principal rivals embarked on their own state-led development in a capitalist direction, they were responding not to imperatives generated by domestic social property relations, but to external military, geopolitical and commercial pressures" (Wood 2009: 55). All considered, downplaying the role of the global sources of Western ascendancy in general and capitalist reliance on colonialism and imperialism in particular would be a serious distortion of the Marxist conception of historical capitalism as much as of history itself. "Globalizing Europe," or the first wave of globalization on which Europe rode to supremacy, means that Europe could not and did not rise by itself. A "much more global, holistic world economic/systemic perspective and theory" is therefore needed (Frank 1998: 334–339). Given this indispensability of the non-European factor in the construction of Europe, world history—in its Marxian connotation of capitalist epochalization—has to be conceived as from the outset internal to all nations, including noncapitalist but not necessarily "pre-capitalist" ones (Chapter 1).

The next consideration, implied by the first, is another forgotten insight, that capitalism hinders development outside its heartland. World history is not only about triumphant strides of capitalism and its transformative power, as viewed through Marx's lens. It is also about capitalism's socioeconomic failures in many of its (former) colonies. Or, more precisely, the logical function of capitalist accumulation entails exploitation, domination, and sabotage, which hamper national development on the peripheries. The widely assumed correlation between capitalism and development is dubious; too often the reality turns out to be capitalism and *under*development. Pockets of successful "late development" outside the historical communist territories are rather exceptional. The economic takeoff in South Korea and Taiwan among so-called Asian tigers, for example, depended on the aid and markets of the United States. Insofar as such pockets cannot alter the basic pattern of a global system polarized between rich and poor countries, the main propositions of dependency theory, as earlier noted, continue to hold up.

Consequent on imperial greed and colonial brutality, global integration and polarization have been the same process. The "extirpation, enslavement and entombment in mines of the aboriginal population," the "conquest and looting of India," and the "conversion of Africa into a preserve for the commercial hunting of black-skins" had wrecked the societies and lives of the "lesser breed" (Marx 1867/1971: 915). These incidents were also accompanied by some lasting ecological and environmental devastations (Davis: part III). A mechanism of the process that deprived the colonized people of their development potentials was the formation of a gross disproportion between an evergrowing volume of manufactured exports from Europe and an evergrowing volume of land-intensive products and minerals from its suppliers on the other continents. Financialization of the home economies as well as financial control abroad in its colonies and semicolonies gave Europe a "decisive advantage in the struggle over all other resources" (Arrighi 2007: 272).[3] It remains the case today that the core of the global system banks on the peripheries staying peripheral.

The twentieth-century Chinese communists learned about this logical function of capitalism as imperialism from China's own experience since the mid-nineteenth century. The illusion of modernization through imitating the West had been thoroughly crushed by the violent slicing of the country by the imperialist powers in collaboration with a local comprador class, which was itself a product of semi-coloniality. Any prospect of a homegrown, strong national capitalism, liberal or otherwise, was blocked. It was not until after 1949 that new China began to develop most impressively. This happened only because of its ability to break free from the colonial logic of capitalism that hindered development, through revolutionary transformations of class and social relations, and the fashioning of a socialist "developmental state." In debating a hypothetical "incipient capitalism" that might have surfaced as early as the Northern Song of the eleventh to twelfth century (Dirlik 1978), those who concurred with a schematized "stage theory" in effect translated the "why not China?" question into a politically charged, counterfactual conjecture. Plausible or not, it is certainly not unreasonable to maintain, as did the Chinese Marxist historians, that foreign intervention was a fatal blockage to China's intrinsically generated "natural course" of development.

The downside of this stance is that it can go too far in overlooking both internal barriers to, and indigenous agencies for, progressive modern change. The one-sidedness here parallels that of the crude "sinocentric" outlook, which may unintentionally lead to overlooking imperialism's crimes. Against complacency in either direction it should be affirmed that "colonialism and modernity are indivisible features of the history of industrial capitalism" and that "the modernity of non-European colonies is as indisputable as the colonial core of European modernity" (Barlow 1997: 1). Hence the clarity of the causal sequence of modern history: it was not the case that backwardness aggravated colonization, nor did revolution bring about underdevelopment. Historical realities have been the other way around. That is, national liberation movements and socialist revolutions took place not where capitalism succeeded but where it utterly failed. As a result, capitalism has not been, and cannot be, a sure path to, let alone the sole form of, modernity and development. If the linkage between capitalism and underdevelopment and, further, between underdevelopment and revolution in peripheral capitalism has been self-evident, then capitalist failures are also what provoke the quest for noncapitalist alternatives.

These considerations lead to a third reflection on raising legitimate questions about China's evolving position in the global system, in the shadow of an inexorable Euro-American hegemony in historical knowledge as well as present ideological contentions. If the supposed necessity or inevitability of industrial capitalism can be rationally refuted, if different peoples in different conditions aspire to different attainments while perceiving "modernity" differently, and if traditions in China have not leaned toward industrialism and urbanism, does it make any sense to apply an initially parochial Western order universally? Is it meaningful or reasonable to ask why China failed? With diverse values, goals, and standards are comparative evaluations even possible? If we are serious about seeking an accurate, non-Western typology of societal systems "in their own right" (Anderson 1974: 548–549), has not the dominant Weberian framing of questions concerning the "great divergence" (if not the whole comparative enterprise under its influence) become invalid?

In thinking through why vibrant economies did not move to industrial capitalism, questions other than "why Europe?" and "why not China?" as discussed in Chapter 2, should be asked. Indeed, if "why Europe?" cannot be adequately addressed without taking into account Europe's atrocities within and without its borders, and if socialism (or "communism" in the usage of a moral economy of the commons) contains elements commendable for the future of humanity, would it not be more worthwhile to ask where the socialist thinking and projects first advanced? Christian socialism and utopian socialism would be cases native to Europe; but there are also forms of a non-Western origin. Even though they failed or were transformed into types of post-socialism, historical communist adventures have been the most daring and the greatest in scope. The idea of socialism cannot be discarded, especially in the crises of our time, which keep forcing on us a choice as sharp as "socialism or barbarism." The socialist variants and counterparts, including welfare social democracies and populist social movements, are the other side of the evolution of the global capitalist system. Socialism, however, is out of the question for disillusioned Marxists who console themselves nowadays by appealing to a self-deceiving orthodoxy of capitalism (rather than the forces of production as such) as a prerequisite for socialism. This is an intellectual retreat and profoundly defeatist. Yet neither the socialist alternative nor the historical understanding of its indigenous or exogenous origins and developments can be renovated without the raising of more accurate and legitimate questions.

In the perspective of a "Eurasian miracle" originating in the "urban revolution" of the Bronze Age affecting the Middle East, India, and China (e.g., in the adoption of scripts and writing) before Europe, for example, Europe possessed only a post-Renaissance "temporary advantage" in a long process of cultural exchange and alteration between East and West. Neither had stable, permanent supremacy (Goody 2010: ch.8). This account matters not only for its recognition of the contributions of the East to scientific progress, industrialization, and modernization or its demystification of European rationality and superiority, but also because of its effort in historicizing "great divergence." The notions of "exchange" and "alteration" denote a dynamic, transcontinental historical movement in which nothing was predestined, not even capitalism, as locally perceived competitive and ecological pressures generated various societal responses in different times and places. Another example would be the ethnohistorical deconstruction of "European diffusionism" (Blaut 1993). The doctrine of the "rest" as subject to the diffusion of a universal civilization from the West is shown to be an ideology of colonialism and its justification. These and similar critiques lead to a fresh terrain where better questions can be asked about nonindustrial, noncapitalist yet modern and progressive cultures and economies, in the manner of not only "what has been" but also "what might have been" and "what might yet be." To engage such questions is "to resist fixed pictures of the social world and make room...for practice" (Hawthorn 1991: 37, 182).

Is then "why Europe?" a wrong question? It is not. The question can and should be legitimately asked without its existing Eurocentric connotation. The related question "why not others?" qualitatively different from "why did others fail?" can also be properly pursued. "Why Europe?" is an important and necessary question about the formation and globalization of capitalism, which has dominated the modern epoch. It requires, however, an acute sense of history. Since the emergence of industrial capitalism was contingent on a unique historical conjunction of specific and unrepeatable conditions, nothing similar can be expected anywhere again. Instead, uneven and compressed development could be possible in the developing world. These issues illustrate a general feature of the world's history of transitory and rotating power centers, which encompasses the rise of the West and the looming return of the East.

What about Eurocentrism? A complication is that the assumption that industrial capitalism (to be conceptually distinguished from capitalism without industrialism and vice versa) is historically superior and indispensable is not exactly Eurocentric but capitalist-centric. Anticapitalism has never been alien to Europe. Certain Euro-universal propositions also cannot be simply discarded, as European modernity since the Enlightenment has involved both destruction and civilization (Horkheimer and Adorno 1972: 92). "Europe" signals struggles for freedom, equality, and fraternity as much as it does colonialism, racism, and imperialism. The rebelling slaves as black Jacobins in the Haitian revolution sang the *Marseillaise* not to emulate their colonizers' model of emancipation but to challenge its failings (Buck-Morss 2009: part I).[4] However, even classical liberalism, arguably the highest attainment in the Enlightenment tradition, is complicit. John Stuart Mill despises the "barbarians" who deserve despotism; and a "master-race democracy" that the liberals cherish characterized the overall relationship between the West and the (post)colonial world (Losurdo 2011: 225–227). The Marxist worldview of the rise and demise of capitalism also has a Eurocentric overtone, but only because of its preoccupation with a Eurogenetic industrial age, a flaw that is simultaneously negated by its own communist internationalism. Also to be recognized is the dilemma of our inherited knowledge and terminology—the modern discourse remains more or less confined to the essential categories initially provided in European historiography and social theories. "European thought is at once both indispensable and inadequate" for historical inquiries and political analysis in non-Western societies (Chakrabarty 2000: 16).[5]

The problem, once again, is not Europe or the West as such but the Eurocentric arrogance and myth of capitalist convergence. Yet a crisis-ridden and polarizing system because of its inherent and unsolvable contradictions does not really converge. Self-readjustments under social pressure or competitive incentives can be only partial or superficial. The disappearance of a socialist bloc has meant the loss of a brake, however ineffective, on the capitalist war and money machines. The fact that socialist revolutions committed errors, fell short, degenerated, or collapsed should not conceal that they had some vastly important successes. And precisely because any socialist undertaking must be regarded as an attempted alternative to capitalist ideas and institutions, it cannot be gauged by capitalist norms. This reminds us that we still lack a hypothesis of postcapitalism in the whole debate. Only with an outlook transcending capitalist modernity can questions about China and the world in history and at present be more fruitfully posed and answered.

The last point of reflection is on the (potential) universality of local experiences of non-Western origin. If it is necessary to ask "why China?" and for that matter "why Asia?" positively, the questions cannot be effective until such universality can be looked for. This would be a project of rehabilitating the "East," which may represent or be represented by the "South," as a symbol of autonomy, energy, creativity, and search for a future of truly universal appeal. The enduring scholarly fascination with the place of China and the East at large in the world is a sign of not only the continuing pursuit of transcultural understanding and global interconnectedness, but also concerns about any potential alternative to capitalist homogenization. As capitalism becomes penetrating while resisted in China, the universal and the contentions over the universal itself play out vividly in struggles across the country for social rights, equality, and justice. This line of reasoning is not about a past "Asian Age," still less has it anything to do with the fashion of chanting about the "rise of China." Confucian revivalism, for example, like so-called Asian values, tends to be conservative, even reactionary, especially in its official versions.[6] Dangerous "Asianization" is not too remote: wartime pan-Asianism would be an example. In a totally different vein, "great Han chauvinism," which Mao and his colleagues in the first Chinese communist generation consistently warned against, could grow in total blindness. All kinds of prejudices embodied in the "race" related "rise" discourse can entrap the relevant debates into either Chinese/Asian particularism/exceptionalism ("cultural authenticity" and "clash of civilizations") or West-centric conformism (*jiegui* and the "end of history"). The AMP-style verdicts about fatal "Asian" deficiencies, Marxist or otherwise, must be overturned. But that cannot be done by any self-orientalization in what Bruce Cumings sees as "a new orientalist craze" (2011: 185). Nor can a one-way globalization solve the problem: nothing would be more vindicating of West-centric capitalism than the capitalist conquest of China, which has been, in culturalist language, "of all the great cultures...the furthest removed from the Western tradition" (Fairbank 1957: 4). More precisely, with the defeat of Chinese socialism, China now "sets the stage for the crystallization of Sinological-orientalism and its capital-logic of the PRC becoming-the-same" (Vukovich 2012: 23). This political "sinological orientalism," however, cannot be countered by cultural "reverse orientalism," which follows the same logic as late capitalism. China's treasured cultural traditions deserve careful revaluation after the twentieth-century revolutionary ruptures. But looking to the East does not validate any nativist fantasies—socialism needs no recourse to prerevolutionary glories.

A stronger, and probably also the only plausible, argument will have to stem from a universalist position about local or localized values awaiting democratic conversation for due recognition in the normative theories of emancipation. Sinified Marxism in the Chinese revolution and, perhaps more controversially, Gandhian democracy in the Indian freedom struggle are two obvious examples. Only thus can the supposed universality of capitalism, secured in a hegemonic and institutionalized ideology yet utterly disproved by the system's perpetual local and global devastation inflicted on societies and nature, be rivaled. However, alternatives, including the aborted ones in the short twentieth century, have yet to be articulated in the universal language of such normative theories in an overdue intellectual enterprise.

Historically, part and parcel of a given political economy and hence necessarily included in a fuller and more accurate understanding of comparative economic development are popular movements from below. One could easily relate rural turmoil in North and South China (Perry 1983; Bernhardt 1992), for example, to peasant rebellions elsewhere, including Europe. In history from below, popular resistance has occurred around the globe before and during an "age of capital." The revolutionary movements from the turn of the twentieth century onward engaged nationalists, communists, and antiwar activists across national and regional borders of East, South, and Southeast Asia (Blackburn 1975; Karl 2002). The idea of Asian universalism, in which nationalism and internationalism intertwined, emerged in response to Western colonialism, Japanese imperialism, and their local collaborators. More generally, from the "three people's principles" and the spirit of Bandung to rights for workers, farmers, women, the minorities, and subaltern groups, shared struggles continue. The pathway of heavy state investment in human capital and government nurturing of "national champion" industries or small business in the "tiger" economies, too, may well teach something about development beyond East Asia. Only through drawing on the common experiences of a "people's Asia" and enhancing their alliance with those of other parts of the world (e.g. Food First, land right, and other transnational popular movements), with regional powers refusing to emulate anything remotely akin to the old colonial practice, might a "Beijing consensus" or "Delhi consensus" begin to make sense.

The communist revolution in China, because of its consciousness of being "part of the world revolution" (as Mao discussed in *On New Democracy* in 1940) and its far-reaching global impacts, is never merely a Chinese event. Because of the nation's oppressed "class" position, the revolution had to be simultaneously nationalist and internationalist. Ernest Gellner is a Marxist when he writes that "only when a nation became a class...did it become politically conscious and activist...[as] a nation-for-itself" (1983: 121). The construction of the subjective "Chinese people" in the process of new nation building is just another case of "we the people" emerging from great social revolutions. The Chinese idea of a "mass line" (and similarly of "democratic centralism" in Maoism in contrast with Stalinism) corresponds to the benchmark process of democratic decisionmaking through solicitation ("from the masses" democratically) and aggregation (centrally made decisions "to the masses" for implementation). As opposed to a "sham" bourgeois democracy on the one hand and statist bureaucratization on the other, this idea also has a universal element of broad participation and self-organization.

If the "right to rebel" is a maxim of the French Declaration of Rights, the same principle is over two thousand years old in the Chinese notion of a "mandate of heaven" justifying revolt against tyranny. Mancur Olson, a mainstream political scientist, finds himself appreciating the Maoist rationale of rectifying bureaucracy through a Cultural Revolution: a "corporate-bargaining state" (as in the Nordic countries) must make a constant effort to curb various "distributional coalitions." Democracy needs periodic upheavals for rebalancing social power (Olson 1982: 42–47; Rose-Ackerman 2003). The Chinese attempts can be rightly linked to the Marxian model of the Paris Commune as "the political form at last discovered under which to work out the economic emancipation of labor." It would replace the game of "deciding once in three or six years which member of the ruling class was to misrepresent the people in Parliament" (Marx [1871]1968: 213). The "Parisian connection" in workers' agitation in Shanghai (Perry 1999) and the images of the Paris Commune in sino-Marxist thought (Meisner 1982: 136–151) are exemplary of the "concrete universal" to be cherished.

A new moral economy as discussed in Chapter 7 could be another case of local contours bearing a universal significance. Its basic assumptions are certainly far broader than such narrow beliefs as the crude "economic man." If the ideology of "exclusive private property" (Hann 1998) or "possessive individualism" (MacPherson 1962) is intrinsic to the Weberian equation of modernity and capitalist rationalization, it is parochial. The wholly individualistic doctrine has found difficulty spreading in many cultures and communities. This fact, even if compromised in the globalization of neoliberalism, not only invalidates capitalist rationality but also competes with it for universality in redefining the modern and rational. The rediscovery in Western academia of a sentimental Adam Smith represents a useful self-critical rethinking from within the system. But again people in the East and their moral economies have been there since long before Smith, and can bring neglected peripheral perspectives and determinants to light beyond "a singular modernity defined by the political economy and culture of capitalism" (Dirlik 2011a:16).

Past and present setbacks notwithstanding, China may strive to lead the way to an imperative global transformation, as the paradigm of capital accumulation has evidently hit its limit. To urgently address climate and environmental crises is inescapable and hence universal, and is where relevant local knowledge might be normatively constructed. A main contribution of the new economic history reviewed in Chapter 2 is that it places ecology in its broadest signification at the center of historical understanding. The possible

Chinese advantage in this regard is twofold. The country's evolving economic structure has always depended in part on a multitude of petty producers and cooperatives; and the revolutionary and reformist transformations of rural China have more or less defied the methods and results of typical third world urbanization. Could not a new kind of "industrious revolution," this time aimed at both needs and freedom, serve to relax the conceptual and discursive rigidity of capitalist modernity? A participatory society as a commons, with direct producers as its subjective and realization of human values through united labor as its objective (Chapter 7), is within the vision of a grand social model. The universalism of this vision lies not in any convergence of development, since a modern world may or may not be urban as we know it. Here comes again the needed strategic clarity of distinction between urbanization and modernization and, further, between modernity and capitalism.

The effort to recast universalism as a Euro-world view from the East requires no cultural uniformity of the region or transregional entities. Such uniformity has never existed; and "Asia" is not generalizable except in its distinguished traditions of not only anti-imperialism and decolonization, but also national development. Neither anything universally appreciable in these traditions nor their denial is of a cultural nature. In the post-Mao era the Chinese revolution, for instance, is disavowed and Maoism demonized as a "native" initiative, but it of course has a Cold War origin and is now loudly welcomed and echoed abroad (Vukovich 2012). Thus, the task of recasting universalism cannot be about cultural uniformity but about commonality in shared political commitment and social desire, and about mutual learning, equal dialogue, and using "Asia as an imaginary anchoring point." Certain ideas and experiences in Asia can indeed be developed "as an alternative horizon, perspective, or method for posing a different set of questions about world history" (Chen 2010: xv). As well-put in a report (unusual for the mainstream mantra of *The Economist*) on "The East Is Grey,"

China "has advantages in addressing its—and the world's—environmental problems" (from political willingness to economic incentives, natural asset of "sunny, windy deserts" to mistakes as lessons from the earlier developers). Building "a zero-carbon energy system is the silver lining of a very dark cloud. If China cannot do it, no one can."[7]

If rethinking Asia necessarily implies questioning the universality of a teleological worldview and world history, and if capitalist "Euromodernity" (Dirlik 2011a) in its universalist pretensions cannot be negated by anything particularistic, then nothing less than a daring socialist alternative gathering strengths on the ground can make the intellectual undoing of long capitalist-centrism and short Cold War mentality achievable. After all, only an epistemological paradigm shift that overturns the perceived universality of the values centered in a Euro-genetic industrial capitalism can beat back the myths and stigma of Oriental defects.

# 9
# Marxism and the Interpretation of China

From a universalist perspective of historical materialism, the position of China in the world and in world history is essentially defined by its relationship with epochal parameters of capitalism. Both entities in question, capitalism in global dominance and China in search of an alternative, are part of an open-ended historical contour. They need to be duly historicized in their interactions and intertwining effects in any rational inquiry and understanding. This is where Marxism appeals by virtue of its powerful global perspective on capitalism and precapitalism, its penetrating critiques of the capitalist crisis, and its logical conclusion about capitalism's eventual demise and replacement by a higher social formation.

The Chinese passages from revolution to reform and into the future have been traced and debated extensively in a scholarship predominantly within a framework of various representations of modernization theory. Marxism has had a notable impact on (if not exactly pioneered) that theory and the knowledge produced under its influence. Insofar as capitalism remains an overriding mode of production in modern times—that differentiates the epoch itself—the enlightenment or for that matter the obscurity of the Marxist outlook is intellectually indispensable. Among the critical issues raised by the Marxist interpretation of China, four interconnected theses will be the focus of the following discussion: the necessity of positioning China in the global political economy; capitalism as neither an inevitable evolutionary stage nor a sustained option for China; the primacy of politics and ideological struggle in development in an era of late capitalism; and the political, rather than cultural, nature of Chinese socialism. Any universal implication that might be drawn from these propositions should surface.

The global system has undergone a long-term financialization and then also a major shift since the 1970s, resulting in the contemporary capitalist crises becoming largely fiscal. Without a fixed gold standard and hence a control mechanism over the international balance of payment, the United States in particular could issue dollars at will, while exporting inflation, deficit, and credit expansion. The liberalization of capital movement and of transactions in the global stock and money markets has meanwhile enabled surplus capital to flow into the developing countries on a massive scale, mostly as short-term, speculative portfolio investments for quick profits. The Chinese reform has proceeded in parallel with capitalist mutation and the onset of neoliberal hegemony, turning itself into a driving force of forming the new spaces and growth centers of the system. In these circumstances, China may still grow bigger economically, but only as a lesser power, and an exploited, bullied, unstable, and probably also explosive and reactionary one. In light of its inimitable contributions to postcommunist globalization as the order of the day, one recalls Marx's fear of counterrevolution in newly converted capitalist regimes (Marx [1858]1983: 345). The People's Republic, on losing its original status with substance and distinction, is in an acute identity crisis.

As China's early reformist attempt at a shallow, selective "relinking" promised in national autonomy and protection fell short, as its political class tried hard to appease global rule makers, and as the communist state's purposeful cultivation of a capitalist market backfired, the reform degenerated into a bureaucratic-capitalist transition. The inroad of casino capital and multinationals alone threatens national economic security and impedes direct producers and small traders, making the country vulnerable to further economic dependency and political incapacity. The rise of social resistance, whether Polanyian or socialist, clarifies the situation: private market cannot be automatically social as widely misconceived in the Chinese official and unofficial media. Concealed in this perception is the reality that market forces and state forces ally and both can be repressive against society. The revolutionary bourgeoisie representing a rising mode of production as analyzed by Marx is long gone in world history.

The progression of two State Council documents exemplifies China's policy strategy. The first, issued in 2005 (no.3), entitled "Encouraging, supporting and guiding the development of private sector" (known as the "old 36 directives"), legitimized the operation of private and foreign enterprises in China's mainstay industries with specified preferential provisions. The second, issued in 2010 (no.13) and similarly titled, identified a dozen more industries open to private and foreign entry, including defense and military, petroleum, nuclear power, and communications. The "new 36 directives" have been quickly and forcefully implemented, complemented also by new measures of financial opening. "China 2030" is an even more comprehensive statement on privatization and liberalization (Chapter 4). Typically, inside China's policy circles, the World Bank is taken as authoritative, as though its preferences override a sovereign state. *China Daily* approvingly reports that the "World Bank urged China to revamp its financial system in a decisive, comprehensive and coordinated manner"; and "the bank also recommends redefining the roles of SOEs and breaking up state monopolies in certain industries, diversifying ownership, lowering entry barriers to private firms."[1] But these recommendations would in effect undermine the entire foundation of the Chinese system, which is what has enabled China to develop rapidly while largely withstanding international antagonism as well as the global and regional financial crises since the 1970s.

Accumulated social discontent from radicalized reforms and resulting political tensions within the party and government culminated in a fierce competition between the so-called Chongqing model and Guangdong model. The difference between the two, in popular discourse, is between "sharing the cake equally" and "making the cake bigger." Before long, however, the Chongqing (distributive) model was crushed in a highly secretive yet public drama fueled by a state-sponsored "rumor machine" in the spring of 2012 (Wang 2012b). The downfall of Bo Xilai, the municipal party secretary, was in news headlines globally. Much of the impetus for this case and unfolding events around it remain conjectural. As they played out, Beijing's information and statements had been so closely echoed in Washington and London that the nature of foreign involvement is also obscure. Negative reports on Chongqing by the Carnegie Endowment for International Peace, the Hoover Institution, and the Rand Corporation had preceded the crackdown.[2] An extraordinary alliance of the Chinese communist power elite, anticommunist factions inside and outside China, and Western governments and press seemed to exist as a phenomenal example of twenty-first-century postmodern politics.

Popular misgiving over the affair, however, is not due only to the lack of evidence against Bo or to the overall uncertainty of judicial independence and fair trial in China. It was obvious that the political motives of the accusers in this case had predetermined the outcome of any investigation. In other words, the persecution of the practitioners and supporters of the model is a matter of "line struggle" (in the Maoist notion) over the future direction of party and country. It is not a matter of personal ambition or corruption but the political stance of communist power. The values of common prosperity the model symbolizes and the social forces behind it, including those also critical of its apparent limitations, are at stake. In April, an open letter addressed to the leaders and signed by "a group of confused communist party members" was briefly circulated on the Internet: Thanks to developments in recent years in Chongqing, "we have seen the return of light of socialism and the original standing of the party....people welcomed the return of the true party and its mass inclination and mass line."[3] The lack of hard evidence for the corruption charge against Bo does itself also pose a problem for the reformers championing the rule of law and procedural justice, according to which one is innocent until proven guilty and has the right to a defense. However, along with arrests and questioning, officials nationally were required to declare loyalty to the center and left-leaning websites were shut down.[4] The atmosphere around the affairs continues to be tense and repressive.

In their local adventure, Bo and his followers tried in particular to restore the spirit of a lost collectivism and ties between the leaders and the led. As indicated in the open letter cited above, the officials in Chongqing were compelled to spend no less than two-thirds of their working hours in the fields with front-line workers, villagers, marginalized groups, and poor households. This might have been the most irritating to those powerful who have alienated the traditional constituents of the party. An Internet commentator puts it thus, "if leaning on popular support can be used to leverage power, is this not the pathway to unleash uncontrollable democratic pressures that would threaten CCP unity and rule"?[5] As Zhao Yuezhi remarks, to stay in power, the party will have to balance the question of social instability against a faltering global economy—all the while living up to some of the rhetoric contained in the Chongqing model. It is perhaps precisely within this context that one can appreciate the front-page layout of the *People's Daily* of April 11, 2012. Rather than the bombshell announcement of Bo's ousting, it led with the following heading: "More than 200,000 Shaanxi officials going to the grass roots." "Since no other region has done a more impressive job in sending officials to attend the grassroots than Bo's Chongqing, the party line was clear: 'Down with Bo Xilai, long live the mass line!'" (Zhao 2012). This optimism may have anticipated a desirable shift with the newly installed leaders in 2013.

In Chongqing, however, things have remained overturned: signs in public squares ban gatherings to sing red
songs, commercial advertising once removed has reoccu-
pied the main television news channel, and "the problems
from prostitution to illegal activities of the wealthy are
creeping back."[6] Yet, "to the extent that Bo was able to
go so far in Chongqing and that his ousting has created
such a grave political crisis, the CCP could not easily bury
his political messages and brush aside the underlying issues
that the Chongqing Model tried to address" (Zhao 2012).
Nationally, as Kerry Brown observes, since Bo was "the
only leader of his generation to truly try to reach across
from the privileged elite zone of power" and speak directly
to people, "his final departure is a huge loss for political
life in China."[7]

To be sure, Chongqing has not represented a new socialist model. On the one hand, the local economy of this giant
mountain city in central China (with 32 million residents,
urban and suburban) has grown faster than the national
average, enabled by earnings and investment from SOEs
(Cui 2011).[8] This source of government revenue is what has
enabled massive public schemes: welfare housing, urban-
rural integrated social security, greening, improving public
transportation, and other *minsheng*-related provisions. The
innovative management of state firms has also helped with
a lower private sector business tax rate of 15 percent, compared with about 25 percent elsewhere in China.[9] On the
other hand, however, circumscribed by its external and internal conditions, Chongqing has pursued a program largely in
line with the national agenda of promoting foreign capital,
export, and market integration. It has not questioned the
teleology of modernization in terms of industrialization and
urbanization. Nor has it offered a vision that transcends
capitalist globalization.

Development in China is at the crossroads, facing on the one
hand the legitimacy or inevitability of a complete capitalist transition and on the other the moral necessity as well

as practical feasibility of a socialist alternative. The former option dominates domestic policy thinking, in which the latter is portrayed, falsely, as a desire to turn back the clock to an ultraleftist political economy. The politics of this division can be spelled out by making the crooked logic of likening Chongqing with the Cultural Revolution straight: as the intended targets of the latter were (still yet to be) "capitalist roaders" and corrupt bureaucrats and such people have now really occupied many leading posts, they are of course threatened. The discursive context is thus that the "Cultural Revolution" can be deployed "as a lethal rhetorical weapon" against critics of the neoliberal policies and elites (Zhao 2008: 56, 323). Indeed, "the few surviving communist regimes are re-inventing themselves as the authoritarian protectors of a new, even more dynamic and efficient, 'capitalism with Asian values.'" And this uncontested hegemony of capitalism is only sustained by the utopian core of capitalist ideology. "Utopias of alternative worlds have been exorcized by the utopia in power, masking itself as pragmatic realism" (Žižek 2009: 77).

Most ironic is the use of Marxism in justifying a utopian capitalism—utopian because of the blindness of capitalist exploitation and destruction, the illusory idealization of an all magical market, and the unfounded assumption that capitalism is necessary or inevitable. But this is an abuse and distortion. Recall what Marx writes about revolution and revolutionary potential in China (Chapter 2), or about the possibility of a Russian transition from communal property to communism (Chapter 3). Marx is crystal clear about the Western European path being unique and confined to Western Europe. There is no inevitability of capitalist development anywhere else, not to mention desirability. In a famous passage written in the late 1870s, he replied to a critic who came to "metamorphose my outline of the genesis of capitalism in western Europe into a historico-philosophical theory of the general course, fatally imposed upon all peoples, regardless of the historical circumstances in which they find themselves placed," but in so doing he "does me too much honor and too much shame at the same time." Marx also mentioned that in *Capital* he had already "made allusion to the fate which overtook the plebeians of ancient Rome."[10] Moreover, the communist revolution in China's own "historical circumstances" has lifted the country categorically from anything comparable to Czarist Russia or any other "precapitalist" societies. Central to the powerful argument of *New Democracy* is precisely that the revolution foreclosed the capitalist path in China.

By the same token, capitalism in its classic forms is also no longer viable. It is not an available option for late development in general or China in particular. As noted, the thesis of capitalism being blocked in China as a work of Western and Japanese imperialism was a consensus among the Chinese Marxists. Newer constraints also abound, from hard, material to soft, moral and cultural ones. Above all, the kind of ecological relief early European capitalism sought in its colonies overseas is obviously unrepeatable (not to mention morally unacceptable). China does engage itself in foreign direct investment but certainly not as a colonial power. Meanwhile, the logic of global capital constantly seeking accumulation through outsourcing sets the ultimate limit. Surplus capital looking for new territories results in geopolitical rivalries, which is a road to international conflict and war. Socialist self-reliance is therefore a choice not just of national security but also of world peace.

Consider also the destruction of a postcommunist transition. In Russia, that transition was "a looting on a grand scale." Capitalism, not organic to Soviet society, was imposed from above and outside; and the imposition, at "the life and death costs" from workers' point of view, "led to wild and anticipated distortions, pathologies and disasters" (Buraway 2009: 34, 62). So it has been for China. Marx, in the letter quoted above, also writes,

> If Russia tries to become a capitalist nation, in imitation of the
> nations of western Europe, and in recent years she has taken a
> great deal of pains in this respect, she will not succeed without first having transformed a good part of her peasants into

proletarians; and after that, once brought into the lap of the capitalist regime, she will be subject to its inexorable laws, like other profane nations.

Every sentence here reads as though written about China today (Chapter 6). And much more follows such a socioeconomic transition, in culture, morality, education, and social relations in general. Rather than enhancing their autonomy and freedom as romanticists promise, the commodification of human values enslaves and corrupts people, even in post-revolutionary societies. In an interview, when asked which countries are the least receptive to his concerns about market fundamentalism, Michael Sandel, who has given public lectures around the world, including Shanghai, responded, "China and the US—no question." Compared with India or Brazil regarding moral limits to markets, "in the US and China, there are strong voices who will challenge the whole idea of there being any limits."[11]

The problems of a capitalism with Chinese characteristics, from exploitation and polarization to greed, fraud and pollution, from market anarchy to state incapacity and repression, are predictable. A widespread "utopia," however, sees the solution of such problems as lying in a wholesale capitalist transformation. But a postcapitalist development would be more realistic, because idealistic capitalism does not exist to offer China a future, and because China's socialist path dependency has not evaporated. If socialism is no longer a coherent metatheory and needs to be reworked so as to accommodate the market, this could be just (one more time) the "finest chance ever offered by history to a people," in the words of Marx on bypassing the fatal vicissitudes of capitalism as quoted in Chapter 3. The historical opportunity to renovate collective legacies can be seized in China, where since the "postsocialist" structural context of reform implies postcapitalism in both logical and historical sequence, socialism may remain "a possible option to which it can return if circumstances so demand" (Dirlik 1989: 377–378).[12]

Such an option is argued to be both more desirable and feasible for China, especially in its immediate conditions of a peculiarly crude, unsettled, contradictory, and confusing process of accumulation. Reorientation, however, requires the socialists to win a political battle. This is the third thesis of this chapter. To be sure, "socialism" is an empty word without an economic foundation—a dominant public sector, for instance, among other components as delineated in Chapter 5. But the laying and guarding of this foundation depend on politics. This dependence is nowhere more illuminating than in the systematic undermining of SOEs and collective land by neoliberal policies. Likewise, even an entirely viable alternative cannot even begin to materialize without political struggle to pave the way for it. Both the radical proposals of overtaking capitalism and the less radical ones of taming wild globalization count on political initiatives from popular movements and possibly also the national governments in the South. China, for example, can contribute to the joint effort of regulating and restricting capital movement as a crisis prevention mechanism, with a long view of socializing monopolies and definancializing economic management the world over (Amin 2013: 24–27). This would improve China's own external conditions as well because of the oppressed "class" position of its modern national identity shared with other developing countries. At issue is no longer growth or energy supply if China will change its developmental pattern and shift focus to its internal market, but a global reordering.[13] Such a change at home, too, implies fierce contentions of interests and power.

Political determination, wisdom, and leadership make all the difference in the quality and clarity of national program and agenda setting. The national trajectory of the PRC illuminates a deterministic role of its political structure and power, of the party and state. The fact that the post-Mao regime has had to deliberately depoliticize Chinese politics or, more specifically, deradicalize or deideologicalize the party to shift course, only reconfirms this point. The reform project is of course itself highly ideological, and the result is the vanishing of a powerful communist party as a revolutionary thinker and organizer, a Gramscian "modern prince". Without discarding the name or wording of its constitution, the party's self-identification is now hardly distinguishable from that of the state. This loss of ideological identity or "statization" of the party, as Wang Hui puts it, deprives the People's Republic of its political soul or commitment inherited from the revolution. The state-party, then, pursuing a political "normalization" of Chinese politics, is all about preserving its own power (Wang 2006). However, precisely because this process is a political work, it should not be irreversible. A fresh leadership taking the office in 2013 does seem to have the opportunity if, and only if, it can read the popular mandate and act in response to it, democratically. That is, without mobilizing social forces to remake socialism, another social revolution may not be avoidable.

"Politics in command" is a most influential idiom of Maoism. More specifically, "all is determined by the party line and cadres," in Mao's words (Gray 1974; Meisner 1982: 94–111). The idea is intimately related to that of mass line and a faith in human agency, of which the "humane elements," the emphasis on the autonomy and creativity of the common people, are "among the great visions of man in the history of human aspirations" (Lindblom 1977: 54–55, 62). "Politics" here entails also the centrality of theoretical, ideological, and discursive struggles. Given the effect of depoliticization in Chinese society, which has been laid bare in the emergence of an all-pervasive monoculture of money fetishism and political cynicism, to reaccentuate politics is to seek a countertransformation of perceptions and structure of feelings. Winning the battle for ideas is then also where the question of subjectivity, agency, and consciousness arises about creating a new popular and historical subject. The social, based on the new moral economy of commons and class alliance symbolized in the generic identity of direct producers, will then have practical means to advocate and organize, and generate alternative pressure mounting on the party and government to reorient.

If Marxism is guilty of economic determinism, "politics in command" would be an invaluable corrective. The "vulgar materialist" reading of Marx with regard to China finds him vindicated on two accounts: the eventual capitalist development in China shows that the country's past adventure with socialism was against the "law of history" and doomed to fail; and making up the missed developmental stage of capitalism is necessary and ideologically legitimate. Market transition with all its vices is thus justified as being "on the side of history". But this, again, is a distortion. As a revolutionary ideology, Marxism has always recognized a need for political precedence. In *The German Ideology,* characteristically Marx and Engels explain why the communist revolution is necessary: "not only because the ruling class cannot be overthrown in any other way, but also because the class overthrowing it can only in a revolution succeed in ridding itself of all the muck of ages and become fitted to found society anew."[14] The ruling class does not depart by itself; and the founders of a new society have to be created through revolutionary education and socialization. This is the case with the dialects of the Chinese revolution.

Based on the Marxist philosophy of active or reactive functions of political movement, ideology and power, a self-consciously Marxist tradition has developed through Lenin and Mao among other revolutionary theorist as well as an eminent school of Western Marxism. From Georg Lukacs's class consciousness to Antonio Gramsci's hegemony, politics commands. Politics also attains primacy over history, as Walter Benjamin remarks, by catalyzing openings from artificial historical closures (in Bensaid 2002: 35). Within the Marxist perspective, history is not itself purposeful but is made by structurally constrained yet morally intentional actors. Such actors could defy certain constraints in transformative politics, as is most compellingly witnessed in those extraordinary historical moments of revolutions. The monumental communist revolution in China has changed Chinese and world history, enabling a modern transformation in contravention of the supposedly universal paradigm of capitalism

It does not matter how truthfully historical materialist the conception of the primacy of politics might be. Often theoretically dismissed in Marxiology, it fits concrete experiences in China. Along with historical indeterminacy and contingency, the implication is that the future of China and the world remains open. For a socialist ambition to make sense in a postcommunist era, this nondeterministic outlook is prerequisite. Strategies can then be devised to preserve the spaces and endeavors not yet dominated by private profit while regaining those already lost so as to reconstruct China's political economy. Whether they can succeed will depend on "line and cadres" of the party drawing strengths from social resistance against further erosion of socialism. That is, committed socialists need to pick themselves up from setbacks and defeats, return to the battleground, and begin from the beginning. Only with a visionary social model and only through common struggles toward it can popular movements, decentralized and experimental, be freed from their existing institutional and ideological chains. Politics is about "plasticity" against "deep structure" rigidity in thinking and acting (Unger 1987).

In essence, Chinese socialism is not a cultural concept of Chineseness but a political one of socialism. This clarification is the last point to be discussed in this chapter concerning the Marxist interpretation of China. From the outset, the modern alternatives initiated in revolutionary China have been political but not cultural in nature. That is, they are not so much about national characteristics as about socialist universality and intended to challenge capitalism, not the West as such. The Sinification of Marxism is a counterexample to the deceptive culturalist narrative about Chinese distinctiveness. In other words, any serious Chinese alternative to capitalist integration has to be a political rather than a cultural project about socialist choice rather than Sinophone preference. This clarification is important also because if cultural particularities are assigned to the Chinese model, the political message of a socialist alternative in China is suppressed. The contention becomes a matter of competition between cultures or civilizations or, often with racist pretensions, between premodernity and modernity. The political unconscious here is that when considered on those terms, the Chinese revolution is revoked politically. The supposedly "cultural" deficiencies turn out to be ideological that China is not "up to" capitalist democracy or in any case is not yet fully modern or is incapable of being so. In the end, the unfolding convergence and divergence between China and the capitalist world cannot be explainable by either the economic power of market standardization or the cultural logic of national identities. There is no such a thing as cultural or economic destiny; nothing is predestined in culture or economy—once again, above a certain threshold of materiality (Chapter 7), politics is in command.

The question of universalism is therefore straightforward. The capitalist universe and epochal conditions make any genuine alternative necessarily universalist. And the socialist Chinese model, as discussed, has to be simultaneously internationalist. The dialectic coherence of singularity and universality of Chinese socialism, which has permanently redrawn the map of world history, is what holds a true universal history "as method and orientation."[15] Needless to add that shared human values, rights, and liberation require no homogeneity of cultures or cultural identities; they instead nurture diversity as well as political pluralism. Consumerism, on the contrary, has a standardizing effect. Market conformity and uniformity deform individualism and diversity, weakening social cohesion and public commitment.

To reject cultural essentialism is not to overlook culture. There are no doubt genuine differences between cultures. Culture is so important that any socioeconomic transformation has also got to be a cultural one. The argument is rather about socialism being not culturally specific, notwithstanding its diverse historical paths or institutions. Collective rationality, as opposed to "possessive individualism," has in one way or another featured traditional moral economy throughout history, West and East. Socialism has deep, wide, and multicultural roots. Seeking a democratic alternative to deficit liberal democracy is also not a cultural project. Democracy understood as the power of the people or people in control of their own destinies is a universal idea. The Chinese, having engaged themselves in a mobilizational "people's democracy" before "normal politics," seem to be more faithful democrats than the formalists in many capitalist democracies. They will not satisfy with mere voting and must find their own ways to bring the people back in and institutionalize political participation, representation, and accountability. National elections are likely to be necessary, but the "minimalist" and antipopulist traditions in Western thought have little appeal in Chinese society. This is a major division, but hardly a cultural one.

That is, democracy is no alien concept to the Chinese political vocabulary but a legitimate and legitimating principle in the communist ideology. The reformers have abandoned mass campaigns but not replaced them with anything significantly more democratic. If a lack of secured liberties and the repression of dissidents make even a "bourgeois democracy" desirable, any cogent discussion of democratization in China still must take its revolutionary and socialist legacies seriously, with their local and cultural specifics. Soviets or councils, committees, public forums, representative congresses, and so on have been functional institutional expressions of a mass line democracy. To be critical of past errors without overlooking truly democratic and universalist aspiration in the Chinese search for democracy is to reject its trivialization and distortion. It is against this backdrop, as argued, that the presumptions and prescription about a choice for China between protracting authoritarianism and a "color revolution" of a sort are misleading (Chapters 4 and 5). So is debating whether China is a candidate for implantation of a ready-made package of electoral and interest-group politics without regard to its own preferences and resources for a democratic change. This insistence on critical appreciation of local knowledge and ethos is, again, not a cultural but a political argument.

Rejecting the global homogenization on the one hand and nativist traditionalism on the other, democracy in China as in other parts of the developing world should and could be more direct, more participatory, more effective, and more social to include also the economic domain. Economic democracy, promoted by Marxists and non-Marxists alike, is Marxist to its core. After all, why should we cherish democracy if it does not deliver public goods to all or stop bankers and gamblers from looting citizens, and if it allows wars and other forms of human and environmental destruction to be committed in its name? Any "democratic" legitimation of exploitation and injustice in the national and global systems must be exposed and rejected. Again, opposing the deformation of democracy in a self-consoling ritual or as an ideological tool of domination does not define a cultural stance. Such deformation is not a "Western sin"—a unified "West" is a myth anyway and successful social democracies could be the hope of a future European social model—but an intrinsic limitation of capitalism.

The history of the PRC can be seen from one point of view as a blending of paradigms of revolution, modernization, and globalization and from another as a combination of the models of late, peripheral, and socialist development. This vast case is weighty enough to negate the teleological fallacy of capitalist modernity, and modernization is not conditioned on capitalism. Whether socialism remains a viable alternative in China will depend on its ability to envision and accomplish what Lenin at the height of New Economic Policy referred to as an "extremely difficult task," an "epoch-making undertaking" of "completing the foundations of socialist economy (particularly in a small-peasant country)."[16] More than 160 years earlier, Marx foresaw it all: the proletarian revolutions, unlike a bourgeois one, would

> consistently engage in self-criticism, and in repeated interruptions of their own course. They return to what has apparently been accomplished in order to begin the task again; with merciless thoroughness

they mock the inadequate, weak and wretched aspects of their first attempts; they seem to throw their opponent to the ground only to see him draw strength from the earth and rise again before them, more colossal than ever; they shrink back again and again before the immensity of their own goals, until the situation is created in which any retreat is impossible, and the conditions themselves cry out: *hic Rhodus, hic salta!* Here is the rose, dance here! (Marx [1852]2005: 62)

This famous passage, so vivid and accurate in its projection, could have been written specifically for the twenty-first-century socialists. The contradictions of historical Chinese socialism need to be looked into squarely, as do the contradictions of post-socialist reforms. China's trial and error is underway, one step forward and two steps back. But has not the situation already been created "in which any retreat is impossible"? Writing a few years after the dissolution of the Soviet Union, Eric Hobsbawm noted that "our assessment of the entire Soviet phenomenon remains provisional" (1998: 242). Something similar might be said about China's socialist and postsocialist transformations as well. If the metahistorical question of whether socialism has a future in China or China has a future in socialism can still be meaningfully asked, the answer would remain a matter of political determination, persuasion, and struggle.

In the darkest days of the Chinese revolution, such as when tens of thousands of workers were slaughtered and the party had to retreat to the countryside to begin from the beginning, in 1927; or when 90 percent of the red areas were lost while the party's urban underground organizations were entirely wiped out, and the red army had to walk 6,000 miles in extreme hardship to build new bases in the north, losing 90 percent of its force along the way, in the mid-1930s, the communists did not despair. They endured exactly what Lenin predicted for Soviet Russia as "a long, stubborn and desperate war of life and death, a war demanding perseverance, discipline, firmness, indomitableness and unity of will,"[17] and marched to victory. The conditions are very different today except "the immensity of their own goals" for the socialists, while the clarity of their tasks and programs, or friends and enemies is no longer there. But political struggle itself is where any answer to our many questions must be sought, for China and thereby for the world.

# Notes

## I  Positioning China in World Capitalist Development

1. In a discussion of "Weber and the question of Chinese modernity," Wang Hui notes that modern social sciences first established in the West rely on a particular social taxonomy and social morphology, including disciplinary classifications. By adopting them we restructure knowledge or reconstruct history based on a particular yet universalized set of categories. This in turn results in our knowledge and history losing their historicity (2011: ch.6).

2. See articles written at the centenary of the revolution in *Global Legal Review* 环球法律评论 5, 2011, Beijing: Chinese Academy of Social Sciences.

3. It apparently depends on how "nation-state" is defined or whether it must be confined to the modern era for any judgment. Mancur Olson, for example, sees China as "among the earliest, if not the earliest, of the nation-states" (1982: 152).

4. Chalmers Johnson tells his fellow Americans that "we are on the brink of losing our democracy for the sake of keeping our empire," in an analysis of "the road to imperial bankruptcy" ("Empire v. Democracy," http://www.tomdispatch.com/post/160594/, Jan 30, 2007).

5. David Harvey's analysis of local mechanisms of capitalist globalization is influenced by Henri Lefebvre's *The Production of Space* in resisting a spatiotemporal perception that "threatens to become fixed, frozen and ossified" (in Lefebvre 1974: 431).

6. Braudel quoted in (Arrighi 2007: 230). See also Immanuel Wallerstein's discussion of "Braudel on capitalism, or everything upside down" in (1991: 207–217).

7. Wang Hui's concept of "interculturality" is a critical development of Jurgen Habermas's "intersubjectivity" limited to individual

interactive behavior and communication within a particular social or linguistic community. It thus fails "to deal with the interactions among members of different linguistic and social-cultural communities" (2011: 305–306).

## 2    Debating History: From "Oriental Society" to "Great Divergence"

1. Indeed, financialization fostered by "the commercialization of war and an incessant armament race" was precisely what made the European path specifically *capitalist* (Arrighi 2007: 230, 266–272, 332).

2. Marx is of the view that "it would be a mistake to place [primitive communities] all on the same level; as in geological formations, these historical forms contain a whole series of primary, secondary, tertiary types, etc." ([1881]1989: 356–357).

3. The Chinese migration mostly to *nanyang* or Southeast Asia over centuries is part of the Asian regional economic history. An obvious and important difference here is that unlike the Europeans, the Chinese overseas had generally not been colonizer-rulers through military conquest.

4. See Rosenthal and Wong (2011: ch.5) and Rawski and Rawski (2008) for the views on local dynamics and efficiency of China's credit markets no less than their European counterparts organized through rigid property rights and formal contracts.

5. See Han (2009: 152ff) for the critiques of silverization in trade by the Ming reformers; Wang (2010) for a critical survey of the Chinese scholarship on China's "premodern" money culture; and Wakeman (2009) for an extensive set of references.

6. The influential "China-centered" approach (Cohen 1984), for instance, while redressing the biases in the asymmetrical binaries between active Western and passive Chinese forces, "rejects theory out of hand for the 'facts'" and "forced its adherents to repeat native pieties" of cultural authenticity (Harootunian 2002: 163).

7. See also, Bairoch (1993) and Maddison (2007). The statistics, however, are not consistent especially on when the "great divergence" began. The gap is as wide as 500 years between ca. 1300 and 1800. A profound difference between these two takings is whether the European industrial revolution has any decisive explanatory power in the story.

8. On the stagnation of real wages in China since the early eighteenth century, see Allen et al. 2011.

9. Similarly, in the case of the Indian subcontinent, highly commercialized regions were not under global competitive or ecological pressures comparable to those that affected Britain. Then the Indians, like the Chinese, "had their own economic and political dynamism." Taking into account agency and choice, however, "the pressures were not such that radical transformations were needed or risky paths had to be pursued" (Parthasarathi 2011: 263).

# 3   Chinese Socialism and Global Capitalism

1. Neil Davidson points out that the Chinese Communist Party was a workers' party before Jiang Jieshi's bloody coup in 1927. Afterward "the CCP had effectively ceased to be a working class party, since its entire urban membership base in that class had been destroyed and had become instead a rural guerrilla organization based on the peasantry" (2012: 252). It might be reasonable to ask a counterfactual question about historical possibilities—if the disastrous "first united front" between the communists and nationalists had not been imposed by the Comintern, would the trajectory and outcome of the revolution have been different? But taking the CCP as a peasant party is confusing more than clarifying. Similarly, Neil Faulkner's depiction of a direct transition of the CCP leadership "from nationalist revolutionaries into a bureaucratic ruling class" (2013: 257) is a sheer oversimplification and serious error in not distinguishing between the Maoist and post-Mao policies.

2. Cf. (Schram 1966). For a case study of the early communist agitation deliberately "cultural," see (Perry 2012).

3. See a marvelous passage in Mao's 1927 report on the peasant movement in Hunan, quoted in Myron Cohen (1993: 151): "The gods? Worship them by all means. But if you had only Lord Guan and the Goddess of Mercy and no peasant association, could you have overthrown the local tyrants and evil gentry? .... You have worshipped them for centuries, and they have not overthrown a single one of the local tyrants and evil gentry for you! Now you want to have your rent reduced. Let me ask how will you go about it? Will you believe in the gods or the peasant association?"

4. Without a revolutionary break, the record of Nehru's regime, for example, was barren of any impulse of meeting even modest requirements of social equality or justice. "No land reform worthy of mention was attempted. No income tax was introduced until 1961. Primary education was grossly neglected. As a party, Congress was controlled by a coalition of rich farmers, traders and urban professionals" (Anderson 2012). Despite its more recent economic development, India has continued to fail its poorest segments, lower castes and classes, and in many aspects also women.

5. Cf. a discussion of the contrast between revolutionary and colonial modernity in Asia (Lin 2006: 52–57).

6. See Mao's speeches at the first Zhengzhou conference (November 2–10, 1958), the Wuchang conference (November 21–27, 1958), the sixth Plenary Session of the eighth Party Congress (November 28 to December 01, 1958), the second Zhengzhou conference (February 27 to March 5, 1959), the Shanghai conference (March 25, to April 01, 1959) and other occasions in June 1959 before the Lushan Conference (July 2–31, 1959). Most of these speeches are collected in (Mao [1958, 1959]1986; [1958, 1959]1999). He emerged from these speeches more sober minded than some of his seemingly more moderate or "conservative" colleagues as was usually portrayed.

7. Wim Wertheim (1995) reports that Chinese demographers in the 1950s privately doubted the accuracy of the census of 1953, upon which calculations of the scale of deaths are often based, because the census was conducted unscientifically, registering "an unbelievable increase of some 30 percent in the period 1947–1953" in the Chinese population. Consequently "the claim that in the 1960s a number between 17 and 29 million people was 'missing' is worthless" if the 600-million figure for 1953 was itself doubtful. Yang Songlin (2013), incorporating the statistician Sun Jingxian's research, further examines China's census data 1955–60, 1958–61, 1964, and 1982, and depicts their methodological inconsistencies, thoroughly discrediting the widely and irresponsibly circulated numbers about famine death. See also Joseph Ball, "And Mao Did Not Want Half of China to Starve to Death: A Key Document in Frank Dikotter's Book *Mao's Great Famine*," http://www.maoists.org/dikottermisinterpretation. htm.

8. An example is India in the last quarter of the nineteenth century. The country experienced both its worst famine in history and largest grain exports, supplying nearly a fifth of Britain's

wheat consumption (Davis 2001: ch.9). The inability of the post-independent Indian government to eradicate extreme poverty along with persistent starvation affecting a large portion of its population is also a shame on its transplanted democracy.

9. Examples are (Hou Yangfang 2003) and (Deng Wei et al. 1997).

10. The puzzle remains unsolved because of the obscure information about China's grain import and export 1959–61, and whether and in what quantity China repaid the Soviet Union part of its debt in grain during the famine period, the role of local governments in the worst-hit provinces, and the extent of confusion on the part of a willful and misinformed central leadership.

11. Commenting on revolutions, French, Russian, and Chinese, Perry Anderson is fair in noting that they "typically accomplish only twenty per cent of what they set out to achieve, at a cost of sixty per cent. But without them there is no leap of society in history" (2011: 120).

12. See Gao Liang 高梁's 2005 research, "Warning against multinationals seizing the opportunity of SOE reforms to annex China's backbone enterprises in the machine manufacturing industry 警惕跨国公司借改制之机吞并我装备制造业骨干企业" (http://www.dajunzk.com/jingtikuag.htm). The alarming figures were used in a petition to the National People's Congress (NPC) in March 2006, signed by a group of concerned citizens, arguing for national autonomy and industrial innovation to prevent "economic colonization."

13. Samir Amin, "The implosion of global capitalism, the challenge for the radical left," speech at Qinghua University, Beijing, December 14, 2012.

# 4   The Politics of China's Self-Positioning

1. James Areddy and James Grimaldi, using data from the Shanghai research firm Hurun Report, "Defying Mao, Rich Chinese Crash the Communist Party," *The Wall Street Journal,* Dec. 26, 2012.

2. According to an expert report, the wealth of the 70 richest members of the legislature rose to $89.8 billion in 2011, a gain of $11.5 billion from 2010, in comparison with the $7.5 billion combined net worth of all 660 top officials in the three branches of the US government (Tyler Cowen, quoting figures from the Hurun Report in "China Fact of the Day," *Marginal Revolution,* Feb. 27, 2012). Much of the *New York Times'* revelation of Premier Wen Jiabao's

family wealth (Oct. 25, and Nov. 24, 2012) along with similar information about other highly placed officials and regulators has been spread as "rumors" in China for a long time. The NPC convention of March 2013 is nicknamed a "parent meeting of the children studying abroad" on the Internet. And in the popular online discussions of corruption and related issues, contrasts are often made between the present and first-generation communist leaders.

3. *The Southern Metropolis Daily* (南方都市报), Dec. 20, 2012.

4. The NPC "may boast more very rich members than any other such body on earth" (James Areddy and James Grimaldi, "Defying Mao," *The Wall Street Journal*, Dec. 26, 2012).

5. Unsure about whether a self-surgery is still possible, he admits that "we are falling like a landslide" (John Garnut, "The Rot Inside," *The Age*, Apr. 14, 2012).

6. High-profile places include the Jilin province and the municipalities of Chengdu and Chongqing. In the Hegang city in Heilongjiang, land speculation was prohibited. Nonspeculative real estate activity was encouraged to achieve affordable housing on the one hand and safeguard arable agricultural land on the other (Wang 2001). More up-to-date reports are currently lacking.

7. Goran Therborn, "If the rulers of the People's Republic were to conclude that China requires a socialist economic base to underpin its national strength, or that further progress along the capitalist road would imperil social cohesion, they still have the power and the resources to change track" (2012: 8–9). For example, Chinese labor costs are estimated to account for only 1 to 3 percent of the final sales price of the iPhone or iPad. Sharp upward retention here is China's goal and also key to its ambitions in all industrial sectors. "Remarkably, few in the western world have understood the depth of this ambition" (Klaus Zimmermann, "Robots Can Solve China's Labor Problem," *Financial Times*, Apr. 16, 2012).

8. Aditya Chakraborty's report begins with the story of one worker in one of Foxconn's factories in Shenzhen: "Tian Yu worked more than 12 hours a day, six days a week. She had to skip meals to do overtime. Then she threw herself from a fourth-floor window" ("The woman who nearly died making your iPad," *The Guardian*, Aug. 5, 2013).

9. *China Labor Bulletin*, Dec. 19, 2012, http://www.clb.org.hk/en/node/110187.

10. Eli Friedman notices the issue in a discussion of workers' strikes in China: "Dispersed, ephemeral, and desubjectivized insurgency

has failed to crystallize any durable forms of counter-hegemonic organization capable of coercing the state or capital at the class level....it is only through an ideological severing of cause from effect at the symbolic level that the state is able to maintain the pretense that workers are in fact 'weak'" ("China in Revolt," *Emancipation Essays* 7–8, 2012, http://jacobinmag.com/2012/08 /china-in-revolt/).

11. *Xinmin Weekly* 682, 2012, 11: 36.
12. See Martin Hart-Landsberg, "China and Neoliberalism," Feb 2, 2012, http://media.lclark.edu/content/hart-landsberg/2012/03/02/china-and-neoliberalism/.
13. See http://www.worldbank.org/content/dam/Worldbank /document/China-2030-complete.pdf.
14. Guo Shuqing, then the Chairman, "Building up a More Open and Inclusive Capital Market," speech at the Asian Financial Forum, http://www.csrc.gov.cn/pub/newsite/bgt/xwdd/201301 /t20130114_220399.htm.
15. Cf. Mark Leonard's introduction to his edited volume *China 3.0: Understanding the New China,* published by the European Council on Foreign Relations: "One group of Chinese intellectuals thinks that the way out of the stability trap is to find ways of institutionalizing Chinese politics. The New Right, which does not believe in removing the roots of inequality, wants to use politics to make it more legitimate," http://ecfr.eu/content/entry /china_3.0.

# 5  Can There Be a Chinese Model?

1. The position I elaborate in this chapter shares the main elements summarized below by Arif Dirlik: China's developmental successes are seen as uniquely "products of the legacy of revolution: an efficient party state with deep roots in the population that has successfully converted itself from an instrument of revolution to a manager of development; a coherent nation that is the product of the organizational and to some extent ideological integration of the nation that the revolution created; a national purpose the search for which had been a motivation for political change since the late Qing; and obsession with sovereignty and autonomy...; a work force, both urban and rural, that had been mobilized and trained to do its utmost in the service of collective goals, national development among them; a highly egalitarian society where encouragement of the pursuit of equality also stimulated civic engagement; and even an entrepreneurial ethic fostered by

the pressure to innovation in the cause of collective welfare that always conflicted with the bureaucratic prerogative of stability and routine; and last but not least, the economic foundation and organization that had been established, modeled on socialist premises, that now had to be converted into a functioning machinery of development within the context of global capitalism" (2011a: 301).

2. Danny Quah: "From 1981 to 2005 China, on a population base of a billion, succeeded in lifting over 600 million of its citizens out of grinding poverty—this is transformation on a scale never before experienced in all of human history, and larger than total poverty reduction on the entire planet. World poverty reduction has taken place on the back of China's poverty reduction" (public lecture at LSE, Oct 12, 2011, http://econ.lse.ac.uk/~dquah/index_own. html).

3. The PRC has a distinguished tradition of providing considerable economic aid to the developing countries, and "China in Africa," for example, is by no means a new phenomenon. Changed however is that while in the past it was all about socialist internationalism and third world solidarity that was complicated also by the Sino-Soviet conflict, today large projects in the African continent managed by Chinese SOEs are motivated mainly by securing energy supply for China, as discussed and debated in a growing literature.

4. Fredric Jameson is reviewing Francis Spufford's *Red Plenty* about the lasting impact of original Soviet idealism.

5. Read a typical cry from manual labor in old China: "I have the misfortune to be born Chinese / And the greater misfortune to be an enslaved worker...like cattle and horses.../ In the past we workers dare not even mention it / But now we have the chance to make the future / Just to talk of liberation is vain / We have to bring it about ourselves / Come workers! Let us hasten to see justice done" (poem by an anonymous worker, *Laodong zhoukan* [*Labor Weekly*] 12: Nov. 5, 1921; quoted in Smith 2002). The year "1949" stands undisputably for liberation in everyday Chinese in new China.

6. Dirlik is thus of the view that to the extent that it is possible to speak of a "Chinese model," 'it is only in the sense of a local version of a modernization paradigm," or a paradigmatic articulation of the contradictions of Chinese development as of global modernity (2011a: 306).

7. The State Statistics Bureau had provided an annual assessment of China's "comprehensive state capacity" for some years by a set

of comparative indicators with the major global economies. The notion is designed to count on the connotations considered positive for national development. For an overview of state capacity, especially the agenda setting power of a functioning state, see (Wang 2003, 2006).

8. See (Lin 2006: ch.3) for a discussion of the rights and wrongs of a verbally redundant "people's democracy" in China.

9. "The majority of accidents involve mines or mining practices, where safety has been preciously compromised by corruption and collusion between local officials and the businesses that run the small private operations; afterward, mine employers and local officials work together to cover up the deaths" (Pai 2012: 78).

10. Referring to "state capitalism" more than socialism, Samir Amin observes that in China today "the Plan remains imperative for the huge infrastructure investments" from massive housing projects for new urban inhabitants to "an unparalleled network of highways, roads, railways, dams, and electric power plants," from opening up the Chinese countryside to developing the country's continental west. "The Plan also remains imperative—at least in part—for the objectives and financial resources of publicly owned enterprises (state, provinces, municipalities)" (2013).

11. The poverty line was set in 2011 at 2,300 *yuan* ($363) per annum, by which standard 128 million were considered in poverty. In July 2011, there were 22.8 million people in the government's urban subsistence security system and 52.4 million in its rural system, plus 5.5 million covered by the "five guarantees" under the collective responsibility and 62.3 million in various state priority schemes of social relief. An unknown number of unregistered people living in poverty are not included in these figures released by the Ministry of Civil Affairs (*People's Daily,* Aug 29 2011).

12. *China news net,* Jan 18, 2013.

13. Ma Jiantang, the bureau chief, admitted that "we feel that our urban Gini coefficient reading based on a survey of urban residents is too low. The main reason is it's hard to access the true figure for the high-income group." As Wang Xiaolu points out, the problem is twofold: many with high-incomes avoid taking the survey, eventually causing part of the high-income group to be omitted. Those survey-takers meanwhile do not necessarily provide a full picture, especially when they have significant gray income or income from extralegal sources. The fact that China suffers

rampant corruption "is the root cause of unreliable income statistics" ("The real problem with those Gini numbers," *CaixinOnline*, http://english.caixin.com/2013–02–04/100489583.html, Feb 5, 2013).

14. It is in the nature of despotism that it should foster single-minded material desires and propagate their havoc, lowering the collective morale (quoted in Daniel A. Bell, "After the Tsunami," *New Republic*, Mar 9, 1998: 25).

15. Marc Blecher observes that "while most authoritarian states seek to insulate themselves from society by repressing it into quiescence, the Maoist state chose instead to rule by activating society It wanted believers, not subjects" (1997: 220).

16. Based on a summary of his many publications, Wang Shaoguang explains some of these ideas in a lecture "Democracy, Chinese style," Sept 18, 2012, http://www.abc.net.au/radionational/programs/bigideas/chinademocracy/4314066 and http://confucius.adelaide.edu.au/gallery/video/2012/Democracy-Chinese_Style.pdf.

17. "On the Soviet textbook of political economy," 1959/60, http://cpc.people.com.cn/GB/64184/64185/189968/11568297.html.

18. In the Chinese debate, apart from the "socialist market," such syntheses as "socialist republicanism," "liberal socialism" and "ecosocialism" are also influential. Many agree that socialism is intrinsically and simultaneously republican, liberal, and environmentalist in its vision and foundation.

# 6   Class, Direct Producers, and the Impasse of Modernization

1. "Analysis of the Classes in Chinese Society," http://www.marxists.org/reference/archive/mao/selected-works/volume-1/mswv1_1.htm. A related text by Mao is "How to Analyze Rural Classes" written in 1933 as a guide to land and rent reforms in the Jiangxi Soviet base area.

2. Echoing Mao, Carl Schmitt insists that a free people must determine for itself this distinction "therein resides the essence of its political existence." Against liberal "political romanticism," for him the political defines the human, and diminishing the political is to diminish humanity. The danger of evading political decisions is that "if a people no longer possesses the energy or the will to maintain itself in the sphere of politics, the latter will not thereby vanish from the world. Only a weak people will disappear" (2007: 49, 53).

3.  See "On the People's Democratic Dictatorship" (1949), http://www. marxists.org/reference/archive/mao/selected-works/volume-4 /mswv4_65.htm.

4.  See Huang (1995) for a sketch especially of rural transformation during 1946 to 1976, from the start of large-scale land reform through socialist reconstruction to the end of the Cultural Revolution. His critique of a perceived discrepancy between "representational and objective realities" in the land reform is controversial.

5.  Sociologists disagree on any single defining factor of income, occupation, or educational attainment. There are also many theoretical difficulties, such as the effect of cultural capital or the "contradictory class locations" concerning splitting domination and exploitation (Bourdieu 1986, ch.2; Wright et al. 1989: 24–28).

6.  Mao was clear that "the serious problem is the education of the peasantry." For, as he explained, the peasant economy is scattered, and the socialization of agriculture will require a long and patient work. Yet "without socialization of agriculture, there can be no complete, consolidated socialism" ([1949]1991: 419).

7.  Chris Hann and Keith Hart describe the global division between rich and poor economies as thus: "Now the cheapest agricultural products come from Brazil, the cheapest manufactures from China, the cheapest information services from India, and the cheapest educated migrant labor from the ruins of the Soviet empire" (2011: 118).

8.  There is a large literature on modern cooperative movements worldwide. For a market friendly model of the movement see the 2012 Declaration of International Summit of Cooperative, http://www.sommetinter2012.coop/site/communication/declaration/en. In a related but more visionary vein, see the "future of work" debate initially influenced by the French thinker Andre Gorz among others around a "third sector" between market and state (e.g., Offe and Heinze 1992; Miller 2010; Rifkin 1995, 2011).

9.  The main arguments of these debates are traced in (Stedman Jones 2004: chs.1–3). For an updated traditional Marxist critique of a "new 'true' socialism," see (Wood 1999).

10. Cui's sources of inspiration are widely drawn: Proudhon, Lassalle, John Stuart Mill, Silvio Gesell, Fernand Braudel, James Meade, Henry George, James Joyce, Charles Sabel, Fei Xiaotong, and Roberto Unger. See his most influential writings in his personal website at Qinghua University, http://www.cui-zy.cn/.

11. Compare the Chinese system with Marx's idea in "The nationalization of the land," written for the *International Herald*

(no. 11, June 15, 1872). Marx argues that agriculture and all other branches of production should be organized "in the most adequate manner," and "national *centralisation of the means of production* will become the national basis of a society composed of associations of free and equal producers, carrying on the social business on a common and rational plan." He sees the project of nationalization of land as a "*Social Necessity*" due to capitalist modernization of agriculture, which requires large-scale farming receptive to modern technology and machinery. Ultimately, however, for him nationalization, as the proletarian state itself, is merely transitional. In a dialectic of the negation of negation, only communal organization or communism is the future. See http://www.marxists.org/archive/marx/works/1872/04/nationali-sation-land.htm.

12. Lenin wrote a series of influential articles between 1911 and 1913 in support of Sun's land policy and "China's democracy and populism," which for him signified "the awakening of Asia," http://www.marxists.org/archive/lenin/works/1913/may/07b.htm.

13. The explanation for the end of communal TVEs through various forms of privatization in the late 1990s remains subject to debate. According to Wen Tiejun, at least in southern Jiangsu, it was because "local state corporatism" aided by various rational mechanisms in engaging village communities had managed to "complete primitive accumulation for local industrialization" (2011: 1). On how the village collectives lost control over their enterprises see, for example, (Naughton 2006: 272–292).

14. The annual pace of reduction since 2008 has been 180 to 200 million *mu*, resulting in a land deficit of 390 million *mu* by 2012 (Yan Yuhua, "Worrying thoughts on our arable land 'red line,'" *China Reform Forum,* Jan 21, 2012, http://www.chinareform.org.cn/economy/Agriculture/Forward/201201/t20120122_132973.htm. According to the World Bank, China's ratio of arable land in hectares per person was only 0.08 in 2009, http://data.worldbank.org/indicator/AG.LND.ARBL.HA.PC.

15. *XinhuaNet,* Feb 7, 2013.

16. According to Chen Xiwen, by the end of 2012, 52.6 percent of China's total population lived in cities and county towns, of which about one-third have no *hukou* or are not formally urban residents. Discounting them China's urbanization rate would be 35.2 percent. Among migrant workers, in 2011, less than 20 percent were ensured for pension and medical care and less than 10 percent for unemployment ("Food, Land and People in Urbanization," 三农中国 http://www.snzg.cn. Apr 12, 2013).

17. "The East Is Grey," *The Economist,* Aug 10, 2013.

18. For the latest example of air pollution, see a report on Beijing in January-February 2013, http://www.guardian.co.uk/world/2013 /feb/16/chinese-struggle-through-airpocalypse-smog. The smog "has become more than a health hazard in China—it has become a symbol of widespread dissatisfaction with the government's growth-first development strategy." The question asked is, "Should growth be paid for by health?"

19. The EPI is annually published by the Yale University Press. See the 2012 reports http://www.epi.yale.edu/epi2012/countryprofiles.

20. He Xuefeng, *Global Times,* Apr 6, 2012, http://opinion.huanqiu. com/roll/2012–04/2586575.html.

21. So far China has managed its agricultural production to keep pace with urban transformation. "This is a remarkable and exceptional result, unparalleled in the countries of the 'capitalist South,' in spite of a major handicap: China's agriculture feeds 22% of the world's population with only 6% of world's arable land" (Amin 2013).

22. China's current geo-sociological "urban" has the following components: the old urban core, upstart cities, new suburban centers of metropolis, the rural fringe of urban transition, and "villages inside the city" (*cheng zhong cun*) (Hsing 2010). There are two kinds of such villages: one refers to those originally agricultural but now encircled by urban expansion—owing to collective land right the residents become rentiers and distribute rent mostly through a shareholding arrangement. The other refers to those hosting migrant workers, which are loosely administered by municipal governments to ensure basic electricity and water supply, hygiene, and service facilities. These provisions, by and large in place, distinguish such "villages" from typical urban slums.

23. The Dalai Lama, for example, consistently differentiates the earlier communist policies from the later ones. In an interview with BBC on June 24, 2012, he reconfirmed his "very good relations" with Mao, "like father and son". He also recounted that he was attracted by the idea of equal distribution in the Marxist theory. http://www.ibtimes.com/dalai-lama-says-mao-considered-him-son-recalls-his-attraction-communism-704140. The Tibetan elites in the end rejected that idea, but that is another story.

24. He developed his work written in the late 1940s (Fei 1992) in many speeches and articles in the 1980s, which has a large following in China, making a notable policy impact.

25. *China Securities News,* www.cs.com.cn, Dec 17, 2012; *China Digital Times,* Feb 21, 2013.

26. "Food sovereignty" is defined thus: "It is essential that food be pro-
    duced through diversified, farmer-based production systems. Food
    sovereignty is the right of peoples to define their own agriculture
    and food policies, to protect and regulate domestic agricultural
    production and trade in order to achieve sustainable development
    objectives, to determine the extent to which they want to be self
    reliant, and to restrict the dumping of products in their market"
    (La Via Campesina, quoted in McMichael 2009: 294). The food
    sovereignty movement in the global south spotlights the relation-
    ship between corporate commercial agriculture and the rural and
    urban crisis of social reproduction caused by accentuated hun-
    ger, poverty and destruction of communities (McMichael 2009:
    304–308). See also (Wittman et al. 2011).
27. Official data show that China has become a net importer since
    2004 at an annual average of 50 million tons of grain varieties,
    running a large trade deficit.
28. *Xinhua Net*, Feb 1, 2013.
29. Transfer of collective land to urban and industrial use amounted to
    160,000 hectares in 2008, 209,000 hectares in 2009, and 428,000
    hectares in 2010. The income from land trading accounted for
    60 percent of local government revenue in the same period (Gao
    2013).
30. See He Xuefeng, *Global Times*, Apr 6, 2012, http://opinion.huan-
    qiu.com/roll/2012–04/2586575.html; and (He 2007).
31. Cui Zhiyuan here introduces the republican-socialist idea of Henry
    George and others, followed by Sun Zhongshan. Huang Qifan, the
    mayor of Chongqing, explains why a government land-banking
    system is the foundation of fiscal equilibrium and urban construc-
    tion in an interview given to *China Business*, Mar 5, 2013.
32. From one perspective, "China remains extremely important
    when considering the continued salience of the agrarian ques-
    tion because, as a consequence of neoliberal globalization, many
    agrarian economies have promoted an agricultural export-
    led strategy, and China is a very important source of demand
    for agricultural exports." The implications of this situation
    are, first, that "rural accumulation in many countries is reli-
    ant on China's ongoing capitalist transition"; and, second, that
    "China's capitalist transition is now a global driver of accumu-
    lation in the North and in the South" (Akram-Lodhi and Kay
    2009: 323–324).
33. For a short summary of Lenin's position see his "The Agrarian
    Program of Social-Democracy in the First Russian Revolution,

1905–07", http://www.marxists.org/archive/lenin/works/1907 /agrprogr/ch01s5.htm. For a comprehensive review of Lenin's work on this question see Howard and King (1988).

34. Li Changping, "Chinese Villages Will Thoroughly Take the Philippine Road," http://chinastudygroup.net/2008/12/chinese-villages-will-thoroughly-take-the-philippine-road/ (Dec 23, 2008). See also *China Left Review* 1, Spring 2008, http://chinaleftreview. org/?page_id=98. "Latin Americanization" is a more common concern in the Chinese debate. See, for example, Wen Tiejun discussed in (Day 2008: 54–55).

35. Chen, *Xinhua Net*, Feb 1, 2013.

36. As established in classical economics by Malthus and Ricardo on the finite resources and diminishing returns: "The productivity of the land set limits to the scale of industrial activity no less than to the level of food consumption. Each of these two great consumers of the produce of the land was necessarily in competition with the other for the use of a factor of production whose supply could not be expanded" (Wrigley 2004: 101–102, 243–245). Modern science and technology may mitigate such limits but cannot transcend them.

# 7  The Rise of the Social: For a Communist Moral Economy

1. Some of the green revolution's detrimental long term consequences began to emerge only after the fact. See, for example, Harvey, "while the green revolution raised productivity and is credited with preventing mass starvation, it did so with all manner of negative environmental and social consequences. The vulnerabilities of monoculture meant heavy investments in oil-based fertilizers and pesticide." In many places it has also consolidated a class of wealthy producers while reducing others to the status of landlessness (2010: 186).

2. E. A. Preobrazhensky used the phrase "primitive socialist accumulation" in the 1920s in debating the New Economic Policy in Soviet Russia. See Miller (1978). That debate, known as the Bukharin debate, was a focus in intellectual search and policy reflections at the beginning of China's market reform.

3. For a more detailed discussion see Lin Chun and Tian Yu Cao, *Reorienting Socialism in the 21st Century: The Chinese Experience and Beyond*, ch. 4, London: Routledge (forthcoming).

4. The foremost classical treatments of the agrarian origins of capitalism within the Marxist perspective are by Engels, *The Peasant Question in France and Germany* (1894), Karl Kausky, *The Agrarian Question* (1899), and Lenin, *The Development of Capitalism in Russia* (1899). Marx focuses on the English path as the most typical. Lenin compares the Prussian and American paths: in the former "pre-capitalist feudal landed property transforms itself into capitalist commodity production, converting its previous labor force of peasants into dependent wage workers"; while in the latter "without feudalism and transition from it; capitalist farming emerged from once-independent smallholders who become increasingly subject to the economic compulsions of commodity relations from the late 18th century" (Bernstein 2010: 30–32). The East Asian path debated among the comparative economic historians is reviewed in Chapters 2 and 7.

5. Polanyi: "To separate labor from other activities of life and to subject it to the laws of the market was to annihilate all organic forms of existence and to replace them by a different type of organization, an atomistic and individualistic one" (1957: 72, 163).

6. The textbook case in reformist liberal economics of early Fordism aiming at enabling workers to purchase the cars they produce is not analogous to the case of direct producers not selling labor as a commodity. But it speaks of direct consumption as a matter of both incentive and justice, which, not fundamentally but still meaningfully, affects the nature of the plant.

7. Mao declared in 1959 that "the fundamental solution for agriculture is mechanization." The notable effort of capital intensification in the 1960s, however, intentionally or unintentionally did not so much save labor as allow for further labor intensification in multiple cropping (Huang 2011: 111).

8. In the case of historical moral economy in England, if the market is where working people are exposed to exploitation, it is also where "they could most easily become organized" (Thompson 1971: 132). In China, uniquely, a decisive factor that remains singularly weightier than the market is party and government involvement in organizing the peasantry.

9. The concept was introduced by Hayami Akira in relation to Tokugawa Japan (in Arrighi 2007: 32–39, 93) and was later borrowed elsewhere to convey different meanings.

10. See also, Xia Mingfang (夏明方), "Real and Fake Adam Smith— Evolution of Rural Economy in Early Modern China in Terms of 'Market without the Social Division of Labor'" ("真假亚当·

斯密—从"没有分工的市场"看近世中国乡村经济的变迁",
*Humanities and Society* (人文与社会), Oct 2012, http://wen.org.
cn/modules/article/view.article.php/3551.

11. As Amin observes, "The Chinese peasantry as a whole is not reactionary because it is not defending the principle of private property, in contrast with the Soviet peasantry, whom the communists never succeeded in turning away from supporting the kulaks in defense of private property" (2013).

12. See, for example, Griffin, Khan, and Ickowitz (2002) and Bramall (2004). Bramall's defense of collective agriculture, however, is done at the cost of being unnecessarily negative about the preceding land reform.

13. See a collective discussion of "China in the 1970s" "70 年代中国", *Open Times* 开放时代 1, 2013.

14. See Elson (1988; 2000) for a conceptual clarification between "socialized market" and "market socialism"; (Schweickart 2011: ch.3) for "economic democracy" central to a socialist market economy. The controversial idea that socialism and market can cohere continues to generate important scholarship; see Lin (2009: 22–27) for selective references.

15. Exclusive intellectual property rights might be required by normal market function, but their limits and absurdity are obvious in any true "knowledge economy" or "information society." However outrageous the current Chinese practices—which are often against formal laws and intended regulations—might be, in principle privatization of knowledge and information is obsolete. Cf. Eben Moglen, "The dotCommunist Manifesto", 2003, http://emoglen. law.columbia.edu/my_pubs/dcm.html.

16. G. D. H. Cole discusses John Stuart Mill's praise for Fourierism, which "assigned in the first place a basic income to all and then distributed the balance of the product in shares to capital, talent or responsibility" (1956: 310). Apart from a regular literature (see Lin 2000: 548–550), see also the BIEN (basic income earth network) news flash http://www.basicincome.org/bien/news.html and its latest issue 26(68), Winter 2013, http://www.basicincome.org /bien/pdf/Flash68.pdf.

17. "Providing adequate food, clean water and basic education for the world's poorest people could be achieved for less than the West spends annually on make-up, ice cream and pet food" (Hann and Hart 2011: 104).

18. As Amartya Sen has pointed out, "starvation is the characteristic of some people not having enough food to eat. It is not the

characteristic of there being not enough food to eat." He sees ownership as one kind of entitlement relation and starvation as "a function of entitlements and not of food availability." Decisive is society's "legal, economic, political, and social characteristics" (1983: 7, 162).

19. See Hussain (2007). China has recently witnessed (1) the emergence of a new social security system; (2) a demographic transition set by the downward fertility rate and its salient feature—the changing age structure of the population and the rise of the dependency ratio of the elderly; and (3) the transformation of an agrarian into an urban economy dominated by industry and services (99). In response the government focuses on the "three pillars" of social security (97–98).

20. The only political—and fundamentally revolutionary—message of *Capital I*, according to Fredric Jameson, is "enforced idleness" of unemployment as a structural feature and source of miseries of capitalism that would engender "a new kind of transformatory politics on a global scale" (2011: 151).

21. On the future of work and leisure debate by the motto of "all shall work, and all shall work less," see Fourier (1996); Gorz (1985); Offe and Heinze (1992); and Rifkin (1995). See also David Graeber, "On The Phenomenon of Bullshit Jobs" (Aug 17, 2013), http://www.strikemag.org/bullshit-jobs/. The assumption of our intrinsic need for work as an essential human instinct is extensively questioned, examined, and reaffirmed in the literature.

22. He writes about the "economic possibilities for our grandchildren": "When the accumulation of wealth is no longer of high social importance, there will be great changes in the code of morals…All kinds of social customs and economic practices…which we now maintain at all costs, however distasteful and unjust they may be in themselves, because they are tremendously useful in promoting the accumulation of capital, we shall then be free, at last, to discard…We shall once more value ends above means and prefer the good to the useful. We shall honor those who can teach us how to pluck the hour and the day virtuously and well" ([1930]1972: 329–331).

23. During the communist effort at land reform in the late 1940s, Mao identified "an agricultural socialist idea of a reactionary, backward and regressive nature, which must be firmly opposed." He used the label "agricultural socialism" to refer to unconditional egalitarianism in land redistribution and likened it to Russian populism and

the land program of the Taiping uprising. He also saw it as a false understanding of socialist construction without industrialization, for "the level of industrial development is a basic indicator of the overall level of the forces of production" (quoted in Bo 2008: 7, 210).

24. Mao wrote and spoke on these ideas on various occasions between 1958 and 1967, for example in a letter to Lin Biao at the very beginning of the Cultural Revolution on May 7, 1966 (http://www. wengewang.org/read.php?tid=24255). A major factor in the background was China's strategic "preparation for attacks and natural disasters" (*bei zhan bei huang*) in response to perceived external threats.

# 8  Toward a Historical Materialist Universalism

1. In addition, already saddled with a huge public debt that included reimbursing the stockholders of the East India Company and paying the costs of the 1857 revolt, India also had to finance British military adventures in Asia and Africa (proxy warfare with Russia on the Afghan frontier and the Indian Army in Egypt, Ethiopia, and the Sudan). Military expenditures thus never made up less than 25 percent of India's annual budget (Davis 2001: ch.10).

2. The debate, initially stimulated by Maurice Dobb in *Studies in the Development of Capitalism* (1946) and carried on in many other works, has culminated in the "Brenner debate" (Aston and Philpin 1985).

3. Domestically, as Harvey notes, "The original accumulation of capital during late medieval times in Europe entailed violence, predation, thievery, fraud and robbery. Through these extra-legal means, pirates, priests and merchants, supplemented by the usurers, assembled enough initial 'money power' to begin to circulate money systematically as capital" (2010: 47).

4. But there could be other choices outside the dichotomy, such as anticolonial traditionalism "between orientalism and nationalism." Such a stance under traditionalist or religious banners has been taken in extremely complicated circumstances. The secular nationalist (and socialist) Ben Bella typically stated that "it's an error to believe our nationalism is the nationalism of the French Revolution....Algerian nationalism and Arab nationalism is

a cultural nationalism essentially based on Islam" (quoted in Yegenoglu 1998: 141). His and similar statements have to be read in context.

5. In response to this predicament, Dipesh Chakrabarty's "provincializing Europe" is a project to have European thought and its genealogy "renewed from and for the margins" (2000: 16).

6. New Confucianism promoted in its official or consumerist forms is a case of self-exoticizing "reverse orientalism." This fake "alternative" is "fraught with contradictions made no less acute by the realities of over 100,000 protests and large-scale demonstrations annually against the daily depredations of capital's reach in China today" (Mazumdar 2009: 71).

7. "China and the Environment: The East Is Grey," *The Economist,* Aug 10, 2013. http://www.economist.com/news/briefing/21583245-china-worlds-worst-polluter-largest-investor-green-energy-its-rise-will-have.

# 9   Marxism and the Interpretation of China

1. *China Daily,* Feb 28, 2012.

2. In a leaked secret report to the US government, Henry Kissinger, after a visit to Chongqing in September 2011, allegedly wrote that "we must destroy the Chongqing model," for "the greatest danger of the Chongqing Model is that it increases the legitimacy and public support for China's government...[and] has ideological attraction...[which] is a threat to US strategic space," http://www.eastbound88.com/showthread.php/2923-Henry-Kissinger-We-must-destroy-the-Chongqing-Model.

3. 一群普通共产党员的困惑, http://opinion.dwnews.com/news/2012–04–09/58693862-all.html.

4. The role of a very extensive Internet politics in China, regulated highly selectively, deserves a separate treatment. It is interesting to note, for example, how much the censors are biased in stifling social critiques. If you google "Wen Jiabao, corruption," tons of information is there about his family grabbing wealth. But if you put in the same words in *Baidu*, China's most used search machine, everything that pops up is about how he fights corruption.

5. Heiko khoo, "After the fall...Bo Xilai and the Crisis in the CPC," Apr 12, 2012, http://www.karlmarx.net/topics/china-1/afterthefallboxilaiandthecrisisinthecpc.

6. Telling the reporter about their feelings, a woman in a red tracksuit said that "95% of us common people support Bo. He was a good leader." And Mr. Shi, a 59-year-old man, said that "now Chongqing people want to take him back." Jonathan Kaiman writes in the *Los Angeles Times* that "Bo's mark will be difficult to erase. Many live in public housing he built and on pension plans he created" (Apr 12, 2012).

7. "Will China's leaders regret Bo Xilai's fall?" BBC News China, Sept. 23, 2013, http://www.bbc.co.uk/news/world-asia-china-24019450. The Bo trial in August 2013 was significant but too new to be treated here.

8. In fact, "Chongqing had been widely lauded as an economic success. Multinational companies, including Hewlett-Packard and Ford, established outposts in Chongqing, creating tens of thousands of jobs. Chongqing's growth is evident in its ubiquitous concrete villages sitting half-demolished among the residential high-rises flanking its freshly paved thoroughfares. The Yangtze River, which cuts through the city, is now traversed by so many bridges that many residents don't know their names" (ibid.).

9. In response to the critics, Huang Qifan, the mayor, clarifies that the municipal government is not guilty of so-called land finance. The existing system since 2002 is about transparent government control over land use, supply, rent and revenue, which is crucial for a stable real estate market and securing public housing construction. The government debt at the rate of 60 percent is also the lowest among local governments in China (*China Review News*, May 5, 2012, http://www.chinareviewnews.com/doc/1020/9/8/0/102098073.html?coluid=45&kindid=0&docid=102098073&mdate=0505113301).

10. Marx's critic was M. Mikhailovsky. The letter was written in French and was translated and published in English for the first time in *The New International* 1(4): 110–111, Nov. 1934 (http://www.marxists.org/history/etol/newspape/ni/vol01/no04/marx.htm).

11. *Financial Times,* Apr 6–7, 2013.

12. Arif Dirlik has later indicated that China has "emerged since the 1990s as one of the cores of the global capitalist economy" (2011b: 7). The question, however, remains as whether this development is still incomplete and reversible.

13. Samir Amin also points out the consequences of China's continuing leaning to the United States, negative toward global social movements, from the Palestinian cause to green politics,

but positive toward capitalist globalization, including intensified global resource competition. China should rectify its position and join the reconstruction of a "Southern front" or "Bandung 2" (2013).

14. Part I, http://www.marxists.org/archive/marx/works/1845/german-ideology/ch01d.htm.

15. For "universal history engages in a double liberation, of the historical phenomena and of our own imagination." (Buck-Morss 2009: 149). See also Daniel Bensaid's caution against the notion (2002: 31–35) if it contains any assumption of linear or homogenous history, or is used without a sense of historicity and politics.

16. "Note of a publicist," Feb 1922, http://www.marxists.org/archive/lenin/works/1922/feb/x01.htm.

17. "Left-Wing" Communism, and Infantile Disorder (1920), http://www.marx2mao.com/Lenin/LWC20.html.

# References

Aglietta, Michel (2008) "Into a New Growth Regime," *New Left Review* 54, Nov/Dec: 61–74.

Akram-Lodhi, A. Haroon, and Cristobal Kay (2009) *Peasants and Globalization: Political Economy, Rural Transformation and the Agrarian Question,* New York: Routledge.

Allen, Robert and Jean-Pascal Bassino, Debin Ma, Christine Moll-Murata, and Jan Luiten van Zanden (2011) "Wages, Prices, and Living Standards in China, 1738–1925: In Comparison with Europe, Japan and India," *Economic History Review* 64(S1): 8–38.

Amin, Samir (1976) *Unequal Development: An Essay on the Social Formations of Peripheral Capitalism,* New York: Monthly Review Press.

——— (1980) *Class and Nation,* New York: Monthly Review Press.

——— (2013) "China 2013," *Monthly Review* 64(10), http://monthlyreview.org/2013/03/01/china-2013.

Anderson, Kevin (2010) *Marx at the Margins: On Nationalism, Ethnicity, and Non-Western Societies,* Chicago: University of Chicago Press.

Anderson, Perry (1974) *Lineages of the Absolutist State,* London: New Left Books.

——— (1992) *A Zone of Engagement,* London: Verso.

——— (2005) *Spectrum,* London: Verso.

——— (2010) "Two Revolutions," *New Left Review* 61, Jan/Feb: 59–96.

——— (2011) "Lucio Magri," *New Left Review* 72, Nov/Dec: 111–121.

——— (2012) "After Nehru," *London Review of Books* 34(15), Aug 2, 2012: 21–36.

Andreas, Joel (2012) "Sino-seismology," *New Left Review* 76, Jul/Aug: 128–135.

Arendt, Hannah (1963) *On Revolution,* New York: Viking.

Arrighi, Giovanni (1994) *The Long Twentieth Century*, London: Verso.
—— (2007) *Adam Smith in Beijing*, London: Verso.
—— (2009) "The Winding Paths of Capital," *New Left Review* 56, Mar/Apr: 61–94.
Arrighi, Giovanni and Takeshi Hamashita and Mark Selden (2003) (eds) *The Resurgence of East Asia: 500, 150 and 50 Year Perspective*, London: Routledge.
Aston, T. H. and C. H. E. Philpin (1985) (eds) *The Brenner Debate: Agrarian Class Struggle and Economic Development in Pre-industrial Europe*, Cambridge: Cambridge University Press.
Avineri, Shlomo (ed) (1969) *Marx on Colonialism and Modernization: His Dispatches and Other Writings on China, India, Mexico, the Middle East and North Africa*, New York: Anchor Books.
Badiou, Alain (2010) *The Communist Hypothesis*, London: Verso.
Bairoch, Paul (1993) *Economics and World History: Myths and Paradoxes*, Chicago: University of Chicago Press.
Ball, Joseph (2006) "Did Mao Really Kill Millions in the Great Leap Forward?" *Monthly Review* http://monthlyreview.org/commentary/did-mao-really-kill-millions-in-the-great-leap-forward.
Banaji, Jairus (2010) *Theory as History: Essays on Modes of Production and Exploitation*, Leiden and Boston: Brill.
Barlow, Tani (1997) (ed) *Formations of Colonial Modernity in East Asia*, Durham, NC: Duke University Press.
Bensaid, Daniel (2002) *Marx for Our Times: Adventures and Misadventures of a Critique*, London: Verso.
Benton, Gregor and Lin Chun (2009) (eds) *Was Mao Really a Monster? The Academic Responses to Chang and Halliday's "Mao: The Unknown Story,"* London: Routledge.
Bernal, Martin (1987) *Black Athena: The Aroasiatic Roots of Classical Civilization*, London: Vintage.
Bernhardt, Kathryn (1992) *Rents, Taxes, and Present Resistance: Lower Yangzi Region, 1840–1950*, Stanford, CA: Stanford University Press.
Bernstein, Henry (2001) "'The Peasantry' in Global Capitalism: Who, Where and Why?" *The Socialist Register* 37: 25–51.
—— (2009) "Agrarian Questions from Transition to Globalization," in Akram-Lodhi and Kay (eds) *Peasants and Globalization: Political Economy, Rural Transformation and the Agrarian Question*, New York: Routledge.
—— (2010) *Class Dynamics of Agrarian Change*, Sterling, VA: Kumarian Press.
—— (2013) "Historical Materialism and Agrarian History," *Journal of Agrarian Change* 13(2): 310–329.
Blackburn, Robin (1975) *Explosion in a Sub-continent: India, Pakistan, Bangladesh, Ceylon*, London: Penguin.

Blaut, James M. (1993) *The Colonizer's Model of the World: Geographical Diffusionism and Eurocentric History*, New York: Guilford Press.

Blecher, Marc (1997) *China against the Tides: Restructuring through Revolution, Radicalism and Reform*, London: Pinter.

Bo, Yibo 薄一波 (2008) *Several Major Decisions and Events in Retrospection* 若干重大决策与事件的回顾, Vols. 1 and 2, Beijing: Central Party History Publisher 中央党史出版社.

Bourdieu, Pierre (1977) *Outline of a Theory of Practice*, Cambridge: Cambridge University Press.

—— (1986) *Distinction: A Social Critique of the Judgment of Taste*, London: Routledge.

Bramall, Chris (2004) "Chinese Land Reform in Long-Run Perspective and in the Wider East Asian Context," *Journal of Agrarian Change* 4(1/2): 107–141.

—— (2009) *Chinese Economic Development*, London: Routledge.

Branstetter, Lee and Nicholas Lardy (2008) "China's Embrace of Globalization," in Loren Brandt and Thomas Rawski (eds) *China's Great Economic Transformation*, Cambridge: Cambridge University Press.

Braudel, Fernand (1980) *On History*, Chicago: University of Chicago Press.

—— (1984) *The Perspective of the World: Civilization and Capitalism, 15th–18th Century*, Vol. 3, London: Fontana Press.

—— (1992) *The Wheels of Commerce: Civilization and Capitalism*, Vol. 2, Berkeley: University of California Press.

Brenner, Robert (2001) "The Low Countries in the Transition to Capitalism," *Journal of Agrarian Change* 1(2), Apr: 169–241.

Brenner, Robert and Chris Isett (2002) "England's Divergence from China's Yangzi Delta: Property Relations, Micro-economics and Patterns of Development," *The Journal of Asian Studies* 61(2), May: 609–662.

Brook, Timothy (ed) (1989) *The Asiatic Mode of Production in China*, Armonk, NY: M. E. Sharpe.

Buck-Morss, Susan (2009) *Hegel, Haiti, and Universal History*, Pittsburgh, PA: University of Pittsburgh Press.

Buck-Morss, Susan (2010) "The Second Time as Farce…Historical Pragmatics and the Untimely Present," in Costas Douzinas and Slavoj Žižek (eds) *The Idea of Communism*, London: Verso: 67–80.

Buraway, Michael (2009) "Working in the Tracks of State Socialism," *Capital and Class* 98: 33–64.

Cartier, Carolyn (2002) "Origins and Evolution of a Geographical Idea: The 'Macroregion' in China," *Modern China* 28(1): 79–143.

Chakrabarty, Dipesh (2000) *Provincializing Europe: Postcolonial Thought and Historical Difference*, Princeton, NJ: Princeton University Press.

Chan, Kam Wing (2012) "Migration and Development in China: Trends, Geography and Current Issues," *Migration and Development* 1(2) Dec: 187–205.

Cheek, Timothy (1998) "From Market to Democracy in China: Gaps in the Civil Society Model," in Juan D. Lindau and Cheek (eds) *Market Economics and Political Change: Comparing China and Mexico*, Lanham, MD: Rowman & Littlefield: 219–254.

Chen, Kuan-Hsing (2010) *Asia as Method*, Durham, NC: Duke University Press.

Cohen, Myron (1993) "Cultural and Political Inventions in Modern China: The Case of the Chinese 'Peasant,'" *Daedalus* 122 (2) Spring: 151–170.

Cohen, Paul (1984), *Discovering History in China: American Historical Writing on the Recent Chinese Past*, New York: Columbia University Press.

Cole, Andrew and D Vance Smith (2010) *The Legitimacy of the Middle Ages: On the Unwritten History of Theory*, Durham, NC: Duke University Press.

Cole, G. D. H. (1956) *Socialist Thought: The Forerunners, 1789–1850 (A History of Socialist Thought Vol.1)*, London: Macmillan.

Cui, Zhiyuan 崔之元 (1996) "Angang Constitution and Post-Fordism" "鞍钢宪法与后福特主义", *Raading 读书*, 1: 11–12.

—— (2005) "Liberal Socialism and the Future of China: A Petty Bourgeois Manifesto," in Tian Yu Cao (ed) *The Chinese Model of Modern Development*, London: Routledge: 157–174.

—— (2011) "Partial Intimations of the Coming Whole: The Chongqing Experiment in Light of the Theories of Henry George, James Meade, and Antonio Gramsci," *Modern China* 37(6), November: 646–660.

Cumings, Bruce (2011) "The 'Rise of China'?" in Katherine Lynch, Robert Marks, and Paul Pickowicz (eds) *Radicalism, Revolution, and Reform in Modern China*, Lanham, MD: Lexington: 185–208.

Dahl, Robert (1985) *A Preface to Economic Democracy*, Cambridge: Polity.

—— (1989) *Democracy and Its Critics*, New Haven, CT: Yale University Press.

Dallmayr, Fred and Zhao Tingyang (2012) *Contemporary Chinese Political Thought: Debates and Perspectives*, Lexington: University Press of Kentucky.

Davidson, Neil (2012) *How Revolutionary Were the Bourgeois Revolutions?* Chicago: Haymarket Books.

Davis, Mike (2001) *Late Victorian Holocausts: El Nino Famines and the Making of the Third World,* London: Verso.

Dawson, Raymond (1964) *The Legacy of China,* Oxford: Clarendon.

Day, Alexander (2008) "The End of the Peasant? New Rural Reconstruction in China", *Boundary 2,* Summer: 49–73.

Day, Alexander (2013) *The Peasant in Postsocialist China: History, Politics, and Capitalism,* Cambridge: Cambridge University Press.

Deng, Wei, Gu Xingyuan, and Zha Bo (1997) "Changes and Trends of China's Mortality Rates,"邓伟, 顾杏元, 查波, "中国人口死亡率的变化及趋势", *The Chinese Journal of Health Statistics* 中国卫生统计, 14(3): 31–33.

Dirlik, Arif (1978) *Revolution and History: The Origins of Marxist Historiography in China, 1919–1937,* Berkeley: University of California Press.

—— (1989) "Postsocialism? Reflections on 'Socialism with Chinese Characteristics,'" in Dirlik and Maurice Meisner (eds) *Marxism and the Chinese Experience,* Armonk, NY: M. E. Sharpe.

—— (1994) *After the Revolution: Waking to Global Capitalism,* Middletown, CT: Wesleyan University Press.

—— (2011a) *Culture and History in Post-Revolutionary China: The Perspective of Global Modernity,* Hong Kong: The Chinese University Press.

—— (2011b) "Back to the Future: Contemporary China in the Perspective of Its Past, circa 1980," *Boundary 2,* 38(1), Spring: 7–52.

Douzinas, Costas (2010) "*Adikia:* On Communism and Rights," in Costas Douzinas and Slavoj Žižek (eds) *The Idea of Communism,* London: Verso: 81–100.

Dreze, Jean and Amartya Sen (2002) *India: Development and Participation,* Oxford: Oxford University Press.

Du, Jianguo 杜建国 (2012) "Do Not Underestimate China's High End Manufacturing," 别低估中国高端制造业, *Global Times* 环球时报, 23 July.

Duara, Prasenjit (1997) *Rescuing History from the Nation: Questioning Narratives of Modern China,* Chicago: University of Chicago Press.

—— (2009) *The Global and Regional in China's Nation-Foundation,* London: Routledge.

—— (2010) *Culture, Power, and the State: Rural North China, 1900–1942,* Stanford, CA: Stanford University Press.

Eagleton, Terry (2010) "Communism: Lear or Gonzalo?" in Costas Douzinas and Slavoj Žižek (eds) *The Idea of Communism*, London: Verso: 101–110.

—— (2011) *Why Marx Was Right*, New Haven, CT: Yale University Press.

Elson, Diane (1988) "Market Socialism or Socialism of the Market," *New Left Review*, Nov/Dec: 3–44.

—— (2000) "Socialized Market, Not Market Socialism", *The Socialist Register* 36: 67–85.

Elvin, Mark (1973) *The Pattern of the Chinese Past*, London: Methuen.

Elvin, Mark (2004) "Some Reflections on the Use of 'Styles of Scientific Thinking' to Disaggregate and Sharpen Comparisons between China and Europe from Song to mid-Qing times," *History of Technology* 25: 53–103.

Elvin, Mark (2008) "The Historian as Haruspex," *New Left Review* 52, Jul/Aug: 83–109.

Engels, Friedrich ([1849]1977) "The Magyar struggle," in Karl Marx and Friedrich Engels *Collected Works*, Vol. 8, New York: International Publishers: 227–238.

Epstein, S. R. (2000) *Freedom and Growth: The Rise of States and Markets in Europe, 1300–1750*, London: Routledge.

Ertman, Thomas (1997) *Birth of the Leviathan: Building States and Regimes in Medieval and Early Modern Europe*, Cambridge: Cambridge University Press.

Evans, Peter (1995) *Embedded Autonomy: States and Industrial Transformation*, Princeton, NJ: Princeton University Press.

Fairbank, John King (1957) *Chinese Thought and Institutions*, Chicago: University of Chicago Press.

Faulkner, Neil (2013) *A Marxist History of the World: From Neanderthals to Neoliberals*, London: Pluto.

Fei, Xiaotong (1992), *From the Soil: The Foundations of Chinese Society*, translated and introduced by Gary Hamilton and Wang Zheng, Berkeley: University of California Press.

Fiskin, James, Baogang He, Robert Luskin, and Alice Siu (2010) "Deliberative Democracy in an Unlikely Place: Deliberative Polling in China," *British Journal of Political Science*, 40(2): 435–448.

Fourier, Charles (1996) *The Theory of the Four Movements*, Gareth Stedman Jones and Ian Patterson (eds), Cambridge: Cambridge University Press.

Frank, Andre Gunder (1978) *Dependent Accumulation and Underdevelopment*, New York: Monthly Review Press.

———— (1998) *ReOrient: Global Economy in the Asian Age*, Berkeley: University of California Press.

Friedman, Eli and Ching Kwan Lee (2010) "Remaking the World of Chinese Labor: A 30-Year Retrospective," *British Journal of Industrial Relations* 48(3), Sep: 507–533.

Fukuyama, Francis (2011) *The Origins of Political Order: From Prehuman Times to the French Revolution*, London: Profile.

Gao, Liang 高梁 (2013) "Changing Developmental Pattern Requires Systematic Thinking 转变发展方式需要系统性的思考," *Political Economy Review 政治经济学评论* 3.

Gao, Mobo (2008), *The Battle for China's Past: Mao and the Cultural Revolution*, London: Pluto.

Gellner, Ernest (1983) *Nations and Nationalism*, Oxford: Blackwell.

Glete, Jan (2001) *War and the State in Early Modern Europe: Spain, the Dutch Republic and Sweden as Fiscal-military States, 1500–1660*, London: Routledge.

Goldstone, Jack (2008), *Why Europe? The Rise of the West in World History, 1500–1850*, Maidenhead, Berkshire: McGraw-Hill Education.

Goody, Jack (2006) *The Theft of History*, Cambridge: Cambridge University Press.

———— (2010) *The Eurasian Miracle*, Cambridge: Polity.

Gorz, Andre (1985) *Path to Paradise: On the Liberation from Work*, London: Pluto.

Gramsci, Antonio (1971) *Selections from the Prison Notebooks of Antonio Gramsci*, Quintin Hoare and Geoffrey Nowell-Smith (eds) London: Lawrence and Wishart.

Gray, Jack (1974) "Politics in Command: The Maoist Theory of Social Change and Economic Growth," *Political Quarterly* 45(1): 26–48.

Griffin, Keith, A. R. Khan, and Amy Ickowitz (2002) "Poverty and Distribution of Land," *Journal of Agrarian Change* 2(3): 2002: 279–330.

Guo, Sujian (2006) *The Political Economy of Asian Transition from Communism*, Aldershot: Ashgate.

Han, Dongping (1999) "The *hukou* System and China's Rural Development," *Journal of Developing Areas*, 33(3): 355–378.

Han, Yuhai 韩毓海 (2009) *Who Made the History of Past 500 Years: China and the World since 1500;五百年来谁著史*, Beijing: Jiuzhou Publisher 九州出版社.

Hann, Chris M. (1998) (ed) *Property Relations: Renewing the Anthropological Tradition*, Cambridge: Cambridge University Press.

Hann, Chris and Keith Hart (2011) *Economic Anthropology,* Cambridge: Polity.

Hardt, Michael (2010) "Production of the Common," in stas Douzinas and Slavoj Žižek (eds) *The Idea of Communism,* London: Verso, 131–144.

Hardt, Michael and Antonio Negri (2005), *Multitude: War and Democracy in the Age of Empire,* London: *Penguin.*

Harootunian, Harry (2002) "Postcoloniality's Unconscious/Area Studies' Desire," in Masao Miyoshi and Harootunian (eds) *Learning Places: The Afterlives of Area Studies,* Durham, NC: Duke University Press: 150–174.

Harvey, David (2001) "Globalization and the spatial fix", *Geographische Revue* 2: 23–30.

Harvey, David (2005) *A Brief History of Neoliberalism,* Oxford: Oxford University Press.

Harvey, David (2006) *Spaces of Global Capitalism: Towards a Theory of Uneven Geographical Development,* London: Verso.

Harvey, David (2010) *The Enigma of Capital and the Crises of Capitalism,* Oxford: Oxford University Press.

Hawthorn, Geoffrey (1991) *Plausible Worlds: Possibilities and Understanding in History and the Social Sciences,* Cambridge: Cambridge University Press.

He, Xuefeng (2007) "New Rural Construction and the Chinese Path," *Chinese Sociology and Anthropology* 39(4): 26–38.

He, Xuefeng贺雨峰 (2010) *The Logic of Land Right: Wither China's Rural Land System?* 地权的逻辑：中国农村土地制度向何处去? Beijing: University of Political Science and Law Press中国政法大学出版社.

Heilmann, Sebastian and Elizabeth Perry (2011) (eds) *Mao's Invisible Hand: The Political Foundations of Adaptive Governance in China,* Cambridge, MA: Harvard University Press.

Hess, Charlotte and Elinor Ostrom (2007) "Introduction: An Overview of the Knowledge Commons," in Charlott and Ostrom (eds) *Understanding Knowledge as a Commons: From Theory to Practice,* Cambridge, MA: MIT Press: 3–26.

Hindess, Barry and Hirst, Paul (1977) *Pre-Capitalist Modes of Production,* London: Routledge.

Hoare, Quintin and Geoffrey Nowell-Smith (1971) (eds) *Selections from the Prison Notebooks of Antonio Gramsci,* London: Lawrence and Wishart.

Hobsbawm, Eric ([1964]2011, "Marx on Pre-Capitalist formations", in *How to Change the World: Marx and Marxism 1840–2011,* London: Little, Brown: 127–175.

—— (1994) *The Age of Extremes: The Short Twentieth Century,* London: Weidenfeld & Nicolson.

—— (1998) *On History,* New York: The New Press.

—— (2012) *How to Change the World: Reflections on Marx and Marxism,* New Haven, CT: Yale University Press.

Hodgson, Marshall (1974) *The Venture of Islam (vol.3): The Gunpower Empires and Modern Times,* Chicago: University of Chicago Press.

Horkheimer, Max and Adorno, Theodor (1972) *Dialectic of Enlightenment,* New York: Herder and Herder.

Hou, Yangfang (2003) "The Gross National Death Rate in Republic China," 侯杨方, "民国时期中国人口的死亡率", *The Chinese Journal of Population Science* 中国人口科学 (5).

Hough, Jerry (1977) *The Soviet Union and Social Science Theory,* Cambridge: Harvard University Press.

Howard, Michael C. and John E. King (1988) "Lenin's Political Economy, 1905–1914: The Prussian and American Paths to the Development of Capitalism in Russia," *Historical Refletions/ Reflexions Historiques* 15(3): 497–521.

Howell, Jude (2012) "Civil Society, Corporatism and Capitalism in China," *Journal of Comparative Asian Development* 11(2), Dec: 271–297.

Hsing, You-Tien (2010) *The Great Urban Transformation: Politics of Land and Property in China,* Oxford: Oxford University Press.

Hsueh, Roselyn (2011) *China's Regulatory State: A New Strategy for Globalization,* Ithaca, NY: Cornell University Press.

Huang, Philip C. C. (1990) *The Peasant Family and Rural Development in the Yangzi Delta, 1350–1988,* Stanford, CA: Stanford University Press.

—— (1995) "Rural Class Struggle in the Chinese Revolution: Representational and Objective Realities from the Land Reform to the Cultural Revolution," *Modern China* 21(1): 105–143.

—— (2011) "China's New-Age Small Farms and Their Vertical Integration: Agribusiness or Co-ops?" *Modern China* 37(2): 107–134.

—— (黄宗智) (2012a) "Introduction" to *China's Hidden Agrarian Revolution* 中国的隐性农业革命导论, Beijing: The Law Press 法律出版社.

—— (黄宗智) (2012b) "The Basic Unit of China's Economy, Past and Present: The Family or the Individual?" "中国过去和现在的基本经济单位：家庭还是个人？" *Scholarship Frontier* 学术前沿 3: 76–93.

Huntington, Samuel (1968) *Political Order in Changing Societies,* New Haven, CT: Yale University Press.

Hussain, Athar (2007) "Social Security in Transition," in Vivienne Shue and Christine Wong (eds) *Paying for Progress in China: Public Finance, Human Welfare and Changing Patterns of Inequality*, London: Routledge: 96–116.

Jacques, Martin (2011) *When China Rules the World: The End of the Western World and the Birth of a New Global Order*, London: Penguin.

Jameson, Fredric (2011) *Representing* Capital: *A Reading of Volume One*, London: Verso.

—— (2012) "Red Plenty," *New Left Review* 75, May/Jun: 119–127.

Jin, Xiaoding (2009) "A Critique of Jung Chang and Jon Halliday, Mao: The Unknown Story," in Gregor Benton and Lin Chun (eds) *Was Mao Really a Monster? The Academic Responses to Chang and Halliday's "Mao: The Unknown Story,"* London: Routledge: 135–161.

Jossa, Bruno (2005) "Marx, Marxism and the Cooperative Movement," *Cambridge Journal of Economics* 29: 3–18.

Kaiwar, Vasant (2009) "Hybrid and Alternative Modernities: A Critical Perspective on Postcolonial Studies and the Project of Provincializing Europe," in Sucheta Mazumdar, Vasant Kaiwar, and Thierry Labica (eds) *From Orientalism to Postcolonialism: Asia, Europe and the Lineages of Difference*, London: Routledge: 206–238.

Karl, Rebecca (2002) *Staging the World: Chinese Nationalism at the Turn of the Twentieth Century*, Durham, NC: Duke University Press.

Keynes, John Maynard ([1930]1972) "Economic Possibilities for Our Grandchildren," in *Essays in Persuasion*, London: Macmillan.

Kuruvilla, Sarosh, Ching Kwan Lee, and Mary Gallagher (2011) (eds) *From Iron Rice Bowl to Informalization: Markets, Workers, and the State in Changing China*, Ithac, NY: Cornell University Press.

Laclau, Ernesto and Chantal Mouffe (1985) *Hegemony and Socialist Strategy: Towards a Radical Democratic Politics*, London: Verso.

Lee, Chin Kwan (2007) *Against the Law: Labor Protests in China's Rustbell and Sunbell*, Berkeley: University of California Press.

Lefebvre, Henri (1974) *The Production of Space*, Oxford: Blackwell.

Leibold, James (2012) "Toward a Second Generation of Ethnic Policies?" *China Brief* 12(13), 6 July.

Lenin, Vladimir ([1905]1972) "Petty-Bourgeois and Proletarian Socialism", *Proletary* 24, 7 Nov, *Collected Works*, Vol. 9, Moscow: Progress Publisher, http://www.marxists.org/archive/lenin/works/1905/oct/25.htm.

—— ([1913]1977a) "The Awakening of Asia," *Pravda*, in *Collected Works*, Vol. 19, Moscow: Progress Publisher: 65–66.

—— ([1913]1977b) "Backward Europe and Advanced China," *Pravda*, in *Collected Works*, Vol. 19, Moscow: Progress Publisher: 99–100.

——— ([1920]1964) *"Left-Wing" Communism: An Infantile Disorder, Collected Works* 31, http://www.marxists.org/archive/lenin/works/1920/lwc/.

Leonard Mark (ed) (2012) *China 3.0,* London: The European Council on Foreign Relations.

Levy, Marion J. (1963) *The Family Revolution in Modern China,* New York: Octagon Books.

Li, Bozhong (李伯重) (2003) *The Economic History of Jiangnan in Multiple Perspectives,* 多视角看江南经济史, Beijing: Sanlian Publisher 三联书店.

Li, Qiang, Chen Yulin, and Liu Jingming (2012) "A Study of the 'Dynamic Advance Model' of China's Urban and Township Expansion," "中国城镇化'推进模式'研究", *Xinhua Digest* 新华文摘 20: 25–29.

Lieberman, Victor (2009) *Strange Parallels vol.2, Mainland Mirrors: Europe, Japan, China, South Asia, and the Islands; Southeast Asia in Global Context, c.800–1830,* Cambridge: Cambridge University Press.

Lin, Chun (2000) "Participation and Recognition: The Transforming of (un)employment in China," *New Political Science* 22(4): 529–552.

——— (2005) "What Is China's "Comparative Advantage"? in T. Y. Cao (ed) *The Chinese Model of Modern Development,* London: Routledge, 264–276.

——— (2006) *The Transformation of Chinese Socialism,* Durham, NC: Duke University Press.

——— (2008a) "Against Privatization in China: A Historical and Empirical Argument," *Journal of Chinese Political Science,* 13(1): 1–27.

——— (2008b) "In Defence of a Participatory Socialism," "为参与社会主义一辩," *The Leader* 领导者, Winter: 151–160.

——— (2009) "Challenging Privatization: A Conceptual and Theoretical Argument," *Journal of Chinese Political Science,* 14(1): 21–48.

Lindblom, Charles (1977) *Politics and Markets: The World's Political-Economic Systems,* New York: Basic Books.

Losurdo, Dominico (2011) *Liberalism: A Counter History,* London: Verso.

Lowe, Donald (1966) *The Function of "China" in Marx, Lenin and Mao,* Berkeley: University of California University Press.

Lu, Qiyuan 卢麒元 (2012) "Reflections and Conclusions on the Economic System since the 14th Party Congress" ("对十四大以来经济制度与政策的思考与总结"), *Hong Kong Economic Journal Monthly* vol. 427.

Lv, Xinyu，吕新雨 (2007) "Rural Construction, Nation State and China's Path of Modernization," "乡村建设、民族国家与中国的现代化道路," in Huang Ping 黄平(ed) *Earthbound China and Cultural Self-consciousness 乡土中国与文化自觉,* Beijing: Sanlian Publisher 三联书店.

—— 吕新雨 (2012a) "City and Country in the Chinese and Western Perspectives," "中西视野中的城市与乡村," *Tianxia 天下* 4.

—— 吕新雨 (2012b) *The Rural World and Revolution: Three Critical Essays on Neoliberalism in China 乡村与革命 – 中国新自由主义批判三书,* Shanghai: East China Normal University Press 华东师范大学出版社.

Lynch, Catherine (2011) "Radical Visions of Time in Modern China: The Utopianism of Mao Zedong and Liang Shuming," in Lynch, Robert Marks, and Paul Pickowicz (eds) *Radicalism, Revolution, and Reform in Modern China,* Lanham, MD: Lexington: 29–54.

Ma, Jun (2012), "Accountability without Elections," in Mark Leonard (ed) *China 3.0,* London: the European Council on Foreign Relations: 80–88.

Ma, Shexiang 马社香 (2012) *An Oral History of Cooperative Movement in China's Agriculture 中国农业合作化运动口述史,* Beijing: Central Documentary Compilation Publisher 中央文献出版社,

MacPherson, C. B. (1962) *The Political Theory of Possessive Individualism: Hobbes to Locke,* Oxford: Oxford University Press.

Maddison, Angus (2007) *The World Economy: A Millennial Perspective: Historical Statistics,* Brussels: OECD.

Mann, Michael (1986) *The Sources of Social Power, Vol. I: A History of Power from the Beginning to AD 1760,* Cambridge: Cambridge University Press.

Mao, Zedong ([1939]1991) "The Chinese Revolution and the Chinese Communist Party," *Selected Works II,* Beijing: People's Publishing House.

—— ([1944]1983) "To Qin Bangxian," Aug 31, in *Selected letters of Mao,* Beijing: People's Publishing House.

—— ([1949]1991) "On the People's Democratic Dictatorship," *Selected Works IV,* Beijing: People's Publishing House.

—— ([1955]1991) "The Socialist Upsurge in China's Countryside," *Selected Works V,* Beijing: People's Publishing House.

—— ([1958, 1959]1986) *Selective Writings of Mao Zedong,* Vol. 8, Beijing: Renmin Publishing House.

—— ([1958, 1959]1999) *Selective Reading of Mao Zedong,* Vol. 2, Beijing: Renmin Publishing House.

—— ([1959]1977) *A Critique of Soviet Economics*, New York: Monthly Review Press.

Marx, Karl (1844) *Economic and Philosophical Manuscripts*, http://www.marxists.org/archive/marx/works/1844/manuscripts/labour.htm.

—— ([1852]2005) *The 18th Brumaire of Louis Bonaparte*, New York: Mondial.

—— ([1853]1979a) "Revolution in China and in Europe," *Marx/Engels Collected Works*, Vol. 12, New York: International Publishers: 93–100.

—— ([1853]1979b) "The Future Results of British Rule in India," *Marx/Engels Collected Works*, Vol. 12, New York: International Publishers: 217–221.

—— ([1857]1964) *Pre-Capitalist Economic Formations*, London: Lawrence and Wishart.

—— ([1857-]1973) *Grundrisse: Foundations of the Critique of Political Economy*, New York: Penguin.

—— ([1858]1983) "To Engels," *Marx/Engels Collected Works*, Vol. 40, New York: International Publishers: 345–346.

——([1861]1989) *Economic Manuscript of 1861–63*, in *Marx/Engels Collected Works*, Vol. 31, New York: International Publishers.

—— (1867) *Preface to the first German edition of Capital*, http://www.marxists.org/archive/marx/works/1867-c1/p1.htm.

—— ([1867]1971) *Capital I: A Critical Analysis of Capitalist Production*, London: George Allen & Unwin.

—— ([1871]1968) *The Civil War in France*, New York: International Publishers.

—— ([1874]1989) "Notes on Bakunin's book *Statehood and Anarchy*," *Marx/Engels Collected Works*, Vol. 24, New York: International Publishers: 485–526.

——([1877]1942) "Letter to the editorial board of *the Otechestvenniye Zapiski*," in *Marx and Engels Selected Correspondence: 1846–1895*, New York: International Publishers: 352: 353.

—— ([1881]1989) "First Draft of Letter to Vera Zasulich," *Marx/Engels Collected Works*, Vol.24, New York: International Publishers, Vol. 24: 346–358.

—— ([1894]1993) *Capital III: A Critique of Political Economy*, London: Penguin.

Marx, Karl and Friedrich Engels ([1846]1968) *The German Ideology*, Moscow: Progress Publishers.

—— ([1848]1998) *The Communist Manifesto*, London: Verso.

Masioli, Itelvina and Paul Nicholson (2011) "Seeing Like a Peasant: Voices from La Via Campesina," in Hannah Wittman et al (eds)

*Food Sovereignty: Reconnecting Food, Nature and Community*, Oxford: Pambazuka Press: 33–44.

Mazumdar, Sucheta (2009) "Locating China, Positioning America: Politics of the Civilizational Model of World History," in Mazumdar, Vasant Kaiwar, and Thierry Labica (eds) *From Orientalism to Postcolonialism: Asia, Europe and the Lineages of Difference*, London: Routledge.

McMichael, Philip (2009) "Food Sovereignty, Social Reproduction and the Agrarian Question," in Akram-Lodhi and Kay, *Peasants and Globalization: Political Economy, Rural Transformation and the Agrarian Question*, New York: Routledge: 288–312.

Meisner, Maurice (1963) "The Despotism of Concepts: Wittfogel and Marx on China," *The China Quarterly* 16, Oct-Dec: 99–111.

—— (1982) *Marxism, Maoism, and Utopianism: Eight Essays*, Madison: University of Wisconsin Press.

—— (1989a) "Marx, Mao and Deng on the Division of Labor in History," in Arif Dirlik and Maurice Meisner (eds) *Marxism and the Chinese Experience*, Armonk, NY: M. E, Sharpe: 79–116.

—— (1989b) "The Deradicalization of Chinese Socialism," in Arif Dirlik and Maurice Meisner (eds) *Marxism and the Chinese Experience*, Armonk, NY: M. E, Sharpe: 341–361.

—— (1996) *The Deng Xiaoping Era: An Inquiry into the Fate of Chinese Socialism, 1978–94*, New York: Hill & Wang.

—— (1999) "The Significance of the Chinese Revolution in World History," London: *LSE Asia Research Centre Working Papers* 1.

—— (2007) "Capitalism, Communism, and Democracy in China: A Review Essay," *The Progressive* 71:11, November.

Meszaros, Istvan (2008) *The Challenge and Burden of Historical Time*, New York: Monthly Review Press.

Miller, Ethan (2010) "Solidarity Economy: Key Concepts and Issues," in Emily Kawano, Tom Masterson, and Jonathan Teller-Ellsberg (eds) *Solidarity Economy I: Building Alternatives for People and Planet*, Amherst, MA: Center for Popular Economics: 25–42.

Miller, James (1978) "A Note on Primitive Accumulation in Marx and Preobrazhensky," *Soviet Studies* 30(3), July: 384–393.

Mills, C. Wright (1951) *White Collar: The American Middle Classes*, Oxford: Oxford University Press.

Moore, Barrington (1966) *Social Origins of Dictatorship and Democracy: Lord and Peasant in the Making of the Modern World*, Boston, MA: Beacon.

Naughton, Barry (2006) *The Chinese Economy: Transitions and Growth*, Cambridge, MA: MIT Press.

Needham, Joseph (1976) *Science and Civilization in China*, Vol. 3, Cambridge: Cambridge University Press.

Nolan, Peter (1976) "Collectivization in China: Some Comparisons with the USSR," *Journal of Peasant Studies* 3(2): 192–220.

—— (2011) "Who Are We? Who Are They?" *New Perspectives Quarterly* 28(3), Summer, http://www.digitalnpq.org/archive/2011_summer/17_nolan.html.

—— (2012) *Is China Buying the World?* Cambridge: Polity.

—— (2013) "Imperial Archipelagos: China, Western Colonialism and the Law of the Sea," *New Left Review* 80, Mar/Apr: 77–95.

Offe, Claus and Ulrich Preuss (1991) "Democratic Institutions and Moral Resources," in David Held (ed) *Political Theory Today*, Stanford, CA: Stanford University Press: 143–171.

Offe, Claus and Rolf Heinze (1992) *Beyond Employment: Time, Work and the Informal Economy*, Cambridge: Polity.

Oi, Jean C (1992) "Fiscal Reform and the Economic Foundations of Local State Corporatism in China," *World Politics* 45(1), Oct: 99–126.

Olson, Mancur (1982) *The Rise and Decline of Nations: Economic Growth, Stagflation, and Social Rigidities*, New Haven, CT: Yale University Press.

Pai, Hsiao-Hung (2012) *Scattered Sand: The Story of China's Rural Migrants*, London: Verso.

Panitch, Leo and Sam Gindin (2012) *The Making of Global Capitalism: The Political Economy of American Empire*, London: Verso.

Parthasarathi, Prasannan (2011) *Why Europe Grew Rich and Asia Did Not: Global Economic Divergence, 1600–1850*, Cambridge: Cambridge University Press.

Patnaik, Utsa (2002) "On Famine and Measuring 'famine deaths,'" in Sujata Patel, Jasodhara Bagchi, and Krishna Raj (eds) *Thinking Social Science in India: Essays in Honor of Alice Thorner*, London: Sage.

Patnaik, Utsa and Sam Moyo (2011) *The Agrarian Question in the Neoliberal Era: Primitive Accumulation and the Peasantry*, Oxford: Pambazuka Press.

Pearson, Margaret M. (2007) "Governing the Chinese Economy: Regulatory Reform in the Service of the State," *Public Administration Review*, 67(4): 718–730.

Perry, Elizabeth (1983) *Rebels and Revolutionaries in North China, 1845–1945*, Stanford, CA: Stanford University Press.

—— (1999) "From Paris to the Paris of the East and Back: Workers as Citizens in Modern Shanghai," *Comparative Studies in Society and History* 41(2), Apr: 348–373.

—— (2012) *Anyuan: Mining China's Revolutionary Tradition,* Berkeley: University of California Press.

Polanyi, Karl (1957) *The Great Transformation: The Political and Economic Origins of Our Time,* 2nd edn. Boston, MA: Beacon.

Pomeranz, Kenneth (2000) *The Great Divergence: Europe, China, and the Making of the Modern World Economy,* Princeton, NJ: Princeton University Press.

—— (2008) "Chinese Development in Long-Run Perspective," *Proceedings of the American Philosophical Society* 152(1) Mar: 83–100.

Poulantzas, Nicos (2008) "Contemporary Classes in Capitalism," in *The Polantzas Reader: Marxism, Law and the State,* London: Verso.

Pun, Ngai and Chris King-Chi Chan (2008) "The Subsumption of Class Discourse in China," *Boundary 2,* 35(2): 75–91.

Pun, Ngai and Jenny Chan (2012) "Global Capital, the State, and Chinese Workers: The Foxconn Experience," *Modern China* 38(4): 383–410.

Pye, Lucien (1992) "Social Science Theories in Search of Chinese Realities," *China Quarterly* 132, Dec: 1161–70.

Qin, Hui and Su Wen 秦晖，苏文 (1996) *Eclogue and Rhapsody: The Guanzhong Model and An Reexamination of Early Modern Society* 田园诗与狂想曲 – 关中模式与前近代社会的再认识，Beijing: Central Compilation and Translation Press 中央编译出版社.

Rapp, John (1987) "The Fate of Marxist Democrats in Leninist Party-States: China's Debate on the Asiatic Mode of Production," *Theory and Society* 16: 709–740.

Rawski, Evelyn and Thomas Rawski (2008) "Economic Change around the Indian Ocean in the Very Long Run," paper presented at the Harvard-Hitotsubashi-Warwick Conference, Venice, July.

Rifkin, Jeremy (1995) *The End of Work: The Decline of the Global Labor Force and the Dawn of the Post-Market Era,* New York: Tarcher.

—— (2011) *The Third Industrial Revolution: How Lateral Power Is Transforming Energy, the Economy, and the World,* London: Palgrave.

Riskin, Carl (1991) "Feeding China: The Experience since 1949," in Jean Dreze and Amartya Sen (eds) *The Political Economy of Hunger* Vol. 3, Oxford: Clarendon: 15–58.

—— (1998) "Seven Questions about the Chinese Famine of 1959–61," *Chinese Economic Review* 9(2), autumn: 111–124.

—— (2012) "Harmony, Crisis, and the Facing of the Lewis Model in China," in Amiya K Bagchi and Anthony D"Costa (eds) *Transformation and Development: The Political Economy of*

*Transition in India and China,* Oxford: Oxford University Press: 152–172.

Rose-Ackerman, Susan (2003) "Was Mancur a Maoist? An Essay on Kleptocracy and Political Stability," *Economics & Politics* 15, Jul: 163–180.

Rosenberg, Justin (1996) "Isaac Deutscher and the Lost History of International Relations," *New Left Review* 215, Jan/Feb: 3–15.

Rosenthal, Jean-Laurent and Wong, Bin (2005) "Another Look at Credit Markets and Investment in China and Europe before the Industrial Revolution," *Yale University Economic History Workshop,*

——— (2011), *Before and Beyond Divergence: The Politics of Economic Change in China and Europe,* Cambridge, MA: Harvard University Press.

Rousset, Pierre (2009), "Marxism(s), Revolution, and the Third World: Thoughts on the Experiences of Successive Generations in Europe and East Asia," in Sucheta Mazumdar et al. (eds) *From Orientalism to Postcolonialism: Asia, Europe and the Lineages of Difference,* London: Routledge: 154–173.

Runciman, W. G. (ed) (1978) *Weber: Selections in Translation,* Cambridge: Cambridge University Press.

Sartori, Giovanni (1987) *The Theory of Democracy Revisited,* Chatham, NJ: Chatham House.

Schmitt, Carl (2007) *The Concept of the Political,* Chicago: University of Chicago Press.

Schram, Stuart (1966) *Mao Tse-Tung,* Harmondsworth: Penguin.

Shultz, Theodore (1964) *Transforming Traditional Agriculture,* New Haven, CT: Yale University Press.

Schumpeter, Joseph (1962) *Capitalism, Socialism and Democracy,* 3rd edn., New York: Harper Torchbooks.

Schweickart, David (2011) *After Capitalism,* 2nd edn. Plymouth: Rowman & Littlefield.

Scott, James (1976) *The Moral Economy of the Peasant: Rebellion and Subsistence in Southeast Asia,* New Haven, CT: Yale University Press.

——— (1985) "Socialism and Small Property—or, Two Cheers for the Petty Bourgeoisie," *Peasant Studies* 12(3): 185–197.

Selden, Mark (1982) "Cooperation and Conflict: Cooperative and Collective Formation in China's Countryside," in Selden and Victor Lippit (eds) *The Transition to Socialism in China,* Armonk, NY: M. E. Sharpe.

Sen, Amartya (1983) *Poverty and Famines: An Essay on Entitlement and Deprivation,* Oxford: Oxford University Press.

——— (2000) *Development as Freedom,* New York: Knopf.

—— (2011) "Quality of Life: India vs. China," *New York Review of Books*, 12 May.

Shanin, Theodore (1983) *Late Marx and the Russian Road: Marx and the Peripheries of Capitalism*, New York: Monthly Review Press.

Shi, Zhengfu and Liu Chang (2012) "Socialization of Property Rights: A Strategy for SOE Reform in China," *Modern China* 38(6): 677–693.

Skinner, William (1977) *The City in Late Imperial China*, Stanford, CA: Stanford University Press.

—— (1985) "The Structure of Chinese history," *Journal of Asian Studies* 44(2), Feb: 271–292.

Skocpol, Theda (1979) *State and Social Revolution: A Comparative Analysis of France, Russia, and China*, Cambridge: Cambridge University Press.

Smith, Adam ([1776]1976) *An Inquiry into the Nature and Causes of the Wealth of Nations*, Chicago: University of Chicago Press.

Smith, Steve A (2002) *Like Cattle and Horses: Nationalism and Labor in Shanghai 1895–1927*, Durham, NC: Duke University Press.

Stedman Jones, Gareth (1975) "Class Struggle and the Industrial Revolution," *New Left Review* 90, Mar/Apr: 35–69.

—— (2004) *An End to Poverty: A Historical Debate*, London: Profile Books.

Strange, Susan (1986) *Casino Capitalism,* Oxford: Wiley-Blackwell.

Sugihara, Kaoru (1996) "Agriculture and Industrialization: The Japanese Experience," in Peter Mathias and John Davis (eds) *Agriculture and Economic Growth*, Oxford: Blackwell, 148–166.

Sugihara, Kaoru (2003) "The East Asian Path of Economic Development: A Long-Term Perspective," in Giovanni Arrighi, Takeshi Hamashita, and Mark Selden (eds) *The Resurgence of East Asia: 500, 150 and 50 Year Perspective*, London: Routledge: 78–123.

Sullivan, Lawrence (1990) "The Controversy over "Feudal Despotism": Politics and Historiography in China, 1978–1982," *The Australian Journal of Chinese Affairs* 23: 1–31.

Therborn, Goran (2012) "Class in the 21st Century", *New Left Review* 78, Nov/Dec: 5–29.

Thompson, Edward P. (1971) "The Moral Economy of the English Crowds in the 18th Century," *Past and Present* 50: 76–136.

Tilly, Charles (1984) *Big Structures, Large Processes, Huge Comparisons*, New York: Russell Sage Foundation.

—— (1992) *Coercion, Capital, and European States, AD 990–1992*, Oxford: Blackwell.

Trotsky, Leon (1959) *The Russian Revolution: The Overthrow of Tsarism and the Triumph of the Soviets*, –F. W. Dupee (ed) New York: Anchor Books.

Unger, Roberto (1987) *Plasticity into Power*, Cambridge: Cambridge University Press.

——— (1997) *Politics: The Central Texts*, London: Verso.

Unger, Roberto and Cui Zhiyuan (1994) "China in the Russian Mirror," *New Left Review* 208, Nov/Dec: 78–87.

van Zanden, Jan Luiten (2011) "Before the Great Divergence: The Modernity of China at the Onset of the Industrial Revolution," *VOX*, 26 Jan, http://www.voxeu.org/index.php?q=node/6051, accessed October 15, 2011.

Veblen, Thorsten (1990) *Imperial Germany and the Industrial Revolution*, New Brunswick, NJ: Transaction.

Vukovich, Daniel (2012) *China and Orientalism: Western Knowledge Production and the P. R. C.*, London: Routledge.

Wade, Robert (1990) *Governing the Market: Economic Theory and the Role of Government in East Asian Industrialization*, Princeton, NJ: Princeton University Press.

Wade, Robert (2004) "The Ringmaster of Doha," *New Left Review* 25, Jan/Feb: 146–152.

Wakeman, Frederic (2009) *Telling Chinese History: A Selection of Essays*, Berkeley: University of California Press.

Wallerstein, Immanuel (1991) *Unthinking Social Science: The Limits of Nineteenth-Century Paradigms*, Cambridge: Polity Press.

——— (1999) *The End of the World as We Know It: Social Science for the 21st Century*, Minneapolis: University of Minnesota Press.

——— (2004) *World-Systems Analysis: An Introduction*, Durham, NC: Duke University Press.

Wang, Gungwu (2006) "Tianxia and Empire: External Chinese Perspective," Inaugural Tsai Lecture, Asian Center, Harvard University, May.

Wang, Hui (2006) "Depoliticized Politics, from East to West," *New Left Review* 41, Sep/Oct: 29–45.

——— (2007) "The Politics of Imagining Asia: A Genealogical analysis," *Inter-Asia Cultural Studies* 8(1): 1–33.

——— (2012a) "Political Repression and the Resurgence of Neoliberalism in China," in Mark Leonard (ed) *China 3.0*, London: The European Council on Foreign Relations: 94–99.

——— (2012b) "The Rumor Machine," *London Review of Books*, 34(9) May: 13–14.

Wang, Shaoguang (2003) "The Problem of State Weakness," *Journal of Democracy* 14(1): 35–42.

—— (2008) "The Great Transformation: The Double Movement in China," *Boundary 2*, 35(2):15–47.

—— (2013) "The Story of Soybeans" "大豆的故事," *Open Times* 开放时代 3.

Wang, Xiaoqiang 王小强 (2001) "Managing Cities as Managing State Asset: Real Estate without Bubbles in Hegang," "把城市作为国有资产来整体经营 鹤岗房地产没有泡沫," *Shanghai State Asset* 上海国资 11.

—— 王小强 (2010) "Only Socialism Can Save China—part 3" "只有社会主义才能救中国—之三," *Sunny Research Advance* 香港传真 9: 1–93.

—— 王小强 (2011) "Only Socialism Can Save China—part 4" "只有社会主义才能救中国—之四," *Sunny Research Advance* 香港传真 44: 1—110.

Watts, Michael (2009) "The Southern Question: Agrarian Questions of Labor and Capital," in Akram-Lodhi and Kay, *Peasants and Globalization: Political Economy, Rural Transformation and the Agrarian Question*, New York: Routledge: 262–288.

Weber, Max (1968a) *The Religion of China*, Glencoe, IL: The Free Press.

—— (1968b) *Economy and Society*, New York: Bedminster.

—— (1978) *Weber: Selections in Translation*, Cambridge: Cambridge University Press.

—— (1986) *The City*, Glencoe, IL: The Free Press.

Wen, Tiejun 温铁军 (2005) *The Sannong Problem and a Fin de Siecle Reflection* 三农问题与世纪反思, Beijing: Sanlian Publisher 三联书店.

—— 温铁军(1999) *An Investigation of Rural China's Basic Economic System* 中国农村基本经济制度调查, Beijing: China Economy Publisher 中国经济出版社.

—— 温铁军 (2011) *Reading Southern Jiangsu* 解读苏南, Suzhou: Suzhou University Press 苏州大学出版社.

Wertheim, Wim (1995) "*Wild Swans* and Mao's Agrarian Strategy," *Australia China Review*, August.

Wittfogel, Karl (1957) *Oriental Despotism: A Comparative Study of Total Power*, New Haven, CT: Yale University Press.

Wittman, Hannah, Annette Aurelie Desmarals and Nettie Wiebe (2010) (eds) *Food Sovereignty: Reconnecting Food, Nature and Community*, Oxford: Pambazuka Press.

Wolf, Eric (2010) *Europe and the People without History*, Berkeley: University of California Press, 2nd edn.

Wong, Bin (1997) *China Transformed: Historical Change and the Limits of European Experience*, Ithaca, NY: Cornell University Press.

Wood, Ellen Meiksins (1999) *The Retreat from Class: A New "True" Socialism*, London: Verso.

——— (2009) "Peasants and the Market Imperative: The Origins of Capitalism," in Akram-Lodhi and Kay, *Peasants and Globalization: Political Economy, Rural Transformation and the Agrarian Question*, New York: Routledge: 37–56.

Wood, Tony (2012) "Collapse as Crucible," *New Left Review* 74, Mar/Apr: 5–38.

Wright, Erik Olin, et al. (1989) *The Debate on Classes*, London: Verso.

Wrigley, A. E. (2004) "Malthus on the Prospects for the Laboring Poor," in A. E. Wrigley (ed) *Poverty, Progress and Population*. Cambridge: Cambridge University Press, 229–248.

Yang, Mao 杨毛 (2009) "No Land Reform, No China's Modernization 没有土地改革就没有中国的现代化," *Sunny Research Advance* 香港传真 38.

Yang, Songlin 杨松林 (2013) *Someone Has to Tell the Truth: On "30 Million of Famine Death"* 总要有人说出真相：关于"饿死三千万"，Haikou: Southern Sea Publishing House 南海出版公司.

Yegenoglu, Meyda (1998) *Colonial Fantasies: Towards a Feminist Reading of Orientalism*, Cambridge: Cambridge University Press.

Zarrow, Peter (2005) *China in War and Revolution, 1895–1949*, London: Routledge.

Zhang, Qian Forrest and John Donaldson (2008) "The Rise of Agrarian Capitalism with Chinese Characteristics: Agricultural Modernization, Agribusiness and Collective Land Rights," *The China Journal* 60: 25–47.

Zhao, Huaquan 赵华荃 (2012) "A Quantitative Analysis and Evaluation of the Mainstay of Public Ownership" (关于公有制主体地位的量化分析和评价), *Contemporary Economic Research* 当代经济研究: 3.

Zhao, Tingyang (2011) *The Tianxia System: Introduction to the Philosophy of World Institutions*, 天下体系：世界制度哲学导论, Beijing: People's University Press, 人民大学出版社.

Zhao, Yuezhi (2008) *Communication in China: Political Economy, Power, and Conflict*, Lanham, MD: Rowman & Littlefield.

Zhao, Yuezhi (2009) "Communication, the Nexus of Class and Nation, and Global Divides: Reflections on China's Post-Revolutionary Experiences," *Nordicom Review*, Jubilee Issue: 91–104.

—— (2012) "The Struggle for Socialism in China: The Bo Xilai Saga and beyond," *Monthly Review*, October: http://monthlyreview.org/2012/10/01/the-struggle-for-socialism-in-china.

Žižek, Slavoj (2009) *First as Tragedy, Then as Farce*, London: Verso.

# Index

Lightning Source UK Ltd.
Milton Keynes UK
UKOW05n2146141014

240083UK00003B/25/P